To the
Baturas —
may this story be as
— meaningful to you as
it is to me.

Rebecca —
Dallas

Surviving the Day

Frank J. Grady

Surviving the Day

AN AMERICAN POW IN JAPAN

Frank J. Grady

& Rebecca Dickson

NAVAL INSTITUTE PRESS

ANNAPOLIS, MARYLAND

Library of Congress Cataloging-in-Publication Data

Grady, Frank J., 1913–1991.
    Surviving the day : an American POW in Japan / Frank J. Grady,
Rebecca Dickson.
        p.   cm.
    Includes bibliographical references (p.) and index.
    ISBN 1-55750-340-0
    1. Grady, Frank J., 1913–1991. 2. World War, 1939–1945—Prisoners
and prisons, Japanese. 3. Prisoners of war—Japan—Biography.
4. Prisoners of war—United States—Biography. I. Dickson,
Rebecca. II. Title.
D804.J3G73 1997
940.54'7252'092—dc21
    [B]   96-51072

Printed in the United States of America on acid-free paper ∞
04 03 02 01 00 99 98 97   9 8 7 6 5 4 3 2
First printing

Frontispiece: Grady Collection

*Dedicated to Lt. Col. Albert H. Easterling and to the
American Defenders of Bataan and Corregidor*

—Frank J. Grady

*To the millions of people who were incarcerated during
World War II, and to Katie, Johnny, Tommy, and Zane*

—Rebecca Dickson

Contents

Preface

From our first meeting, Frank Grady impressed me as a tolerant and kind man; as I learned more about him and came to understand his years as a prisoner of war, I became convinced that I would meet few people as patient and good-hearted as he. Nor do I think I will I meet anyone whose life has more meaningful lessons embedded within it. I met Elizabeth Grady, Frank Grady's second wife, when we served together as election judges in 1984. We had struck up a conversation about the Second World War, and she told me of her experiences in Germany and Austria in July 1937. I was impressed with her account, but she said, in characteristic fashion, "Oh kid, my story's nothing. You ought to hear my husband Frank's story—now *there's* a story about World War II worth telling." After I met him, I discovered that Mrs. Grady was correct: Frank Grady's story is indeed one that deserves airing.

While we worked on this project, Colonel Grady was adamant that we not convey bitterness toward the Japanese people; though he was determined to document some of the ugly events he had witnessed, he knew full well that any people can act inhumanely. This compassion in a man who suffered considerably while held captive by the Japanese sometimes surprises those who hear his account, but it wouldn't be surprising if they had known him. Frank Grady didn't appear to have a resentful bone in his body, despite the fact that in the latter part of his life he wrestled with chronic health problems that originated during his years as a prisoner of war. He was one of the friendliest, most genuine people I have ever met.

I was willing to become Frank Grady's voice on paper because the way he lived and interpreted his life, especially while a POW, is instructive and inspiring. Colonel Grady's account impressed on me the understanding that human behavior can range from disturbingly vicious to mighty wonderful.

For me, the kind, heroic, and resourceful people in this story made this project an ongoing realization that the best of human nature can survive the most torturous conditions. I believe the forbearance and tolerance portrayed in this account are of particular importance right now, given the increasing polarization of American culture. Though many of the people in this book are now dead, they still have a vital story to tell.

I found I could trust Colonel Grady's memory. The majority of the history that we relate is from his recollection. He told me his war experiences over a period of some six months; we made more than thirty interview tapes. In May 1985 we attended the American Defenders of Bataan and Corregidor convention in Albuquerque, New Mexico, where I was able to confirm much of Colonel Grady's account and learn of other POW experiences. I corresponded with several former POWs in Great Britain who added to our account and verified events. Eric Marsden, Colonel Grady's co-officer-in-charge while at the Kamaishi camp, sent me a copy of his Kamaishi affidavit that he presented to British army officials after the war. In its factual detail, it is almost identical to Colonel Grady's account. I also consulted books, historical documents, and experts on the Second World War as I worked on the manuscript. Overall, I found I needed to change very little of the account, which suggests that Colonel Grady's understanding of the events surrounding the war and his imprisonment was clear and accurate more than forty years after the war. As Colonel Grady died some five years before this book went to press, he was not able to read the final draft. He did, however, read and approve the first complete drafts.

As we move into the new century, I suspect that future generations will want to know how humanity endured what we all must hope will remain the most vicious war humankind will ever fight. With Elizabeth Grady, I offer this final version of Frank Grady's POW years as a testimony to human survival and to the multiple faces of the human spirit, and as a tribute to Frank Grady himself, who is deeply missed. It has been an honor to share his voice with him and to commit his story to public memory.

Acknowledgments

I AM GRATEFUL and beholden to the late Frank J. Grady for sharing with me his account of his POW years and for choosing me to help him commit that account to paper. I thank Elizabeth Grady for all her help as I wrote her husband's story; without Mrs. Grady's support, this project would not have been possible. She has also been a dear friend.

I also thank Colonel Grady's daughters, Mary Virginia Grady and Huntley Chamberlain, for their cooperation in this project.

Many people helped me understand what Allied prisoners of war experienced under the Japanese. To former American POWs Sam Blank, James "Pappy" Eggers, Richard "Dick" Francies, Harold Pohl, Irving Strobing, Ed "Tommy" Thomas, and Joe Warren, many thanks for the accounts and observations you shared with me. Several former British POWs also helped me corroborate the details of this account: Gerry Beard, C. John Harvie, John C. Sharp, and H. Robert Yates. Frank A. Iacobucci provided helpful information regarding his brother; I also thank him for allowing us to use a photo of Captain Iacobucci. Eric Marsden helped confirm Colonel Grady's account of his days at Kamaishi—his affidavit was very useful. Jerry Cooper, Olive DeLucia, Lisa Reichert, and Jamie Steinhauser, all of Texas A&M University, helped me uncover information on Lt. Andy James; thanks to each of them for their help. Philip Reed and John Delaney of the Imperial War Museum in London assisted me in finding various British POWs, and I. Asaipillai of the British Ministry of Defense helped me hunt down the full names of several British officers. I am grateful for their help.

Thanks also to Mark Gilderhus for reviewing the manuscript for me, and to William Griswold for teaching me to respect the lessons of history. I am also indebted to Anne Collier, formerly of the Naval Institute Press, who believed that this account was worthy of publication; I also thank Scott

Belliveau for finishing what Ms. Collier began. And many thanks to Anne R. Gibbons for her expert editorial work.

Rachel Dickson provided invaluable editorial suggestions during each and every stage of this project; I am all the more indebted to her. And Steve Welter's suggestions and proofreading of the final drafts were helpful and encouraging. Thanks also to Mark Dickson for his support. And to the many friends who have unwittingly helped me shape my thoughts and writing style, I am grateful to you all. Finally, I must mention Ed and Frances Dickson and Jackie and George Jones, my favorites of the generation that got us through World War II; their fine characters inspired this work.

Surviving the Day

1. Manila: December 1941

TROPICAL AIR HAS a distinctive scent—heavy, languid, and unhurried; the atmosphere was rich with that fragrance where we sat atop the Bayview Hotel in Manila. It was a warm, pleasant night. My boss had treated my wife and me to dinner, and to finish off the night we were enjoying a quiet drink here, high above the bustle of the city below. Manila was a perfect place to be stationed this time of year—no cold northern blasts could reach the Philippine Islands, not even in December.

As a sweet breeze whispered across our table, I asked my boss, Colonel Stowell, about orders that had sent most U.S. military dependents in the Philippines back to wintry North America; Stowell's wife had been among those sent home. He shook his head. It was a shame, he said. The Japanese were no real threat, he declared, and if war did break out between the United States and Japan, we would be engaged in little more than a holding action against the Japanese. Yet certain politicians back Stateside were acting as if we were in danger. Colonel Stowell thought them alarmist. My wife, Virginia, and I agreed. Although the Japanese were acting aggressively throughout East Asia, they knew they were no match for the U.S. military. Virginia and I were so unalarmed about the Japanese that we had received permission for her to stay in the Philippines. I took a sip of my drink—an exquisite concoction of fruit juices and rum—and gazed complacently down at the streets of Manila.

Virginia and I went home that tranquil night of 7 December 1941 a happy couple. Our pleasant dinner with the colonel was symptomatic of our life together—we were a young couple with a future. The U.S. Army Forces in the Far East (USAFFE), under the command of Gen. Douglas MacArthur, was located in Manila, and I was a member of MacArthur's staff. I was proud of my position—I had come a long way in the Army Air Corps. I was a second lieutenant in the Signal Corps (228th Signal Operations Company) at Fort Santiago in Manila and officer-in-charge of the cryptography section there. Virginia worked for the Army Corps of Engineers. We both had interesting jobs, and we lived in one of the most beautiful places in the world. As we turned in that night, we had no earthly worries. The world was our little oyster.

We hadn't been asleep long when the telephone jangled loudly in the dark. This was not unusual; as head of cryptography, I was on twenty-four-hour call. I groaned but rolled out of bed to pick up the phone.

"Sorry to bother you so late, Lieutenant Grady." It was Sgt. Eugene McCann, the night operator in the communications offices. "I'm in the radio room talking to a lieutenant out on Cavite. He's yelling that he needs to talk to MacArthur and he's madder than hell because I won't put him through. He won't calm down, so I told him I'd call you about it."

I looked at my watch. It was almost three o'clock. "Is he crazy? What does he want?"

"I'm not sure. He just keeps yelling that he has to talk to MacArthur. He won't talk to me—he wants to talk to an officer. I couldn't find any officer awake over here."

"I wasn't awake either, McCann," I said dourly.

"I'm sorry, sir."

"Leave it to a navy man to get me up in the middle of the night," I grumbled. I was a loyal army man. The annoying lieutenant was stationed at Cavite Naval Base, some twenty miles away on the southern side of Manila Bay. I shook my head, still half asleep and irritated. Whatever this message was, certainly it could wait until morning. MacArthur was not a man to disturb in the middle of the night. But someone had to take care of the crazy lieutenant out at Cavite.

"All right, McCann. Tell him to keep his pants on. I'll be right there."

I quickly dressed, slipped out the door, and walked across the quiet compound to the communications offices.

I gave McCann a nod as I entered the radio room and took the telephone receiver from him.

"This is Lieutenant Grady. What's the problem?"

The lieutenant on the other end was obviously agitated about something —he managed to identify himself but then he became incomprehensible because he was simultaneously talking to me and several others in the room with him. Finally he spoke to me exclusively. "Let me talk to MacArthur!"

I rolled my eyes at McCann. He nodded at me sympathetically. I started to speak to the lieutenant but he had just begun yelling at someone in the room with him.

When he began talking to me again, I interrupted him. "Lieutenant, do you know what time it is? I'm not going to ring up MacArthur at three in the morning! I can get hold of his chief of staff General Sutherland if it's important." I let my voice become sarcastic. "But maybe you could tell us what you want to say to MacArthur so we can decide whether to wake him up for you." I grinned at McCann as I finished speaking. I was at least going to have some fun with the obnoxious navy man at this time of night.

But the lieutenant didn't notice my sarcasm. "Well, damn! Let me talk to *somebody!*" he cried. Someone was yelling at the lieutenant on the other end of the phone. After shouting back at him, the lieutenant returned to me. He was still yelling so loudly that McCann could hear every word as he stood next to me. "Listen Grady, you get me somebody to talk to! MacArthur or Sutherland or somebody—somebody important! We're at war! We're under attack!"

The indulgent smile on my face quickly froze. McCann and I stared at one another, wondering if we had heard correctly. War? So suddenly? I must have asked the lieutenant to repeat himself, because he yelled the words again. "We're at war!"

The lieutenant's report tumbled out brokenly after that. He didn't know much, only that it was a sneak attack and that it was going badly for the Americans. It was unbelievable. While we slept in the Philippines, thousands of miles to the east, across the Pacific Ocean and the earth's international date line, our forces in Hawaii were being bombed by the Japanese at a romantic sounding place called Pearl Harbor, a naval base outside Honolulu. No wonder the lieutenant was yelling. We Americans at that moment were joining the cataclysm that so many other countries were already caught in, the holocaust of World War II.

I put through a call to Gen. Richard Sutherland's office.

THERE WERE THOUSANDS of American service personnel in the Philippines when the Japanese attacked Pearl Harbor. Many of them were there for the same reason I was. The dismal U.S. economy of the 1930s had made the military look better than ever before. My path to the Philippines had begun in 1935 in Chicago. I had a job, but the work was menial and the mood in Chicago bleak. The U.S. Army offered promise that American industry could not. It guaranteed jobs and provided its personnel with a place to stay, food to eat, and a certain measure of prestige. Like many others, I didn't think much about what it meant to be a soldier—I just wanted a job with potential for advancement. I enlisted with the Army Air Corps, the precursor to today's air force, and received training as a radio and communications specialist. I was given an assignment at Fort Monmouth, New Jersey.

But New Jersey seemed awfully tame to me and several of my Air Corps buddies. At a bar one night three of us realized that we were sitting on the best chance we'd ever have to travel. The Army Air Corps, we told each other excitedly, sent enlisted men to exotic lands and paid them to go! After a few beers, we thought foreign travel sounded fabulous. The next day, the three of us volunteered to go overseas together. At that time, the United States had three foreign theaters for us to choose from: the Panama Department, the Hawaii Department, and the Philippine Department. As we were getting the trip for free, we decided to go as far as Uncle Sam would send us— we requested assignment to the Philippine Islands.

We arrived in Manila in January 1936.

The Philippines in the 1930s were a paradise for U.S. service personnel. Wherever one was stationed—at Clark Field or Fort Stotsenburg in Central Luzon, at Fort Santiago, Nichols Field, or Fort McKinley in the Manila area, or at Fort Mills on Corregidor—a good life, one unavailable back home, was within reach. Thus, few of us Americans thought of the States, except in distant or idealized ways. The islands were beautiful, a collection of lush green jewels surrounded by azure waters. The climate was uncomfortably hot only in summer, and when the temperatures soared, there were always weekend passes to cool mountain retreats or to bedazzling beaches. Bars, resorts, and restaurants welcomed Americans and their dollars, and those dollars went much further in the Philippines than they did in the States. Good food, alcohol, music, dancing, and native prostitutes abounded —even a private could afford them.

In retrospect, of course, I realize we were taking advantage of the Filipinos. The majority of Filipinos in the 1930s had never known anything but poverty. They were uneducated and poorly housed; many were malnourished and work was hard to come by. But predictably enough, the inequitable economy made life all the more pleasant for Americans in the country. Hungry Filipinos considered themselves lucky to land a job in an American military household, be it as a cook, shoe shiner, or toilet cleaner. Thus a resident maid cost pennies a day, a houseboy even less.

Not every Filipino was suffering, though. The United States had taken over the Philippines in 1898, but a wealthy Spanish and mestizo class that had ruled there for centuries still lived on the islands. Due to what was virtually slave labor on the part of many native Filipinos, the Spanish and mestizos enjoyed fine homes and grounds. They put on grand parties. And we U.S. service personnel were invited to those parties, for when the United States took over the area, this elite class became friendly with their new overlords. The poverty sometimes reminded us that ours was not a perfect world, but we learned to imitate our wealthy hosts in their attitude toward economic inequity: we wore invisible blinders that shielded us from the suffering around us. We basked in the sun, unconcerned about tomorrow, savoring this delightful today.

After taking several correspondence courses, I was awarded my officer's commission in September 1940, some six months after Virginia and I married, and, at age twenty-seven, I was happier than I had ever been.

But September 1940 was a time of ominous changes around the world. President Roosevelt had called to active duty all the reserves and, for the first time in the history of the United States, Congress had enacted a peacetime draft the month before. In the previous year, Adolf Hitler had attacked Poland, and the Nazi military machine had rolled over Denmark, Norway, Belgium, and Holland. By June 1940 the Nazis controlled France and much of Europe. It seemed only a matter of weeks before their incessant bombing of Britain would prevail there as well. And then the world's spotlight shifted to Japan when it signed the Tripartite Pact with Germany and Italy in September 1940.

Of course, Japan had long been a source of alarm for the Western allies. In the late nineteenth century, Japan began establishing itself as an economic power. After World War I, Japan seized former German holdings in China via the Versailles settlement; those holdings proved lucrative footholds in resource-rich Asia, and the Japanese wanted more influence in the area. Added to this was growing political extremism in Japan. As the economic and social devastation of the 1930s reached the country, it seemed to many Japanese citizens that a strong hand would best help the country meet its problems. A strong hand is often a military one, and Japan found its in a string of military officers who encouraged expansion of the Japanese holdings by invading Manchuria. Japan attacked Chinese forces in Manchuria in 1931, and by 1932 Japan had considerable holdings in China. Japanese military leaders had a plan: they declared that if Japan and, more broadly, all East Asians, could reclaim Asia from Western powers, they would create a successful empire dominated by Asians, specifically the Japanese. Japanese leaders named this empire-to-be the Greater East Asia Co-Prosperity Sphere.

British and U.S. leaders were disturbed by Japanese militarism, but the economic problems that both countries faced throughout the 1930s left them unwilling to act upon events in remote East Asia. In 1932 the United States condemned Japan's actions in Manchuria and refused to recognize their territorial gains there, but they did little more. After Japan's full-out war with China erupted in 1937, the United States became more severe in its condemnations of Japan's aggression, but they did not punish Japan with economic sanctions until 1939, when Britain, the Netherlands, and the United States cut off shipments of scrap iron, steel, and petroleum to Japan. By then, the military extremists were firmly in control of Japan, with Lt. Gen. Hideki Tojo at the helm. Tojo's answer to these economic sanctions in late 1941 was to attack the mighty United States at Pearl Harbor.

I learned the story of Japan's road to war long after the events of December 1941. Up until that night, Japanese leaders such as Tojo meant little to me and to most Americans. Two oceans on either side of the North American continent served as a security blanket for the American people that extended to the Philippines. Even though we knew the Japanese must control the Philippines and its trade routes to complete their dominion of the Pacific, those of us stationed there were almost as unconcerned about the threat the Axis represented as the typical American in Chicago—we were convinced the Japanese were no match for us. The United States had sent thousands of new troops to Manila since MacArthur took command of USAFFE in July 1941; the force had almost doubled, to over nineteen thousand U.S. military personnel by 30 November 1941. New planes had arrived at Philippine airfields. There were thirty-five B-17 bombers and about a hundred P-40 fighters as December began.[1] And there was more of everything on the way—more guns, more planes, more ships, more troops; they were to arrive in mid-December or early January.

These reinforcements left us all the more confident that we could quickly defeat the Japanese. But what few of us noticed was that many of our arms were old—some dated from before World War I—and many of the new planes lacked vital parts that rendered them undependable in the air or simply inoperable. We never considered that the new U.S. troops arriving to reinforce the Philippines were young and inexperienced in battle, as many of us were. And our air warning system was primitive. There were seven radar sets in the Philippines, but five of them weren't functioning in early December 1941. Thus our enemy aircraft sighting system depended primarily on men strategically placed around the islands who were to keep their eyes peeled for enemy planes.[2] Obviously the system was not foolproof. And the impoverished Filipino army was even less prepared for battle than we were—many Filipino soldiers did not have guns and in fact had never fired one. They trained with sticks fashioned to look like rifles or swords, and the few guns they had were outdated. They had few trucks and thus no viable form of mass transport. And the language barrier between the Americans and the Filipinos compounded these problems.

But again, none of this mattered. We all believed that a strong Filipino army wasn't important, for the U.S. forces would quickly quell any outbreak of hostilities in the area. And should the Japanese somehow take the Philippines, they would still have to take Indonesia from the British and Dutch—dominion of the Pacific was simply too formidable a task. But even if military personnel had been nervous about Japan, no one would have worried about an attack on Hawaii. The Philippines, an American outpost closer to Japan, was a much likelier target. But we actually expected the first strike to take place against a ship, as in the previous war.[3] Therefore only the navy was officially on alert that night of 7 December 1941.

In retrospect, it should have been obvious to any officer in the Signal Corps in late 1941 that war was inevitable. I had been USAFFE's custodian of codes and ciphers long enough to know that talks between Japan and the United States were breaking down. The Signal Intelligence Service had begun in 1929—this unit monitored and intercepted military and diplomatic messages that were transmitted by the Japanese to various locales across the Pacific. The Japanese, of course, communicated by code, but one of their diplomatic codes had been broken by cryptanalysts in Washington. One of our jobs in the code room was to encode the intercepted messages in our own secure codes so the Japanese would not know we were monitoring their communications.[4] It was painstaking work, as between the two codes everything was gibberish to us and needed to be checked digit by digit for accuracy. We then sent all this on to Washington, D.C., where a top secret deciphering unit decoded them. Two or three days later, we received the decoded Japanese text—which was collectively known as MAGIC—for USAFFE command to peruse.

Every day I delivered these decoded Japanese transmissions to another officer, Maj. Joe Sherr, who passed them on to MacArthur, and I couldn't help but wonder what the Japanese were saying to one another. One decoded message that came in struck me as particularly odd. As I handed the transcripts over to Sherr, I asked him what he made of it.

Sherr took the decoded text from me and read the mysterious line aloud: "The East Winds will blow favorably on 8 December." He shook his head. "I don't know. It's probably a code within a code. Sometimes we just can't figure out what they're saying. Their language is too different."

That same day in early December, I gave Sherr decoded transmissions from U.S. spies all over the Pacific.[5] They reported that personnel at Japanese embassies were burning papers, files, and books in their offices. Many Japanese diplomats seemed to be leaving their various posts at Java, Singapore, Sumatra, and Manila. None of us realized the significance of all this until later, but in retrospect the meaning of that Japanese transmission is obvious. The message about the wind was not a code within a code, it was in fact a simple announcement veiled in almost poetic language. The Japanese military would strike against the Western world on 8 December (the seventh on the other side of the international dateline) and Japanese diplomats should take steps to protect themselves and any classified information.[6]

After fifty years, our collective naïveté still amazes me. The possibility that our never-never land in the Philippines might be in danger did not faze us. With the potential for what we thought would be a quick and tidy victory over the Japanese, patriotism soared. Whether we were with the army or the navy, we were all cocky. We were the U.S. armed forces, the insurmountable force in the Pacific. We could beat anybody. Let the Japanese just try to take us on—we'd show them! These fighting words were unleashed over smooth drinks in the languid atmosphere of Manila nightspots or at indulgent garden parties; such tough boasts mingled improbably with the parasols, pavilions, and pints of beer that surrounded us. There has probably never been a group of human beings more ready for a fall.

IN THOSE EARLY HOURS of 8 December, there was nothing we could do for those at Pearl Harbor but monitor radio reports and dazedly pass them on to our superiors.

War. A devastating sneak attack on Pearl Harbor. We had been wrong. So wrong.

After calling General Sutherland's office, I stood in the quiet telephone area a few minutes before returning to the radio room. There was a lone Filipino man operating the switchboard at that hour. The young man, a boy really, looked up at me. He was obviously wondering what an attack on Pearl Harbor meant. I ignored his questioning eyes and looked over at the couch where another Filipino youth was curled up asleep. "Who's that?" I asked.

The young Filipino said, "My companion. He works at o-six-hundred." Sleeping peacefully before going on duty. I wondered how long it would be before any of us would be able to sleep peacefully again. "Well, you'd better wake him up," I said. "Get ready for more work than you've ever had before. You won't recognize that board in a little bit."

I went back into the radio room and stood behind Cpl. Donald Sollenberger, the radio operator on duty, as he typed out a message from his counterpart in Honolulu. The message wasn't encoded.[7] There wasn't any reason to hide what was happening at Pearl Harbor—the Japanese certainly knew what was going on there. The report was chilling:

I don't know how many enemy airplanes there are. . . . They're sure bombing the hell out of us. I don't know how much longer I'll be able to stay on the air, because they're getting pretty close and they'll knock my antenna out and I'm through. But as long as I can, I'll tell you what's happening. They've hit at least one of our battleships—someone ran by saying that it's sinking.

After these alarming words, Sollenberger quit typing after punching out the letters CUL—see you later. Our connection in Hawaii had stopped transmitting.

We waited tensely for the transmission to begin again. By this time, a crowd of us stood behind Sollenberger in the radio room, as men arriving for early morning duty heard the news of the attack. When we spoke, we did so in hushed tones. But we didn't speak much. Mostly we stood, awestruck and afraid.

A few minutes later the operator in Hawaii sent through another message, but on a weaker signal:

They've hit the station—another bomb fell just outside. I still have a partial antenna. They're dive-bombing us with guns blasting. There's nothing we can do. It looks like all our battleships are on fire. Many wounded. I think the duty officer is dead.

He paused again, or a break came in the transmission, but he managed to come back again:

They've hit our planes. They're all burning. It's chaos here. None of us knew what was happening when they hit us. We were all asleep.

He continued sending information about Japanese bombers and American losses a bit longer; then the signal died again.

This time he didn't come back.

And there was nothing we could do, nothing at all. We monitored the reports of death and destruction, but we could not send any help. Most of our military "help" was located in Hawaii, the U.S. stronghold of the Pacific. The Japanese knew exactly what they were doing, attacking Pearl Harbor early on a Sunday. It was where all our battleships were docked and the home of hundreds of planes—even our aircraft carriers called Pearl Harbor home (though none of them were in port during the attack).[8] The Philippines had planes at Clark Field, and some smaller warships and submarines were at Cavite and Subic Bay, but the battleships and aircraft carriers were in Hawaii. Hawaii had seemed so safe, so unapproachable without detection—this security combined with Pearl Harbor's relative nearness to the United States had persuaded American leaders that Hawaii, not the Philippines, was the best place for the main Pacific military installation. And yet the Japanese had slipped in without waking anyone until the bombs were falling.

Had their risky attack failed, heads would have rolled in the Japanese military. But the maneuver had succeeded, beyond their most ambitious dreams, certainly beyond any U.S. leader's nightmares. And now we in the Philippines were in more danger than the Americans in Honolulu were. Our supply line from the States had suddenly become thousands of miles longer, and our reinforcements in Hawaii were demolished. It was obvious where the Japanese would turn next. They were destroying U.S. naval and air forces with one goal in sight: domination of the Pacific. To do this, the Japanese would need to control the Philippine Islands. We all knew it wouldn't be long before we too would receive a visit from our Japanese neighbors. When that radio operator quit transmitting from Pearl Harbor, I was more afraid than I had ever been in my life.

I walked back into the telephone room. Both telephone operators were working hard now over the lit-up switchboard. I saw through the windows that it was still dark. That was reassuring; the Japanese probably wouldn't attack at night. But the sun would soon be rising. If I had been outside, I probably would have searched the horizon for their approach.

Soon messages began pouring in from all over the Pacific. I had been right in thinking there would be no more sleep in this tropical paradise. This tranquil little corner of the world would soon be embroiled in some of the most brutal fighting in history. Lovely Manila would become a battlefield. And those of us in the Philippines would soon not recognize our lives or our world.

2. Retreat

THE SUN ROSE that 8 December to a world buzzing with the news of war. Two men entered the communications rooms early that morning with heavy boxes—they removed the tops to reveal a cache of handguns. We were each issued one and told to wear it at all times. I was not certain what help the guns would be if we were victims of a bombing, but the cold steel of the revolvers on our hips did make the war real to us.

A squadron of Japanese bombers paid their first visit to the Philippines that morning. They bombed Baguio, a mountain resort. The town had little military importance—there were some barracks there, but no planes and only limited personnel; we suffered no real damage from that initial attack. Early that same morning, Maj. Gen. Lewis Brereton, who was in command of the Far East Air Force, alerted his heavy bomber pilots at Clark Field, a key U.S. airfield about fifty miles north of Manila, to be ready to take off at any moment; Brereton wanted them to attack the Japanese at Formosa (now Taiwan). But Brereton did not order them to take off because he believed MacArthur and Sutherland wanted him to stand by until he had their release. There was also some confusion between Brereton, Sutherland, and MacArthur as to what the U.S. response to Pearl Harbor should be.[1] The outcome of all this hesitation and confusion was that our B-17 pilots were poised to take off with their bombs but many weren't allowed off the ground, so they sat next to their planes as the sun climbed higher into the sky.

By 11:30 A.M., some ten hours after the first bombs fell at Pearl Harbor, Clark Field got crowded. A chase squadron returned to the airfield after a futile effort to catch the Japanese who had bombed Baguio. Those pilots left their planes lined up for refueling next to some of the B-17s. Another squadron of unarmed heavy bombers returned to be loaded for the attack on Formosa; those planes had been ordered aloft to protect them from a bombing of the airfield. Several other miscellaneous aircraft arrived and also lined up for refueling.[2] By then it was almost noon. All morning the B-17 pilots had heard false alarms and unreliable rumors while waiting for further orders; they were frustrated, hot, and hungry. They went into the mess hall to eat lunch, leaving their planes lined up for a quick takeoff.

About that same time, observers on the Filipino coast radioed Manila and Clark Field that a large number of Japanese bombers were headed toward Luzon, the large island on which Manila and Clark Field sit. The air raid sirens went off in Manila, screaming out their warning across the city for the first time. But no sirens went off at Clark Field. Apparently the radio operators were hungry, too—they had heard false alarms all morning and had had enough. They went to have lunch. So no one was in the radio room to hear that enemy planes were on their way.[3]

The result was that even though we all knew about Pearl Harbor, and the Philippines had already been attacked, it happened again: the Japanese managed to sneak up on another major U.S. military base.

They arrived at noon, several squadrons of them. At Clark Field the planes that were lined up for fueling were plump sitting ducks for the Japanese to first bomb and then strafe. Given that huge tanks of fuel were stored at the airfield and many of the planes were full of fuel and bombs, Clark Field was soon a mass of flame, a giant funeral pyre. Only a few planes got off the ground, and those that did inflicted only negligible damage on the Japanese, for many Zeros had flown in with the Japanese bombers, and they destroyed most of the airborne P-40s in moments. That same noon hour the Japanese bombed Iba Field and Fort Stotsenburg, causing immense damage there as well.[4] It took hours to get the fires at the various bases out and far longer to attend to the many casualties.

That eighth of December had just become bleaker for all of us, for in bombing Clark Field and Iba, the Japanese had effectively wiped out half of our air power in the Philippines. Several times that morning I had heard men claiming that we still had a chance against the Japanese: "Yeah, well we've still got Clark Field and Cavite." By that afternoon we didn't have Clark—our B-17s were charred cinders and many pilots were dead or wounded.

We lost 18 B-17s that day. Fifty-three P-40s were destroyed and 3 P-35s, along with some 25 to 30 other planes. Eighty men were killed, and 150 were wounded.[5] And then we got more bad news as the facts from Pearl Harbor trickled in. The Japanese strike had destroyed or severely damaged 8 battleships and 10 other vessels; those that were reparable would be out of commission for months. In addition, 349 aircraft had been destroyed or damaged. And the human toll was high: 2,345 servicemen killed, 1,247 wounded, and 103 civilian casualties. The only good news was that our 4 aircraft carriers based at Pearl Harbor had escaped damage.[6] In contrast, the Japanese had suffered only minimal damage.

Not a bad twenty-four hours for the Japanese military.

IN THE CRYPTOGRAPHY department, scores of messages came in and went out that day, all of them requiring deciphering or encoding. None of us went home that night, so we were awake when the Japanese came back. At about two in the morning, the air raid sirens in Manila went off again. But this time the Japanese planes were headed toward the city, not Clark Field.

It was the first time I heard Japanese planes overhead, and the first time I felt the walls shake as they rumbled above us. But those of us at Fort Santiago were safe that night; the bombers' target was Nichols Field, a small airfield just outside the city. The Japanese planes dropped some bombs there and then took a swipe at Fort William McKinley, which was just south of Manila. It was a quick strike, and though it did little damage, it too went unanswered.

Japan's next move was inevitable. At dawn on the tenth, Japanese infantry landed on the north coast of Luzon. Lt. Gen. Jonathan Wainwright and his North Luzon Force were to defend the area, but they were not pre-pared or equipped for battle. This was partially because the Japanese sur-prised us once again—any invasion of the Philippines was expected to come from Lingayen Gulf or the South China Sea. There were simply not enough troops to stop the northern incursion because most of Wainwright's forces were at Lingayen Gulf, more than a hundred miles away, waiting for the Japanese.[7] Two days later Japanese troops also landed at Legaspi in southern Luzon. We were being surrounded.

At noon on the tenth, Japanese bombers came back to Manila. When we in the cryptography office heard the alarms, I ran outside for no real reason—I had a morbid desire, I suppose, to watch the Japanese drop bombs on us. I saw one squadron of planes headed toward Nichols Field, while an-other was directly overhead. I was momentarily alarmed, thinking they might cut loose over our offices in Fort Santiago, but it was soon obvious they had another target in mind—Cavite Naval Yard. It took the planes only a few minutes to cover the miles between Manila and Cavite on the other end of the bay. Once over the naval base, they released their bombs. I could not see them fall, but I knew they had been dropped because the sound traveled across the water to where I stood, an echo of the destruction taking place at the shipyard. After a few minutes, I saw giant plumes of smoke on the horizon—soon it appeared as if the entire point was ablaze.

I think perhaps the Japanese were more thorough in their attack upon the navy base than they were any place else, for Cavite was finished when the fires were finally extinguished. The entire base had blown up or burned. There was no rebuilding possible there. On another horizon, Nichols and Nielson airfields were burning as well, both crippled beyond quick repair. Only Manila stood untouched, a city of thousands left to watch forlornly as three of the major military installations protecting them went up in smoke.

After disabling Cavite and the airfields, the Japanese turned their atten-tion to Manila, the capital of the Philippines. The bombings became an almost predictable event—the Japanese bombers had destroyed Clark and Nichols and Cavite at noon, and they usually came back at noon to hit Manila. Our only response was to turn on air raid sirens and engage in some antiaircraft fire. There was no sense in sending a lone plane up to challenge the Zeros and bombers, for it would only be shot down, and we had so few planes left. Planes were reserved for reconnaissance and the transport of personnel and supplies.

By this time, just about everyone in the Philippines was terrified of the approaching Japanese. With each Japanese bombing or land advance, myths grew about them. People said they were machines because they didn't make mistakes as we did; they were efficiency and might in military form. Others believed they were unfeeling monsters who killed without remorse. These myths were juxtaposed against inescapable facts. While we had been jinxed with faulty equipment, untrained troops, and a lack of cooperation and coordination between commands, the Japanese war machine clicked and purred and always, always moved forward. Between the myths and the facts of the Japanese, the racist seeds that have long plagued many white Americans sprouted and began to grow. Very soon after Pearl Harbor, it was difficult to tell which was greater: our fear of the Japanese military, or our hatred of the Japanese race.

WITH THE JAPANESE infantry invading, MacArthur and his generals reverted to War Plan Orange, a blueprint originally put together years before for the defense of the Philippines. The plan called for a defense of central Luzon and Manila. If this proved infeasible—as it was by mid-December 1941—U.S. and Filipino forces were to withdraw from the north and south into Bataan Peninsula, a bulbous portion of Luzon Island that jutted out into the South China Sea. From Bataan, U.S. and Filipino forces were to defend the Philippine Islands until reinforcements arrived. USAFFE command would withdraw from Manila to Corregidor; Manila would then be declared an open city. The idea seemed a sound one, for Bataan was capped by Mount Bataan and the Mariveles Mountains, which provided high ground for troops, and there were many towns on the peninsula that would serve as strategic battlegrounds. The Japanese would not easily take the jungle area from the U.S. and Filipino forces.

Across from Bataan, some two miles to the south, sits Corregidor, a small island at the entrance to Manila Bay. This island would shelter officers, administrative and hospital personnel, and any U.S. military families still in the Philippines. Under the cover of darkness on Christmas Eve, MacArthur and his staff, including my wife and me, boarded the transport boat *Don Esteban* and headed for Corregidor.

Luzon Island, The Philippines, 1941

It was an eerie feeling that night as we pulled out of Manila. I stood on deck and watched as we drew away from what had been my home for six years. The city was blacked out because the Japanese were still bombing the area, but the blackout hardly seemed necessary: a heavy cloud of smoke shrouded the city, for half the city seemed to be burning. As the U.S. forces pulled out of Manila, we blew up boats, bridges, and buildings—anything we had to leave behind that the Japanese might find useful. The naval fuel storage tanks had been torched that day, and they still burned as our transport pulled away from the docks. That afternoon I had seen panicked Filipinos in the streets, rushing to stock up on as many supplies as possible before the Japanese arrived. Later, as Virginia and I walked toward the dock, we saw white towels and flags fluttering in windows of houses, apartments, and shops. And now, as we pulled away, a smoky stillness blanketed the dark city in a dreamlike quality; it had become a smudged image that I almost expected to disappear without much more than a quiet rustling into nothingness.

I boarded the boat bound for Corregidor with a higher rank. I had been a second lieutenant when Pearl Harbor had occurred, with no expectation of a promotion in the near future. But in October 1941 MacArthur had been promoted from a two-star general to a three-star general. This sort of promotion eventually filters down to all administrative personnel, as any general with an additional star feels he deserves higher-ranked aides, and so do each of the officers under him. So my fellow officer in the cryptography department, Joe Iacobucci, and I suddenly found ourselves first lieutenants. We were promoted again just before leaving for Corregidor, which made us captains. I did not protest the promotions, but I had done nothing special to earn them.

Very soon after General MacArthur and his staff pulled out of Manila, the North Luzon Forces, under General Wainwright, withdrew into Bataan, and the South Luzon Forces under Maj. Gen. George Parker moved up to meet them. The maneuver was one of the few successful tactics performed by U.S. forces in the Philippines in 1941. The Japanese fought hard to block Wainwright and Parker from withdrawing into Bataan Peninsula, but they slipped through; the U.S. and Filipino troops held back the Japanese long enough to blow up some bridges behind them and thus make the Japanese seizure of Manila more difficult.[8] Manila was then declared an open city, undefended because it was indefensible. The nonmilitary citizens of Manila, including some three thousand U.S. and Allied civilians, were left to their fate under the Japanese.

CORREGIDOR IS A small island, only three miles long and one mile wide. It is essentially a rock—an eroding mountain actually—that had been separated from the larger island of Luzon long ago. It is covered with lush trees and vegetation, which would help hide military activities. It is shaped like a tadpole, with its tail facing inward toward Manila. The tail is the island's only flat area, where there was a small airfield and the 92d Garage area; planes were stored and repaired there. On the other side of Corregidor, or "the Rock," as it came to be called, were our major gun batteries, which faced the open sea. That was the way the U.S. military had expected an enemy to come, and so the guns were embedded in cement, facing that direction. There were twenty-three gun batteries on Corregidor and most of them were old guns—built at the turn of the century. The guns worked efficiently enough, but if an enemy came from the opposite direction, attacked from above, or shelled us from Bataan, many of them would be useless.[9]

The island was divided into four areas: Topside, Middleside, Bottomside, and the Malinta Tunnel. Topside was the high ground on the west side of the island and the site of Fort Mills. Middleside was a plateau on which the officers' quarters, hospital, and other buildings were located. Bottomside was the low area between Malinta Hill and the main part of the island; there were docks and a small town there. For an army hurrying to put together a defense, Corregidor's most important feature was the Malinta Tunnel. In the 1930s the United States completed blasting out the tunnel for storage of equipment and ammunition. It was a huge tunnel, with many laterals and more space than anyone thought we would ever need. It was so large that a streetcar system ran through it to transport supplies. Air ducts went up through the rock, and fans operated to keep air moving in the dank corridors. We had radio reception equipment on top of Malinta Hill, a dependable water supply, and generators for power. There was also a three-hundred-bed hospital lodged in one of the Tunnel's laterals.

In an emergency, Malinta Tunnel was to be used as a massive bomb shelter. This was an emergency, so the Tunnel became home to thousands of people. Although it wasn't comfortable—it was, after all, a damp, dark cavern—the Tunnel was sheltered by tons of rock and was, therefore, the safest place in the Philippines. Virginia and I were both assigned living space there, but we were quartered separately. Crowded with civilians and military personnel, the Tunnel was divided into men's and women's sections. There were also several laterals devoted to administrative offices. Blankets hung over wires strung across the corridors, and hastily erected wooden partitions separated quarters and offices. Those flimsy blankets and planks provided the only privacy anyone had.

When we first moved to the island, MacArthur's offices and USAFFE headquarters were set up on Topside, as were the communications offices and other administrative units. We put the cryptography room in the basement of the Mile-Long Barracks near MacArthur's headquarters on Topside. By 29 December we were settled into our new locale and operating smoothly.

The Japanese knew where USAFFE command had withdrawn to, of course, and they were aware that thousands of troops, medical personnel, and civilians were on Corregidor. Thus, while pressuring Bataan with artillery fire and dive-bombing planes, Japanese aircraft also frequently bombed our island fortress. I was down in the Tunnel on an errand on 29 December when the sirens went off, so I watched from a Tunnel entrance as the Japanese planes approached Corregidor. I saw the bombs fall on Topside a few minutes later.

Once the planes departed an hour or so later, people emerged from trenches and buildings and ran for fire-fighting equipment, first aid boxes, and stretchers. I was trying to find transport to get up to the cryptography office, for I knew that at least four of our crypto guys had been there when I left the building before the bombing. I finally got hold of a Jeep and started toward Topside when I saw another Jeep racing toward the Tunnel with a great cloud of dust trailing behind it. It skidded to a stop once the driver saw me and out climbed Joe Iacobucci, my fellow captain in the code room. One of the other officers who worked with us, Lt. Robert Pfaff, was driving. In the back sat Lt. Andy James squashed between three large machines that I recognized as some of our cryptographic devices. All three men looked dazed and were covered with dust, wood splinters, and abrasions.

"What in the world is going on, Joe?" I asked.

Joe was a calm and soft-spoken man; in the months I had known him, I had never seen him lose his temper. Now he was gazing at me wildly, his eyes defiant. He excitedly told me that the crypto office had been badly damaged, and he had taken the initiative to move our office down to the Tunnel.

As Joe told me this, Pfaff and James stood grimly with arms folded across their chests. I learned later that they all looked defiant because they expected me to argue protocol with them; officially, I was the officer-in-charge of the code room, and therefore I should make final decisions about office moves. But I had no reason to argue with them. We turned back toward the Tunnel and began moving our crypto equipment into an empty lateral.

As we worked, Joe, Pfaff, and James reported that there had been massive destruction up Topside. According to the three of them, many buildings on Topside had been blown to smithereens. When we later climbed into the Jeep to get the rest of the machines, a thought struck me—there had been four men in the crypto room when I had left. "Where's McCann?" I asked. Joe answered as he turned over the engine. "He left before the bombing and was off duty, sleeping." McCann had taken up a bunk in those same Mile-Long Barracks where the crypto office was, and those, I saw a few moments later, had indeed been blown to smithereens. Up until then, none of the men I worked with had been hurt—we were office personnel, after all. But for the first time, one of our own guys might have been hit, and our little realm, the code room, had been badly damaged.

James spoke up from the back seat. "MacArthur's moving into the Tunnel, his aides, everyone. I'll bet that tunnel gets mighty damned crowded now." We would remember that prophecy later.

I record that day, partly because it was the day we moved into the Tunnel, but primarily because it was when Joe, Pfaff, James, and I came to an understanding with each other. Joe and I had taken an instant liking to one another when he had arrived several months before. When we brought Pfaff and James in from the Coastal Artillery to help us out, we discovered the two of them to be efficient, quick, and enthusiastic workers. But up until that day, I had been in charge, the experienced officer in the code room. I had taught Joe much about code work, and we had in turn taught Pfaff and James when they joined us. This changed the day Joe moved the code room; we became equals. Joe acted quickly and decisively, and Pfaff and James supported him in that decision. The three of them proved themselves dependable officers whom I wouldn't have to command—they would instead help me command and keep communications up and running. We became firm friends after that, not just friendly coworkers.

That same day, MacArthur moved USAFFE headquarters into the Tunnel. We set up the crypto department in a lateral adjacent to his, along with the other communications offices, the radio room, and message center. "Offices" is an extravagant term for these areas, as only a scrawled sign designated which cordoned-off area was which.

As James had predicted, the Tunnel did become "mighty damned crowded"—MacArthur's retinue of aides took up one entire lateral, which forced the ever-increasing numbers of military personnel and civilians into a smaller area. Cots and bunks lined every available wall of the gloomy Tunnel. We in the code room made our sleeping quarters the cryptography area itself. We figured we might as well; we could only nap for a few hours each day anyway because we had so much work to do. We were still encoding the intercepted Japanese transmissions, and we had the volumes of correspondence between USAFFE, Washington, and the commanders in the Pacific to encode, decode, and pass along to their various recipients. There were twenty-four hours of work a day, and we were only seven in the crypto room. We had been eight, but McCann had indeed been hit while in the barracks on Middleside; one of his legs had been badly wounded. McCann never returned to work with us. We crypto personnel visited him in the hospital during off hours.

Though Virginia and I were extremely busy, we did meet every afternoon. She was quartered in the women's section of the Tunnel, but she wasn't idle (as many civilians were). Virginia wanted to keep occupied, so she had gone to work for the army engineers again; they had set up operations on Corregidor and were glad for her help.

As we moved into January 1942, the noon bombings on Corregidor became as predictable as they had been in Manila. One noontime I was near MacArthur's office after delivering a message when I heard the air raid sirens go off. As I walked past a tunnel entrance, I heard excited voices and drew closer to see what was happening. I saw MacArthur standing outside the Tunnel. He was watching the skies as the alarms sounded. Around him buzzed several of his aides, imploring him to return to the safety of the Tunnel and observe the bombing from there. MacArthur calmly told them that this was impossible, that he could see better from where he stood. He advised his aides to go inside and leave him alone. His aides withdrew into the Tunnel to stand next to me.

We watched as a lone Japanese plane dropped a parachute, checking air and weather conditions before the first squadron of bombers struck. It was a reconnaissance plane, a "Photo Joe" as we called them; the Photo Joe was taking pictures of our installations along with checking the weather. A few minutes later, a squadron of bombers arrived and began methodically dropping their bombs on Topside and Middleside. An occasional errant bomb landed in the vicinity of the Tunnel, which brought a chorus of yells from MacArthur's aides that he should withdraw, but MacArthur ignored them and stayed out there alone watching the planes. From where I was just inside the Tunnel I could not see exactly what was happening up there on Middleside, but MacArthur could.

Once the Japanese had finished their work, MacArthur returned to the Tunnel, nodded to various personnel at the entrance and passed on to his offices. From there, as I found out later when he handed me a message to encode, he wrote up a detailed account of Japanese bombing tactics for President Roosevelt and Army Chief of Staff Gen. George Marshall. He was eventually commended for that eyewitness report.

There were many enlisted men and officers in the Philippines and elsewhere who could not tolerate MacArthur's arrogance. They felt he lacked the courage to do anything but send out orders from the safety of the Tunnel or, later, from Australia. But I could never call him "Dugout Doug" after seeing him that day outside the Tunnel. That he was haughty and self-seeking there is no doubt, and perhaps he made some strategic errors in defending the Philippines in 1941–42. Equally, there is no doubt that he was a courageous man. Others remember him for his egotistical "I shall return" gaffe; I see him as he stood alone in the midst of a bombing, studying his enemy's tactics. No one can know another's thoughts, but MacArthur impressed me that day as a man very alone, full of silent despair and fury, but in his stance there was a grim determination as well. Whatever history's verdict on Douglas MacArthur ultimately is, this memory will remain with me. He was a complicated man, and during that bombing, a very solitary one.

FOOD AND MEDICAL supplies had been transferred to Bataan, along with guns, equipment, and ammunition, before the U.S. and Filipino troops moved there. Radio and telephone communications were hurriedly put together in the jungles. But the move, like just about everything else we did in those early months of the war, was chaotic and incomplete. Supplies did not arrive intact; medicine stores were inadequate; and most important, there wasn't enough food stockpiled. By late January the food shortages on Bataan became alarmingly obvious. The story I most frequently heard to account for this was that the confused quartermaster who had been in charge of stockpiling food supplies on Bataan and Corregidor had hesitated to move too much food out of Manila. He was worried about the civilians there starving, which was noble of him, but the result was that the military began to do so.

It was a slow process, of course; at first, we were cut back to two small meals a day, which was bearable. In late January, however, those two meals were cut to one, and we were left irritable and weak for lack of food. A noncombatant could still tolerate this, but it was a different story for a soldier who needed to be tougher than he had ever been in his life. The battle on Bataan was already weakening Wainwright's troops, and the food shortage made things much worse.

But as humans will do in such a predicament, we gave ourselves reason to hope. Immediately after Pearl Harbor, rumors began to circulate that help was on the way, and at first I frequently found myself scanning the horizon, looking for the convoy of ships that was to save us. These rumors were reinforced by words of support and hope from Washington. On 28 December a Navy Department message announced that a plan was in the making to help defend the Philippines. The troops had also heard radio reports from San Francisco that announced Roosevelt's promises of "protection" of the troops in the Philippines, and Chief of Staff Marshall had himself sent a message about help being sent to the Philippines.[10] America was standing by us, the story was, and it was only a matter of time before reinforcements arrived.

MacArthur added to these stories. In mid-January he sent an encouraging message to the troops on Bataan, part of which was as follows: "Help is on its way from the United States. Thousands of troops and hundreds of planes are being dispatched. The exact time of arrival of reinforcements is unknown, as they will have to fight through Japanese. . . . It is imperative that our troops hold until these reinforcements arrive."[11]

Whether MacArthur made up the report is unknown. But the result was that nearly everyone searched the horizons when they could, looking for ships and discussing the delectable foods the convoy was supposedly bringing to us.

After several weeks, I stopped joining such discussions. We officers in the crypto room did the final encoding and decoding of all transmissions pertaining to events in the Pacific, and we knew there was no convoy coming to save the beleaguered troops in the Philippines. It was empty scuttlebutt, encouraged by MacArthur and others to give the troops something to grasp onto during a bombing raid or while under artillery fire. War Plan Orange began to take on a hopeless cast. Without air or naval power, it provided for only a short defense of the islands until reinforcements arrived. If we received no outside help, we were doomed.

Perhaps U.S. leaders had no choice. Perhaps they did have to deal with Hitler before they could turn westward. Certainly it would have been a dangerous and costly project to break the Japanese blockade of the Philippines; Americans would indeed have had to "fight through Japanese" with supplies and reinforcements. And the United States was unaccustomed to fighting a major war in the Pacific, so maybe it made sense that no help was forthcoming. We in the Philippines were too far away and in unfamiliar territory —America just wasn't looking in our direction. But we Americans on Bataan and Corregidor could not imagine the problems in Europe taking precedence over us, the trapped, outnumbered, and outgunned defenders of the Philippines. Yet that is exactly what happened. We were stuck on a back burner, left to heat up slowly as the tropical summer approached. Our country had abandoned us to our collective fate.

For many, it was a diseased and wounded fate. Bataan, a peninsula that few Americans had heard of before 1942, was proving a disaster area. Not long after we abandoned Manila, we learned that Bataan was no place to fight a war. Though the Japanese had a difficult time forging forward in the undergrowth, the jungle was just as dense and unyielding to Americans and Filipinos, and this impenetrable foliage was alive with mosquitoes. Malaria victims soon filled the makeshift hospitals. The men were starving, and nothing was clean, not the hospital, not the water, not the food, nothing. Dysentery became standard on Bataan, and it went untreated for lack of medicine. We also discovered that a hot jungle is a perfect incubator for disease; many ill-fed men who came down with cholera, beriberi, malaria, and dengue fever simply couldn't get well. By February it was obvious that as many men were dying of disease, starvation, and inadequately tended wounds as were dying from Japanese fire.

And yet the soldiers on Bataan continued to hold. Hong Kong had fallen at Christmas to the Japanese, and in January the Japanese were pushing at

Malaysia and Dutch Indonesia. Singapore had surrendered on 16 February, and Bali fell a few days later, leaving the Japanese in control of most of Southeast Asia. Everywhere the Japanese armies went that winter, they were victorious. Except in the Philippines. Our orders from Washington were to hold until July, and the U.S. and Filipino forces were determined somehow to meet that command.

In the midst of our disaster in the Philippines, there was one bright episode: a romance. My buddy Joe Iacobucci had met the love of his life, Phyllis Arnold, a nurse, while steaming to the Philippines in the fall of 1941. Though they had only known each other a few months, love will flourish in the harshest of conditions, and they decided to marry—I stood as Joe's best man as he avowed his love for Phyllis on Valentine's Day 1942.[12] They didn't have much of a honeymoon, but their love gave all of us hope as we worked and lived in the Tunnel.

About the time of Joe's wedding, talk began to circulate that MacArthur would withdraw from the Philippines. In late February, he received orders to leave the Philippines; Roosevelt himself sent the message telling MacArthur to go to Australia. MacArthur protested the order on receiving it. He called me to his office in the Tunnel and gave me a message to encode; I was not to send the message immediately, but to hold it ready and bring all drafts of the message back to him. In the message, he objected to the president's order, saying that morale was low among the troops and would ebb even lower if he were to leave. They would view it as abandonment.

"What they're saying of me isn't true, Frank," MacArthur said that day. MacArthur was referring to the rumors that had been circulating for weeks that he intended to withdraw to Australia. MacArthur went on: "I did not request this. Australia is not the place for me. I will remain here and fight this war."

MacArthur often thought aloud with his aides; I had learned not to say anything when he did. After he had fallen silent, I left with his message. Later that day, after I had encoded his message, MacArthur called me back to his office. He had changed his mind. I was to send a revised message in which he said he would leave the Philippines, but he requested that his departure date be left up to him.[13] Roosevelt agreed to this. All this was done in secrecy—for as long as possible, MacArthur did not want the troops to know he was leaving.

In the second week of March, MacArthur faced his defeat in the Philippines. He, his family, and aides boarded several PT boats that would carry them on the first leg of their journey to Australia. And once MacArthur was gone, the troops finally realized that no help was coming. The enlisted men began murmuring among themselves that the high-ranking officers were deserting, leaving them to face the Japanese. A mute, hungry despair settled over all of us.

After MacArthur's departure, Wainwright inherited the command of the ailing U.S. and Filipino forces. He toured the front lines on Bataan every day, pumping up morale—he had been doing this for weeks. Wainwright was far more popular with the troops than MacArthur was. They knew Wainwright wasn't going anywhere. If the defenders of Bataan and Corregidor fell, Wainwright would fall with them.

By early March there were thousands of Filipinos and Americans in the Malinta Tunnel, and with each bombardment more people would slip into the giant bomb shelter to share the limited oxygen with us. The air was heavy. Even when empty of people, the Tunnel was faintly malodorous; with thousands of sweating bodies in there, the atmosphere was foul, one giant latrine. During every bombing, the air became thicker and more difficult to bear, for the laterals were filled with dust and smoke. To compound matters, the overworked fans, powered by vulnerable generators outside the Tunnel, were turned off during air raids. Without the fans to help move the air, temperatures escalated in those crowded corridors.

The sound was deafening during the bombing raids—it was as if the very earth were angry with us and trying to shake us loose from our sanity by sending up tremors from the bowels of the mountain. When bombs hit close by, the dim light provided by naked bulbs would flicker, threatening to blink out and leave us groveling in complete darkness.

And yet our enclosed hell was far preferable to what our comrades endured outside the rock walls. By March many of the troops on Corregidor were left with little shelter. Much of the greenery had been blasted from the island by bombings and shellings, leaving the men to sleep in narrow slit trenches with the stars overhead. The stress upon them was incredible, and some snapped; there were a few dead bodies in foxholes that weren't caused by Japanese bombs or strafing of the area. Few of us considered the suicides cowardly acts. The fear on Corregidor and on Bataan was a pervasive, almost palpable entity, and it would sometimes well up, becoming a giant hand to slap down a vulnerable human being caught considering the future. No one can promise unflinching bravery when caught in a thundering chaos. This I learned on Corregidor.

I WAS ONE of the Tunnel Rats—such was our name to those unprotected personnel on Bataan and outside the Tunnel on Corregidor. But I was a lucky Tunnel Rat. While we were on Corregidor, I had a regular break from the Tunnel's filthy air and crowds. The other communications officers and I took turns going across to the town of Mariveles on Bataan to deliver and pick up messages; I went over about twice a week. Although these crossings were somewhat risky—we were easy targets for a strafing plane or a Japanese shell—I enjoyed them. Between attacks, the sea and sky were calm and clear, and a light fresh wind swept the stench of the dark Tunnel from my mind as we crossed the three-mile stretch of water.

While at Mariveles wharf one day, I had to face my special status both as a Tunnel Rat and as a captain who had been promoted for no real reason. I ran into a lieutenant I had known before the war who was working communications at sector headquarters. On seeing me, he stared incredulously.

"How in the goddamned world did you become a captain?"

I self-consciously explained that I was a captain because of promotions higher up.

The lieutenant glared at me angrily. "I'm still a second lieutenant! I'm over here in the open taking bombs while you're in the Tunnel taking messages!"

I didn't say a word. He was right. But I could not make him a captain, much as he deserved it. All of the men on the beaches deserved promotions, but they would probably get none. Real heroism during wartime is rarely recognized.

The lieutenant turned away, shaking his head and cursing. I returned to the security of the Tunnel, feeling ashamed and unworthy, but also tremendously relieved to be back in the best bomb shelter in the Philippines. That lieutenant, who had once been my friend, would never be able to address the injustice of the system. After surviving the war, he suffered a mental collapse upon returning to the States and was permanently institutionalized.[14]

3. Bataan and Corregidor

COL. THEODORE TEAGUE, one of my superior officers, spent much time in the communications section on Bataan and felt that we in the Tunnel should have a taste of what the U.S. forces were enduring in that sweltering undergrowth. Thus he assigned each of his officers in the Tunnel to Bataan for several days. My assignment came in early March—I left the crypto section under Joe's command and set out for Bataan with a sidearm, a mosquito bar, and a bedroll.

On Bataan I found two sergeants waiting to take me to the communications officer. Before climbing into their Jeep, I looked back at Corregidor. With its security blanket of heavy rock, the Malinta Tunnel seemed a secure hole in which to hide from the war. No wonder the personnel on Bataan called us Tunnel Rats. As I heard the sound of exploding shells, I suspected I would miss that tunnel.

As we drove inland along the vine-tangled roads, the battle sounds grew louder. At one point, a shrill rushing sound followed by a deafening roar arose off to the side of us, which made me yell out from the back of the Jeep. I thought sure it was only a matter of seconds before we would be hit by a descending shell. I automatically dropped my head onto my forearms and looked up from that position at the driver and his companion. They did not seem concerned that we were about to be blown to bits. Instead, the sergeant in the passenger seat turned toward me and calmly explained that there was nothing to fear.

"It's the one you can't hear that will kill you, sir. If you hear the whistle, it's already over your head. That one was a long ways off."

I stared at him incredulously. When all was *silent* I should worry? I wouldn't be able to hear a shell with my name on it? After a long moment of staring blankly at the man, I asked him, "How long have you been here, sergeant?" It was the only thing I could think of to say.

"Since it started, sir."

I was going to ask how he kept his sanity when I jumped at another whistling blast.

The sergeant smiled indulgently at me. "That's our guys shootin' back, sir." He pointed toward a clump of trees just behind us in which our artillery and men were presumably hidden. I wondered how he could tell which ear-popping whistle came from whom, but I didn't want to appear any more foolish than I already did.

"Doesn't the noise get to you?" I asked instead.

"We don't hear it anymore, sir," the sergeant said politely as he turned to face forward again.

But that wasn't entirely true. There was a mysterious sound that both sergeants heard, which was fortunate for all of us. Somehow they knew that the Japanese were answering the shelling of the nearby U.S. battery. Though we heard no whistling sounds, the driver began to veer wildly back and forth to avoid the shells that were exploding in the foliage around us. The Japanese did not have us targeted; they were firing arbitrarily toward the U.S. battery from a distant hill. But the sergeant behind the wheel seemed to divine where the shells would land and somehow avoided them.

On one, though, he apparently was not sure of the shell's direction and he screeched the Jeep to a halt. Both sergeants piled out, yelling at me to take cover. I bailed out and took refuge in the undergrowth next to a tree just as a shell exploded about twenty-five feet behind the Jeep. In a stunned state of panic, I was showered with flying dirt and debris. After a second, I lifted my head and looked wildly around me for the two sergeants. They were already getting up from behind a rock and running back toward the

Jeep. I scrambled to do the same and probably moved faster than I ever had in my life—I did not want to be left behind in that jungle.

"Everything all right, sir?" yelled the driver as I jumped in and he shoved the Jeep into gear.

"I think so," I yelled back and we were off again, rushing along the track as fast as the sergeant dared.

Neither of the sergeants was particularly shaken over the close call. It soon became obvious why—before we were out of the shells' reach, we had to jump out of the Jeep two more times. The sergeants were calm because they had to be. One learned to take in stride such daily brushes with mutilation or death, or go berserk. It amazes me that more soldiers did not go mad on Bataan, and I speak as one who experienced for only four days what they endured for over four months. I should add that while I was there, the shelling activity was relatively quiet.

As I alighted at the communications "office" (it was a hut buried in the undergrowth), the driver assured me I would get used to the chaos. "Just remember," he said. "If you can hear 'em, you're OK." I wanted to ask how he knew when to bail out of the Jeep, but I was still too stunned to speak much. The sergeants both saluted me and wished me luck. I did not see either of them again. I have often wondered if they survived Bataan.

The next four days were rather like the forty-minute drive in from the beach. I was constantly jumping at events that left the regulars on Bataan unmoved. And when I wasn't startled by nearby shelling, I was appalled by the conditions in which the men were fighting. The troops had been receiving fewer rations than we noncombatants in the Tunnel, which to me was unimaginable. They were fighting a war on less than a thousand calories a day. Earlier in the year the cooks had killed all their pack horses and mules to add protein to their meals, but that meat had already been eaten.[1] Almost everyone complained of the "trots"—dysentery—and yet they continued fighting, for most men did not consider a mild case of dysentery a reason to quit the field. As a result, the front lines were an open toilet and smelled of it. The mats they slept on were crawling with lice and fleas, and there was no water for bathing.

Most chilling of all was the lack of medical facilities and supplies. A "hospital" was usually a row of beds under a canopy of trees; the doctors operated in small, impossibly unsanitary huts. There was no morphine for men who had just lost an eye, an arm, or a leg, and little disinfectant to sterilize wounds, leaving wounded men to develop gangrene in the steaming jungle. There were few medicines to help fight malaria and none to combat dengue fever, and no insecticides to control the millions of hungry mosquitoes carrying the diseases. Bataan was a foul, chaotic mess. Only the nights were relatively peaceful there, when I slept as best I could under my mosquito bar in the foxhole I had dug. By day I performed basic communications tasks—operating a radio and doing simple field enciphering and decoding. And all the time I was uneasy as I witnessed the slow defeat of an army, a damned good army, but one that had been doomed ever since the Japanese cut off U.S. supply lines to the Pacific.

After four days there in that steaming hell, I returned to Corregidor depressed and shaken. I was a Tunnel Rat, I reflected with mingled shame and relief, and went back to my tasks as a cryptographer, three miles distant from exploding shells, crippling malaria, and slow starvation.

As March came to an end, the situation on Bataan became intolerable. The Japanese had received fresh troops, more guns, and additional air power in March, and with this new strength, they were finally defeating the starving army that opposed them. There were so many high explosives dropped on the jungle that the damp undergrowth finally caught fire. The troops, who now had no place to hide and no defense against the aircraft and burning jungle, were backed up on the beaches, caught between water and fire. The death rate was abominably high, the casualty rate much higher. There were no alternatives left for the forces on Bataan.

Shortly after midnight on 9 April 1942, the army blew up its ammunition stores. A few hours later, over 76,000 men—11,500 Americans and 65,000 Filipinos—stood behind white flags and waited for the Japanese to take them prisoner.[2]

Maj. Gen. Edward King ordered the surrender of the troops on Bataan in hopes of saving thousands of lives. But the chaotic violence of Bataan just grew worse after the surrender. The Japanese suddenly had a big problem on their hands: how to deal with their 76,000 prisoners of war so they could begin their assault on Corregidor. For the forces on Corregidor had not surrendered with King's troops, which infuriated the Japanese military. The Japanese could not afford to lose time and precious momentum after their victory on Bataan—they had already lost too much momentum because of the stubborn American and Filipino stand in the Philippines. They wanted to move posthaste into the positions that the U.S. defenders had held. To do this, they first had to remove the very real obstacle of those 76,000 POWs. The Japanese military performed this feat by marching the American and Filipino troops out of the peninsula; as they forced our troops along the fifty-five-mile route, the Japanese army committed some of the most atrocious acts of World War II.

I learned much later that the Geneva Convention was a controversial issue for the Japanese. Prompted by the events of World War I, representatives from forty-seven nations met in Geneva, Switzerland, in 1929 to agree as to how prisoners of war would be treated. The Japanese delegate to the conference signed what has become known as the Geneva Convention Relative to the Treatment of Prisoners of War, but the Japanese government never ratified the document.[3] As we would discover, Japan had an altogether different attitude toward POWs than did other nations represented at the conference. Prisoners of war didn't really exist in their definition of military activity; a good soldier by Japanese standards either won the battle, died trying, or committed suicide before being taken prisoner. They believed that a prisoner of war was a coward, and many Japanese soldiers felt they had the right to treat him as such.

The Japanese military apparently had no respect for ailing soldiers, either, for they turned out the sick and wounded from the hospitals on Bataan and forced them to join their healthier comrades in the march. Many of the former patients died within sight of the hospital, while others died in the following days. Few former hospital inmates survived the movement of men from Bataan Peninsula to Camp O'Donnell, the first POW camp in the Philippines.

The movement of prisoners was in a single direction—out of the peninsula to the town of San Fernando, a distance of more than fifty-five miles. Trucks were supposed to help transport the prisoners, but only a few were provided. The vast majority of the men, whether wounded, sick, malnourished, or simply exhausted, began a long trek that has since become known as the Bataan Death March. I did not experience or witness the march, and my description reflects only what I heard and read later from survivors of that week's ordeal.

The prisoners were first lined up and searched. Japanese guards took whatever valuables the POWs had, and many prisoners who had had the forethought to grab a blanket or a mat were relieved of them along with their mosquito bars and any food. Most men walked empty-handed and bare-headed under the hot sun with perhaps only a canteen or mess kit attached to their belts. The Japanese gave little food or fresh water to their prisoners, partly because there were far more prisoners than the Japanese had expected. They had expected to take ten thousand POWs, not seventy-six thousand.[4] But even when the POWs had access to water, often their Japanese guards refused to allow them to fill their canteens or get a drink.

The prisoners quickly discovered why the Japanese were such an efficient and well-organized fighting force. Japanese soldiers were literally whipped into form via a strict military discipline. To enforce their authority, each rank held unquestionable power over the lesser ranks. Captains had the right to strike lieutenants and all enlisted men; the lieutenants could pommel any enlisted man; a sergeant might beat on a corporal, and so on. As prison guards were usually of the lowest ranks, they were the most bullied. Many of them were looking for a victim they themselves could beat on. They found their victims in their prisoners of war.

This authority system, combined with the Japanese notion of honor, was particularly unfortunate for the POWs. Honor was the magic word to the Japanese military man: if anyone insulted his honor, it was his duty to retaliate. And during the Bataan Death March just about any action by a POW could be construed as dishonorable. If a POW looked at a guard, he might be hit. Asking for water or food could be deadly, as a Japanese soldier might interpret such a request as an insult to his honor and act accordingly. Any prisoner who fell behind because of disease, wounds, fatigue, starvation, or heat prostration was risking his life in doing so, for Japanese soldiers might kick him, bayonet him, or simply shoot him. Men who were given no water under the hot sun had no choice but to drink from fetid ditches, some of which were contaminated by the corpses of prisoners who had already succumbed to disease or dehydration or who had been murdered by a guard. The "honorable" guards had the guns, and they acted with practical impunity.

I later heard from survivors of the march that they watched as comrades were forced to dig shallow trenches in the hot sun and then were beheaded while they stood in them. Others were forced to eat or lie in their own excrement as punishment for having dysentery, while still others were shot and their bodies left in the road to be run over by trucks and trampled by delirious prisoners and resentful guards. Perhaps the taste of blood or the smell of it can stir up a hunger for more blood. This is what it did to the Japanese army on Bataan.[5]

Some prisoners received help from Filipino civilians who risked beatings and death to offer food and water to the struggling men. Other acts of heroism occurred. POWs who saw what was happening to the ill prisoners helped them, which usually meant they had to drag them along, for few in that ragtag group were strong enough to carry another man.

The Death March lasted about a week. Those who survived it arrived in San Fernando, a town that sits in the entryway to Bataan Peninsula. Once there, the prisoners were loaded onto boxcars that were meant to carry at maximum forty men; twice that many and more were packed into each car, and each train door was slammed shut and locked on the outside for the slow thirty-mile trip to the town of Capas. Once at Capas, those who survived the stifling train ride—and some did not—marched the final seven miles to O'Donnell. Of the roughly seventy-six thousand Filipinos and Americans who began the march, thousands died. No one knows the exact number of dead because no one knows exactly how many surrendered at Bataan, but it is certain that many did not make it to San Fernando.[6]

As the Death March was taking place, the Japanese proceeded to regroup and prepare for their assault on the last U.S. bastion in Manila Bay. They set up their guns with an efficiency of purpose—150 Japanese batteries were soon aimed at Corregidor. The shelling began just after the surrender on Bataan, and for the next four weeks it continued, night and day. Japanese planes based at Manila and Cavite bombed the island several times a day, not just at noontime. One of their goals was to strip the island of all remaining vegetation so U.S. gun placements would be revealed; this they did in a matter of days. Outside Malinta Tunnel our exposed troops dug in, tossing back shells as they could, but the Japanese had a tremendous advantage: there was no foliage to hide the U.S. guns anymore, and the Japanese above us in the Mariveles Mountains could look down into the weapons pits of Corregidor. Our gun batteries were blown to pieces, one by one.[7]

Wainwright still left the Tunnel every day to join the men at the fortifications and gun batteries up on Middleside and Topside, but it was not to build up morale anymore. Hope had long since died. He spent time with

the troops every day as a demonstration of his solidarity with them. Few
spoke of it, but a sense of the inevitable was in the air: we too would soon
fall the way of Bataan. Washington's expectations and MacArthur's orders,
all given from a safe distance, did not matter anymore—we could not possibly continue until July.

As APRIL CAME to an end, I became frantic about Virginia. We hoped that
she, as a civilian and a woman, would fare better under the Japanese, but
both of us wanted to get her out of the Philippines if possible. We had
agreed that the safest way for her to leave was on a submarine, so every time
I heard of one coming in, I tried to get her aboard. But there were always
people with higher priority who were allowed to board first. By the end of
April, Corregidor shook with constant bombings and shellings, and Virginia
was still in the Tunnel. About this time, MacArthur sent a message that two
navy PBYs were being sent to pick up a specialist on Japanese language and
military strategy whom he had had to leave behind when he left Corregidor.
I got permission for Virginia to leave on one of those planes. On 30 April
she collected her few belongings and we went together to the pier on the far
side of the island. Several motorboats were waiting to take the group to the
PBYs that rested on the dark water out of reach of the shells.

Our goodbye was brief. There was little to say and no way to express our
thoughts and fears—neither of us tried. We simply clung to one another in
the twilight for a few moments. Up until then we had been afforded some
meager relief in knowing each other's whereabouts and affairs in the Tunnel.
Now we would no longer have that. After a few moments we released each
other and I helped her into the boat. The motors churned to life and the
crafts began to slide away from the dock. Once free, they turned to the open
sea. A last wave and Virginia was gone.

The PBYs made it to Mindanao, the southernmost Philippine island.
But when they tried to take off the next night, the plane Virginia was on had
mechanical problems and was left behind. The passengers took refuge at a
hidden airfield at Malaybalay where they waited for another transport to
Australia. The last message I received concerning her was that a daredevil
American pilot, Col. Denny Gunn, was flying in to pick them up. I could
only hope he would succeed; I was powerless to do much else. I tried not to
think often of Virginia, for such thoughts only led to worry and fear, and I

had seen what that had done to so many in the Tunnel. But I wasn't very successful at keeping her from my mind.

The twenty-ninth of April was the Japanese emperor's birthday, and the Japanese celebrated by bombing the hell out of Corregidor. The entire mountain shook—several times that interminable day I suspected that it was no longer the Japanese who were responsible for the Rock's shaking and deafening roar, but the very earth itself. Such fury, I thought, could only be the earth's anger—we had to be in the throes of an unending earthquake. I was certain it could get no worse than this. I was wrong.

The first week of May became a suspended time in our lives during which we awaited the inevitable. On 4 May the Japanese struck the island hard again, with a fury that spelled the end for us. Sixteen thousand shells exploded on Corregidor that day.[8] The Tunnel was more packed than ever. The generators that powered the fans inside the Tunnel were only on sporadically because the shells kept knocking out the power, which left the air a foul, visible vapor of smoke and sweat and dust and urine. In the last hour of 5 May, I threaded my way past people of all sizes and ranks, civilians and soldiers alike, all of us Tunnel Rats, until I got to Wainwright's offices. Wainwright had sent for me.

Gen. Jonathan Wainwright, one of the most dedicated U.S. leaders this century has seen, was suffering. He had always been thin; his nickname was in fact "Skinny" Wainwright. Now, after months on the Rock, he was a scarecrow. It was not only the malnutrition that weakened him; it was the worry and responsibility of his command.

When I entered his office, he reached wearily for an envelope lying on his desk. "I have a message for you to encode, Frank." After saying that, he fell silent while gazing down at the envelope in his hand. We remained that way for several minutes before he finally cleared his throat. "Encode it and hold onto it—don't send it without my direct order. I'll tell you when to send it. When you're finished encoding it, bring back every draft. I want to have it all—every scrap. And nobody else is to see or hear of it."

I had a feeling I knew what it was.

Once back in my section, I opened the envelope and found what I expected: Wainwright's surrender message to Roosevelt. Wainwright was a realist and a compassionate man. He had no choice but to be the first general to surrender a U.S. army. We had heard by then of the Death March from

Filipino informants. We knew, as Wainwright did, that we could not expect compassion from the Japanese if we showed the white flag, but the carnage on Corregidor simply had to stop.

Wainwright's last communication with the States was poignant:

> With broken heart and head bowed in sadness but not in shame I report to Your Excellency that today I must arrange terms for the surrender of the fortified islands of Manila Bay. . . .
>
> There is a limit of human endurance and that limit has long since been past [sic]. Without prospect of relief I feel it is my duty to my country and to my gallant troops to end this useless effusion of blood and human sacrifice.
>
> If you agree, Mr. President, please say to the nation that my troops and I have accomplished all that is humanly possible and that we have upheld the best traditions of the United States and its Army.
>
> May God bless and preserve you and guide you and the nation in the effort to ultimate victory.
>
> With profound regret and with continued pride in my gallant troops I go to meet the Japanese commander. Good-by, Mr. President.[9]

I sat staring blankly into the crowded tunnel when I finished encoding the message. We had all known that we would soon fall the way of the British and the Dutch in Southeast Asia, but that calamity had always been in the future. I thought about what this meant for the U.S. forces in the Pacific and the country as a whole. I thought about Wainwright, the broken man who would soon meet with Lt. Gen. Masaharu Homma, the Japanese commander, and arrange our surrender. But mostly I wondered how this message would change my life and what it would be like to be a prisoner of war.

It was many minutes before I stood, wiped the tears from my eyes, and returned with all the drafts to Wainwright. It was just a few minutes after midnight, a new day.

Wainwright silently accepted the drafts and dismissed me, but I lingered. Because Wainwright was an approachable man, I asked him when he would release the message. His answer surprised me. "I don't know. Maybe never. I just may not have to send this message, Frank." He gazed at me defiantly. "Something may come through. I'm not sending anything until we're certain of something." Wainwright was hopeful to the end, even after he had composed his surrender message.

I left Wainwright's office without further comment. While I sympathized with the general, I had pressing practical matters to address. I had a responsibility to protect the security of our cryptographic devices. The machines in our department were some of the most technically advanced of the time; if the Japanese were to capture one of them, America's cryptographic security would be jeopardized. We in the crypto area were determined that this would not happen and had a plan to prevent their capture. But we needed time, and that last message had to be sent first.

As I walked back to our lateral, I passed the finance "office." I was surprised to find a number of enlisted men and lieutenants laughing and tossing bits of paper into the air. The bits of paper turned out to be shredded Filipino pesos. I discovered they were acting on a rumor then circulating in the Tunnel, one that the finance personnel apparently took seriously. According to just about everyone, the Japanese would kill on sight any enemy soldier with Filipino money on him and take the money.

The rumor made sense to us. If Japanese guards would kill a man for pausing to relieve himself while on the Death March, why wouldn't they kill enemy soldiers to get the Filipino money they carried? So that day the finance officer, Col. John Vance, had pulled out the stores of Filipino money and, with the help of some very willing aides, they were gleefully cutting and tearing up packs of hundred-peso notes and tossing the bits of paper toward the dark stone ceilings of the Tunnel. The shredded money cascaded down softly, settling on their shoulders and on the ground around their feet. By the time I arrived, the cut pesos were piled up ankle deep.

A lieutenant called to me as I stood there. "Come on, Captain, have some of the fun!" He tossed a wad of pesos at me. I hesitated, preoccupied with my responsibilities, then grinned and began to tear it up, peso by peso. I began to laugh. When I finished with that packet and had tossed the pieces toward the ceiling, I reached for another wad and a pair of scissors in order to work more efficiently. I was there for an hour or more, for we had some two million pesos to destroy that night.[10]

It was a delicious act of release, tearing up all that currency. Money represented a civilized world, and that world had deserted us. We in turn vindictively bade it a final adieu as we tossed those shreds of paper upward. Money, we all agreed, certainly wouldn't matter where we were going.

Or so we thought.

When I got back to my lateral, I saw a friend of mine who had come to deliver a message from his commanding officer to Wainwright's staff. Duck

—it was the only name I ever knew him by—spotted me in the communications lateral and walked toward me.

I was surprised and alarmed by his appearance. Happy-go-lucky Duck had looked robust and confident before the war began; now his face was thin and wan, his body emaciated. Duck was part of the artillery and had been on Corregidor's beaches for the last several days. I said hello and figured that would be the end of our encounter, as both of us were preoccupied. But as he started to leave, Duck turned back to me with an anguished look on his face. He obviously needed to talk to someone; I listened as he began to describe the battle outside.

Corregidor, Duck said, was a hellish, barren place where one sometimes couldn't tell day from night because of the smoke. But the smoke served a purpose. Since the foliage was gone, it was their only cover during the day. But now the Japanese were landing on the island, and they were fighting on the beaches. Duck lowered his voice then. "I saw dead bodies on the beaches after Bataan. They'd been gunned down by the Japs when they tried to swim over from Bataan." I remember his voice dropped to a whisper. "They're still washing up on shore. The water around them's red—dirt red. And now there's dead Americans and Japs all over the beaches." Tears were trickling down his dirty face. "Jesus. Jesus, Frank. Jesus Christ, it's so bad."

Duck began to weep openly then. I stood helplessly beside him while he wept. After a few minutes, as I tried to comfort him, he collected himself and wiped his eyes. Then he saluted me, his friend, said goodbye, and turned and moved away through the crowded Tunnel.

I never saw Duck again. He returned to fight on the beaches of Corregidor and was killed sometime before dawn, a mutual friend much later reported, when a shell hit his slit trench.

THE JAPANESE LANDED on Corregidor at Monkey Point about midnight that night. The first invasion troops suffered tremendous casualties at the hands of the marines and other U.S. troops protecting the point, but the Japanese kept coming in increasing numbers until the defense was broken and the Japanese wave pushed forward onto Corregidor. I heard the news of the landings about one-thirty in the morning from the terror-stricken crowd in the main lateral and became all the more concerned as I stood watching over the machines that two of the men were still using to decode messages.

Even though we were going under, I thought wryly, Washington and others still had things to say to us.

I wandered pensively through our area, fretting about those machines. It was dark still, but at daybreak the Japanese would probably be at the entrances of the Tunnel. I returned to Wainwright's office and asked for permission to release the message to the radio area. He refused. There just might be a chance, he said. I walked away, but returned an hour later. Wainwright still refused.

The Japanese were by then fighting their way up to the approaches of the Tunnel. About a half an hour later, I went to see Wainwright again. He had just finished talking to several of his aides when I appeared. He looked utterly exhausted and ill. He nodded at me. "Send it, Frank."

I hurried back through the crammed corridor and finished the final encoding of the message, then passed it on to the radio room while feeling a tremendous sense of relief mingled with deep melancholy. Until I passed it on, the message was only a duty to be fulfilled, a final task. Once it was off, the U.S. army in the Philippines had officially and fully surrendered.

It was by then about five in the morning. We didn't have much time, so we in the crypto section immediately went to work. Once the final message was sent, we grabbed as many heavy objects and sledge hammers as we could find to ensure the security of the devices. With a certain amount of gusto, we pulverized those encoders and decoders. We also destroyed several typewriters and adding machines to make the jigsaw puzzle all the more impossible to piece back together. We then gathered up the pieces into buckets and went in separate directions, scattering the cryptographic shards behind the concrete walls that stood in front of the stone sides of the tunnel.

After we finished destroying and scattering those machines, we had completed our responsibilities in the Signal Corps. We returned to our section and listened to the battle rage outside. It was by then about nine o'clock in the morning. We had all removed our handguns, not wanting to be caught with them and taken as a hostile prisoner. Men and women were openly crying in the corridors while slumped against the walls; others mumbled incoherently to themselves, while still others stood or sat silently.

The men in the communications area had not destroyed all of the transmitters; one was still intact. Sgt. Irving Strobing, a radio operator, decided to take advantage of the idle moments and the still-operating machine. No one objected to the content of the message; the Japanese could listen to the terse words and be damned. The message summed up the feelings of all of us at that point:

> We've got about fifty-five minutes and I feel sick at my stomach. I am really low down. They are around now smashing rifles. They bring in the wounded every minute. We will be waiting for you guys to help. . . .
>
> General Wainwright is a right guy and we are willing to go on for him, but shells were dropping all night, faster than hell. Damage terrific. Too much for guys to take. Enemy heavy cross-shelling and bombing. They have got us all around and from [the] skies. . . .
>
> Corregidor used to be a nice place, but it's haunted now. Withstood a terrific pounding.
>
> Just made broadcast to Manila to arrange meeting for surrender. . . . I can't say much. Can't think at all. I can hardly think. . . .
>
> The jig is up. Everyone is bawling like a baby. They are piling dead and wounded in our tunnel. Arm's weak from pounding [Morse code] key, long hours, no rest, short rations, tired.
>
> I know now how a mouse feels. Caught in a trap waiting for guys to come along and finish it up. . . .
>
> My name [is] Irving Strobing. Get this to my mother, Mrs. Minnie Strobing . . . Brooklyn, N.Y. . . . My love to Pa, Joe, Sue, Mac, Garry, Joy and Paul. Also to all family and friends. God bless 'em all. Hope they be there when I come home. Tell Joe, wherever he is, go give 'em hell for us. My love [to] you all. God bless you and keep you. Love. Sign my name and tell my mother how you heard from me.[11]

There was no answer to his message. Washington had not yet received news of our surrender and would not for several more hours as the news passed slowly from Honolulu to San Francisco to the capital. But it made little difference when they received the news. There was nothing they could do. Even if they had some consoling words for us, we had no way to receive them now. Our machines were destroyed; after Strobing was finished with it, we also destroyed the machine he had been using. Then all of us on Corregidor were off the air.

Late that morning white flags went up at all entrances to the Tunnel. General Wainwright left for his meeting with General Homma to negotiate our surrender. The hot sun climbed to the middle of the sky, and with it a Japanese tank rolled up to the Tunnel entrance next to the cryptographic section and pointed its impressive gun barrel down the lateral. We stared at it blankly, disoriented. Basic training had never taught us how to surrender, how to act the role of the vanquished. I remember vaguely saying to no one in particular that I hoped they wouldn't give us a demonstration of the tank's fire power. They didn't. But a few Japanese soldiers appeared with rifles pointed at us and took up positions next to the tank. We raised our hands above our heads and waited for the worst, but it didn't happen. They simply stood there, apparently awaiting further orders. After our initial fear of them wore off, most of us found a place to sit with our backs against the cold concrete walls and wait for whatever our conquerors planned to do next. It was their move. We were now their prisoners of war, and our country, to which we had sworn our allegiance, didn't even know we had surrendered.

It was the sixth of May 1942.

4. From the 92d Garage to Bilibid

T HOUGH WE WERE now prisoners of war, we didn't leave the Tunnel. The terms of surrender of the Philippine forces had to be agreed upon, and this took longer than anyone expected. Wainwright had played one last card before his meeting with Homma. When he saw that the fall of Corregidor was imminent, Wainwright sent messages to Gen. William Sharp in the south and Colonels John Horan and Guillermo Nakar in the north.[1] Wainwright released his command of the Southern Forces, which included Batangas in southern Luzon and the island of Mindanao, to Sharp, and relinquished command of northern Luzon and Baguio to the two colonels there. Sharp, Horan, and Nakar were to turn to MacArthur in Australia for further orders. Thus, all Wainwright had to surrender on 6 May was the small island of Corregidor.

When Homma fully understood that Wainwright no longer controlled all the forces in the Philippines, he was furious. Homma had not fought for so long simply to win several thousand more POWs; he had expected Wainwright to surrender all the islands to him. Homma refused to accept Wainwright's terms—he heatedly informed Wainwright that if Wainwright could not surrender all the U.S. forces in the Philippines, then we would all return to our guns and the fighting would continue until each and every island of the Philippines was under Japanese control.

Wainwright was finally beaten. He had no alternative but to accept Homma's terms; he could not allow the senseless slaughter of his troops to continue. He signed a full surrender document and then was taken to Manila to broadcast a surrender message to Horan and Nakar in the north. One of his aides, Col. Jesse Traywick, was sent south to tell Sharp to surrender all troops under his command to the Japanese.[2]

While the high command of both armies settled the details of our surrender, we of lesser rank had nothing to do. Defeat had seemed such a frightening fate before it happened, yet our surrender was innocuous and anticlimactic in those first days. Those of us who had been in the crowded Tunnel were still there, milling about, waiting for something to happen. Troops who had defended the beaches wandered about as we did. Our surrender seemed unreal, the dark quiet after a nightmare. We had seen little of the Japanese after their tank's first thrust into the Tunnel—our enemies had withdrawn to their own camps and waited, as we did, for their leaders to come to terms with the new turn of events.

Finally, on 8 May several Japanese officers entered our part of the Tunnel and issued orders to us in Japanese. We emerged from the Tunnel with our hands atop our heads and joined the troops outside. We were a subdued column as we marched down from the Tunnel, squinting our eyes against the bright sunlight while white flags fluttered in the breeze along the route. Corregidor was eerily quiet; after weeks of incessant bombardment, the stillness was unfamiliar. We saw dead bodies lying among the battle debris as we marched.

Joe and I walked side by side, and unlike the majority of the new prisoners of war, we weren't empty-handed. We didn't have any food, but we did have a change of clothes, a blanket, a mosquito bar, a half-tent, and other items in each of the large rucksacks we carried.

We marched out to the 92d Garage area, which would be our home for the next two weeks. By the time all of us were there, there were 12,000 POWs in the garage area; some 8,700 were American, the rest Filipino.[3] The area had been meant to house planes, not people, so there were no toilets and no kitchen. There was no shelter from the hot sun or rain, and the concrete pavement made miserable beds. The garage area was big enough to accommodate a large number of us, but nobody was comfortable. We did have access to clean water, though.

What was most curious about our first prison camp was the fact that the Japanese allowed us to wander around the area unhindered. This was at first a surprise, but we found that it made sense. There was no need to watch over unarmed POWs on a barren island that was surrounded by Japanese-held territory. So there were few guards among us. As we wandered on the beaches, Joe and I learned that some POWs were finding K-rations around the still-standing beach fortifications; the rations had been left when the Americans fled the Japanese. We began to look for them as well. The rations weren't very tasty, but given that our captors had not yet fed us, we thought ourselves lucky to have them.

While searching for K-rations one day, I came across some Japanese soldiers who were operating a large oven. I wondered what they were doing and drew closer; the soldiers noticed me, but ignored me. Around the mouth of the large oven was a platform on which two Japanese stood. Two other soldiers hauled a Japanese corpse from a cart and dragged it toward the oven. They handed it up to the soldiers above, who then unceremoniously shoved it into the oven. I noticed that the bodies had no right arms. At a smaller oven nearby, another detail of soldiers was at work cutting the right arms from corpses. They tossed the severed appendages into the smaller oven. From this oven, a soldier was scooping out portions of the ashes and indiscriminately dumping them into small wooden boxes, to which he attached some sort of metal tag—it served the same purpose, I suppose, as American dog tags. The box was then placed aside in a high pile of such boxes, which attested to the heavy losses the Japanese had suffered in the battle for Corregidor. Each of the men in the unit worked quickly and quietly, releasing the fallen warriors to ash and atmosphere without much visible reflection. They hadn't the time to be pensive over their dead; there were too many bodies to attend to.

Our captors began to feed us after we had been in the garage area for several days—we got small amounts of rice twice a day. Many of the new POWs were then put to work. Most cleaned up the battlefield—Joe and I participated in one of these details—while a few worked burial details, or rather cremation details. All the Japanese bodies had already been gathered up, but there were still fast-decaying Filipino and American corpses on the beaches four days after the last shots were fired.

The Japanese also had started taking down our names and serial numbers for their records. We were all assigned a number. Guards lined us up one day and painted our numbers on the backs of our shirts for quick identification. The numbering was arbitrary; we received it according to where we stood in line. I was number 1045.

Once the Japanese knew each prisoner's name, rank, and former duties, they began interrogating anyone they thought might have useful information. One of the matters they pursued was the location of the Philippine treasury. They wanted to lay their hands on the silver and gold ingots they believed had been dumped overboard into Manila Bay just before the U.S. forces on Corregidor surrendered. As Joe and I were Signal Corps officers, the Japanese thought we might have relayed a message to someone that designated the waterlogged location of the treasury. They had set up their headquarters and interrogation rooms in the Tunnel, and the two of us were called up there about the fifteenth of May.

We walked into our former home with a Japanese guard who marched us down to the hospital lateral, the only area in the Tunnel that had finished rooms and offices. There the Japanese had set up their operations. We came to a stop outside a room with a large glass window through which we could see what was going on inside. In the room, we recognized USAFFE's finance officer, Col. John Vance, seated in front of a large desk. With him were four Japanese, two of them officers. One of the officers, obviously the leader of the group, was deftly twirling a golf club in his hands. I wondered where he had found that; the Japanese must have been doing some foraging for themselves. The door was not closed, so we could hear the Japanese officer's words as he spoke to Vance; he was asking him a question in stilted but correct English. "Where is the Philippine treasury?"

Vance said he did not know.

The officer, upon hearing Vance's response, stopped twirling the club and brought it around in front of him. "You dropped it in the Manila Bay. You tell us where."

Vance shrugged. "Honestly, sir, I do not know. I'm not sure it's even in the bay."

The Japanese officer ordered Vance to stand. Vance stood.

His interrogator then blithely swung the golf club up into the air and slashed it across one of Vance's shins. Vance doubled over and cried out. His interrogator then stepped close to him and spat out several words in Japanese.

Vance stared straight ahead, not moving a muscle or shifting his smarting leg. He said nothing.

The Japanese officer spoke to his subordinates in rapid Japanese, then turned to Vance again and spoke calmly to him in English. "You do know where the treasury is. You must know. You are officer in charge of dollars. Where is it?"

Vance spoke carefully and slowly. "I do not know where it is, sir. No one ever told me where it was sent, sir." He still stared forward, not looking at his interrogators.

The Japanese officer lifted the club again to swing. This time he cracked the club down across Vance's other shin, paused a moment to let his victim register the pain, and then swung up to hit the first leg again.

The interrogation went on in this macabre manner for some time—the tightly controlled questioning and the same negative answers that brought the painful blows across Vance's shins and ankles. The Japanese officer seemed indifferent to his task. He never raised his voice or appeared angry; he might have been hitting a golf ball for all the emotion he displayed while beating the defenseless man in front of him. Vance never told them where the treasury was.

The interrogators obviously wanted an audience, for we watched the entire episode with our guard. We did not know if Vance knew where the treasury was. That was top secret information that only a few people would have access to. When they began with us, they would receive the same answer, for neither Joe nor I knew for certain what had become of the treasury. We had heard the rumors that it had been dumped in Manila Bay; I had even sent some grid coordinates to Washington, but I couldn't be sure they actually indicated the location of the treasury.

Finally, the club-wielding officer released Vance to a guard. Joe and I glanced at one another briefly as we watched Vance stumble out. We had already rehearsed our answers to any questions asked us by the Japanese, and we certainly weren't going to say anything about codes or grid coordinates. If we corroborated each other's stories, maybe our inquisitor would leave the golf club aside. As we were escorted into the room, our guard spoke respectfully to the club-wielding officer, then stepped back. The officer looked Joe and me over briefly; he seemed uninterested in us. He spoke to the other officer and then left the room. With relief, we watched him and his golf club exit the room. Joe was then ordered out into the corridor again, where he was to watch my interrogation, but the door was closed.

The remaining officer asked me in passable English as to my rank and duties.

I gave him my rank and serial number. "I was a clerk," I said. "I delivered messages."

"You worked with Colonel Vance?" the lieutenant asked.

"No."

"You worked with who?"

"I worked with MacArthur's aides and Wainwright's aides."

"What did you do?"

"I was in the Signal Corps. I delivered messages."

The officer scribbled something on a pad in front of him, then nodded. "You tell me where the Philippine treasury is?"

I said I didn't know where it was.

The Japanese officer looked tired. "It is in Manila Bay," he said. "You know that it is in Manila Bay."

"I heard that it was."

He nodded his head, exasperated. "Yes, yes. But where in Manila Bay?"

I shook my head. "I don't know."

My interrogator leaned forward and stared at me intently. "You are officer to deliver messages. Your army sent no message to Washington to tell where is the treasury?"

"No one told us what the messages said. It was against regulations to look. We'd be court-martialed if we did. None of us knew what the messages said."

We went through this basic set of questions two more times—the officer asked the same questions; I gave the same answers. After the third go-round, my interrogator sat silently for a moment, then spoke to one of his subordinates in Japanese. He then looked up at me and without rancor dismissed me. Joe was ordered in as I stepped out. Once outside the room, I leaned against the wall and thanked fortune that not every man in the Japanese army was as zealous in performing his duties as the officer with his golf club.

When Joe emerged later to say that his interrogation had gone as mine had, we felt a bit confident that the Japanese would leave us alone.

But they didn't, not right away. We were interrogated in the same manner for the next week or so. Our interrogators did treat us humanely—we never saw the golf club–wielding officer again. After the first two interrogations, our questioning sessions seemed like mere formalities that various lesser officers had to complete before they could release us to our fates as prisoners of war. No one seemed to think we had anything of value to say. We were happy enough to be thought unimportant—Joe and I had no firm idea where the treasury was, but we did know quite a bit about highly classified cryptographic methods, and we didn't want our self-control tested by any torture measures.

The tedious interrogations turned out to be fortuitous for us. While up at the Tunnel one day, we ran into Joe's wife, Phyllis. The Japanese had left U.S. medical personnel and ailing prisoners in the hospital lateral, so Phyllis, as a nurse, was still there. We met Phyllis as we waited with our guard in the hall for our second set of interrogations. When he first saw her, he wasn't concerned that we were talking to her.

After we all exchanged excited hellos, Joe and Phyllis stepped away from the guard and me, and there they whispered for a few minutes until Phyllis stood back warily as a Japanese officer approached. It was our interrogator, and with his approach, our Japanese guard became nervous. He glared at Phyllis.

"Will you be back here again?" she asked hurriedly.

"Maybe again tomorrow," said Joe.

"I'll try to meet you then," she whispered. She smiled at us and brushed Joe's hand lightly, then withdrew back into the hospital area.

The interrogator said nothing about Phyllis. He interviewed us separately again and then dismissed us.

The next day, sure enough, we were back at the Tunnel to repeat our stories. And just as she had promised, Phyllis met us before our interrogations. She had two bags that she handed to us. Joe peeked inside one as we waited for our interrogator and then smiled. I took a look and saw a five-pound can of Spam and a carton of cigarettes. In the other bag were several bottles of vitamin pills and quinine tablets. Phyllis didn't have time to tell us where she had found the treasures, and I still wonder how she managed to get those goods for us.

After Phyllis stepped away from Joe and started down the dimly lit lateral, she stopped about ten paces away and gazed silently back at her husband. Then she waved her hand, turned, and walked quickly away, back to her own prison. Joe said nothing, but there were tears in his eyes as we walked away with our guard.

That day was our last interrogation. We returned to the garage area with our two precious bags of goods tightly clasped in our arms. We kept them with us constantly; we used the two lumpy bags as pillows at night to protect them from hungry hands. We refrained from opening the Spam just then, as we had several packs of K-rations left. We both agreed we might need the protein more later; wherever we were going likely would not have K-rations sprinkled across a beach that we could roam freely.

The next day, 23 May, three Japanese transport steamers arrived at Corregidor to move us off the island.[4] There were twelve thousand of us in the 92d Garage area, but the Japanese were determined to move us to Manila in one trip, so they squeezed all of us onto the three ships. The ships, we immediately found, were old freighters that reeked of urine and rotting wood; we wondered whether they had once hauled animals. We were first taken by small launches out to the ships, then led to a small opening on the deck and forced one by one down a rope ladder to the dark, damp hold. As there were four thousand men per ship, loading took all day. Joe and I were among the first to load, which we both regretted—it would have been far better to be out in the bright sunlight and clean air than in that dismal place. There was nothing to do but sit against the wall and watch the small area fill up. By the time the boarding was finished, there was barely enough room to sit, let alone lie down. There were no toilets of any kind. We prisoners designated a latrine area in one corner, which, with the crowded conditions and dysentery, added to the already overpowering stench of the ship. When the sun went down, the Japanese slammed the small door above shut, and we were locked within the dark hold with only a few portholes to admit the fading light and some fresh air.

There was no leaving the spot Joe and I had staked out, for if we did, we would lose it—we also might lose some of our precious gear. So we sat in the same place until after dark, sometimes talking, but mostly just sitting silently in the uncomfortable gloom, waiting for the ship to move. Some men smoked, others played cards with the aid of a torch, more than a few cried aloud. The ship did not move that night—the Japanese apparently decided we would stay put until daylight. They did not worry themselves with the fact that a night in that crowded, hot, and stinking hold would be torturous. We were given no food or water. Sleeping was almost out of the question —with the foul atmosphere and constant jostling of some 3,999 other human beings, only short, uncomfortable naps were possible.

It was a restive mass of bodies that welcomed the light of dawn and the ship's first stirrings the next morning. When we finally were free of the docks of Corregidor, there were shouts of relief. The trip to Manila took several hours; although it is not far from Corregidor, the transports were agonizingly slow. We sailed into Manila Bay about midday and then were loaded onto landing barges that pulled us in about a hundred feet from shore. From there, we were ordered to jump into the water and wade in. This was not an unattractive thought; we were all dirty and hot and the idea of jumping in the water was a refreshing one after being in the hold of that stuffy transport ship for twenty-four hours. But Joe and I had something to consider that the majority of the prisoners did not: we had our cumbersome rucksacks to take with us, along with our small bags containing our treasures from Phyllis.

When it came my turn to jump in the water, I immediately found that our worries about our packs were completely justified. The saturated bag tipped me over on my back and left me without any footing in the shoulder-deep water. While the men around me headed for shore, I could only wriggle about like a bug on its back in a puddle. The same thing happened to Joe. We must have presented quite a spectacle for all who cared to watch.

I finally got my feet under me and began the trek toward shore with that heavy pack, cursing it and everything in it. Some time later, I dragged myself up on dry ground. My pack had weighed forty pounds or so before my dip; now it weighed at least twice that. We were all exhausted after wading in, but the guards did not allow anyone to recuperate. I was able to linger long enough so Joe could catch up with me, then the two of us had to fall in behind the other prisoners.

Most of the POWs around us wore their only possessions: slacks, boots, and light shirts—some even wore shorts and no shirt. They carried nothing in their hands or on their backs; their only belongings were the empty mess kits attached to their belts. Some of them preferred traveling that lightly, others had simply not had time to grab any belongings before the Japanese marched us out to the 92d Garage area. While Joe and I marched, we considered dumping our packs. But in the end we held onto them. Neither Joe nor I had any faith in the Japanese commitment to fairness toward enemy prisoners. We figured our packs served as insurance policies of sorts.

While marching along those first few blocks, a rumor circulated through our ranks. "Don't fall out; keep marching no matter what." The guards were said to have just bayoneted a man to death for stopping for a rest. I hoped this was mere scuttlebutt, because my pack was heavy and I was already feeling exhausted. But I kept moving.

The sidewalks through the city were lined with Filipinos. The Japanese wanted to make certain we had an audience to march by on that hot, muggy day, so they had ordered the Filipino civilians out of their homes to watch the defeated defenders of the Philippines. The Filipinos stared at us in despair. Some wailed openly; others only stood silently, with tears shining in their eyes or slipping down their faces. Many of them tried to give us food —they ran to us, offering rice patties or fruit. The guards yelled and struck at adults who tried to give us anything. They were less likely to hit a child, so the Filipinos sent their children scurrying among us, handing us food.

This generosity on the part of the Filipinos for the U.S. POWs confused and infuriated the new conquerors of the islands. They could not understand why an Asian people would show sympathy to this alien Western power. The Japanese military was trying to belittle the U.S. forces, and the Filipinos only cried out in anguish to us. The United States had also been an imperial power in the Philippines, but a working relationship had been fashioned before the war that was better than the Spanish had given them and better than what the Japanese were currently offering. And the Japanese were responsible for the bombings that had so badly damaged Manila. It was this that prompted Filipinos to help their former overlords. They also felt compassion for us as we marched in the hot sun. All of us were tired and hungry; many of us, sick. Some of those who watched us march were looking for loved ones among the Filipino POWs. Women approached Joe and me in our officers' uniforms to ask if we had seen a son, a nephew, a husband. We could only shake our heads.

By the time we reached downtown Manila, we were an exhausted mass of prisoners, for the afternoon heat was setting in. We were dry by then, which made my pack easier to carry, but the heat was now evaporating all my meager energy stores. A division of the Japanese cavalry guarded us and set the pace—that pace was too fast for me. I started to stumble as we rounded the corner by the Bayview Hotel where I had complacently sipped a smooth drink some six months before, convinced that the U.S. armed forces had nothing to worry about in the Japanese. We marched on past that memory, past the Luneta Park area, the Walled City, and the colossal national post office building, and then approached the Santa Cruz bridge that spans the Pasig River. A long hill leads up to the bridge, and it was at that point that I could march no more. I had started with too heavy a load and was not in the same shape as the GIs who had been getting the exercise of fighting a war for five months. Though they were half-starved also, their bodies were more fit than mine.

I tripped once and recovered, only to stumble again under the weight of my bags. I finally collapsed amid confused thoughts and warnings from those around me of the cruelty that I could expect from our Japanese guards if I did not continue. But I could go no further. I dropped out of the line at the side of the road and sank down slowly until I was lying with my cheek against a hot metal grating that covered the gutter. A putrid smell assailed my nostrils, but I no longer cared. Come a bayonet or a beating, I had to rest after marching some four miles in the heat with that heavy pack.

Fortunately, the guards around me were not feeling as rushed or vindictive as the guards had after the surrender on Bataan, and I also had help. A Filipino policeman hurried over to me when he saw me collapse and leaned over me protectively. "Don't move," he whispered. "Be quiet and don't move."

The policeman had little reason to worry about that.

A Japanese guard rode up on horseback. He yelled something down at us that neither of us understood. The guard yelled again, repeating a word that he had used in his last sentence, "bango." My Filipino friend apparently recognized that word, for he told me to roll over and show the guard the number that had been painted on my shirt. The soldier nodded and wrote down my number, then rode away. The policeman remained with me, standing over me like a sentinel.

After I had been lying there for about five minutes, a truck rolled up and four Japanese soldiers leaped out. Two of them grabbed me and with the help of the policeman lifted me into the truck. I noted that the other two Japanese were wearing green armbands. They were carrying cameras and were busy taking pictures of me and my compassionate Japanese captors to present to the folks back home in Japan. The green armbands, I later understood, identified this unit as part of the Japanese propaganda corps. I did not smile for the photos.

I still felt miserable as I bounced around in the back of that truck, but at least I was not marching under the hot sun anymore. The truck moved slowly alongside the troops, stopping every few minutes to pick up another fatigued or ill prisoner. Every time, the four Japanese would jump out, two to help the prisoner in and two to photograph the sympathetic act. It was a slow process, with delays at each step. One pickup yielded a particularly gruesome prisoner. He was so torn up that the photographers did not photograph his rescue, for his pitiable condition would not portray our captors favorably. Since he was not a model, they threw him into the truck bodily, with no concern for his already damaged person. His face was a bloody mess and he was covered with grime. As they tossed him in, I noticed that he was an officer, carrying a heavy pack. He was out cold.

I crawled over to him and turned him on his back. Although his face was covered with blood, I recognized Joe Iacobucci. He had apparently fainted while marching and had keeled over headfirst with nothing to break his fall, thus his torn and bleeding face. An alarming thought struck me, and I began searching among Joe's belongings, only to confirm my fear. His overnight bag, with its precious five-pound can of Spam and carton of cigarettes, was gone.

I would like to say that my only concern at that point was for Joe and his weak and bleeding body, but I cannot. I thought instead of the Spam and cigarettes that I had last seen on his back before I collapsed. I pulled out my handkerchief and canteen, wet it and mopped up his face as best I could. I gave him a drink of water and brought him to after a few minutes. My first question had nothing to do with his health.

"Joe, where is it? Your overnight bag? The Spam?"

Joe looked at me confusedly. When he finally remembered what had happened to him and understood my question, his face seemed to grow pale. He didn't speak for a minute, then swallowed hard.

"I gave it to a GI," he mumbled hoarsely.

A wave of fury overcame me. "You gave it to a GI?" I yelled, grabbing him by the shirt. "You gave it to one of those GIs?! You didn't get it back? We'll never see it again!" Joe winced and turned his head away from me. I released him and continued shouting. Of course I wasn't fair. Joe hadn't known he was going to collapse and certainly had had no time to grab his bag back before falling on his face. But it didn't matter that it wasn't his fault. That precious can of Spam that would have yielded at least ten dinners was in the hands of a hungry GI.

I leaned back against the wall of that bouncing truck, furious and beaten, disgusted with myself, with Joe, and with the whole atrocity that the war represented. I was yelling at my dearest companion, without whom I would have been desperately alone, over a can of processed meat. The vitamins were valuable, yes, but the Spam!—all that protein, and it was probably being devoured that very minute by a couple of half-starved GIs as they marched. And I couldn't blame them. I would have done the same.

I kicked myself, managed to refrain from kicking Joe, and closed my eyes. It was hot. It was humid. I was hungry. The Spam was lost and there was nothing to be done about it. We had lost the Philippines, and there was nothing to be done about that, either. It seemed that ever since the attack on Pearl Harbor, we had been doomed and powerless. I allowed my head to bounce where it would against the truck wall.

The truck came to a final stop before long and we were told to walk the remaining distance. Joe and I climbed out with our heavy packs and began to march again. We eventually entered the gates of Bilibid Prison, which had been built by the Spanish a century before.

It was our latest in a series of ill-suited homes.

5. Cabanatuan

W HEN WE REACHED Bilibid and had recovered enough from the march to move again, Joe and I went in search of our precious overnight bag. We walked through Bilibid countless times, questioning every enlisted man who looked familiar to Joe. But it was useless. We gave up when we realized how ridiculous our question sounded: "Have you seen a GI with a five-pound can of Spam and a carton of cigarettes that belong to us?" We had to face the fact that our treasure was gone.

The loss of that Spam was one of the most depressing events of the entire war for me. It had been a connection with Phyllis and the outside world, and it represented our ability to cope, our ingenuity in the face of hardship. Most important, it was five protein-packed dinners apiece. And we lost it. Joe and I never talked about our lost Spam after our futile search for it; it was too discouraging.

There was one fortuitous event that first day in Manila, though. Soon after our arrival, a GI who had worked with us in the Tunnel found me and asked me if I had any money.

I remember I winced at his question. "Don't talk to me of money. I was one of the idiots who tore up thousands of pesos before we surrendered." In the 92d Garage area, we had learned that pesos were a valuable means of exchange, second only to cigarettes or food itself, and that the guards did not habitually shoot POWs with money on them. They would often steal any pesos they found on a POW, but there were twelve thousand of us and only a handful of them; they couldn't search everyone.

My companion hooted aloud at my answer. "You believed that story? Captain, Vance and them just made that story up to keep guys like me away from the money stores." A devious look passed over his face. "But it didn't work. And I've got even more now. I won some in a poker game on the ship last night." He dug into a pocket of his pack and pulled out a wad of bills that we later found to contain over two hundred pesos. "Here," he said, handing it to me. "Take this. And don't believe all the scuttlebutt you hear from now on, sir."

I stared at the money, dumbfounded. "But what about you? Have you got enough? We could be prisoners for a long time."

He grinned again. "Captain," he said, dropping his voice, "if you knew how much money I have in this pack," he patted his bag lovingly, "you'd say I'm selfish for not giving you more." He laughed quietly, then raised his voice. "You find me after the war and pay me back if you want."

I am eternally grateful to that GI for giving us that money—it helped keep us alive in the coming months. I gave half the wad to Joe, stuffed the other half into my own pocket and felt like a rich man for several days.

In some ways Bilibid was a decent POW camp. We had drinking water, showers, and flush toilets, and we received a thin rice soup three times a day. But there were simply too many of us there. The prison had been built for several hundred criminals, not thousands of POWs. We had to be moved, so in late May, our captors began moving groups of us out of Bilibid.

First we were separated from the Filipino POWs. I learned later that many of them were released by the Japanese, who thought that as Asians, the Filipino soldiers would take their side. (The Japanese were wrong; many Filipino soldiers joined guerrilla movements against them.) Once separated, the U.S. POWs were sent to several different camps on the island. Joe, Pfaff, James, and I were among a large group assigned to the camps being set up at Cabanatuan, a small town about ninety miles north of Manila. It was too far to reach by foot, so we were to go by train. (The Japanese had taken over the Philippine rail system by then.)

On 2 June Japanese guards marched our group of two thousand POWs out of Bilibid and led us to Manila's train station. From there we were loaded into boxcars, barren affairs without seats, lights, running water, toilets, or any other amenities. Animals might have been transported comfortably in such crates, if they had been given food and water; we were given neither. And no compassionate human would ever pack as many animals into a train as our guards did their POWs that day. Most of us had no choice but to stand during the entire trip to Cabanatuan, which took some ten hours. Those who were sick or wounded suffered the crowded conditions with the rest of us. Healthier prisoners made room for the ill so they could sit, but we had no latrines in which to relieve ourselves and soon the boxcars were permeated with a nauseating, diseased odor as sick men defecated or vomited where they were. The tropical sun soon transformed those crowded and unventilated boxcars into a sort of mobile sauna, but we could not exit to cool down, and we ached for water. When we filed out of the train after arriving in Cabanatuan, we discovered several corpses among us. Those men had died where they stood, their lifeless bodies supported by the men tightly packed around them. Most of the dead seemed to have died of their various ailments, but at least one in our car appeared to have actually suffocated.

We arrived in Cabanatuan as night fell, but our journey wasn't over; we were to march to the prison camp, some five miles distant. It was raining fiercely as we started walking and showed no signs of stopping. At first, the march in the storm was a relief. Though we were all quickly soaked to the bone, at least we had room to move and fresh air to breathe. But soon the walking was difficult—the dirt road had become a mire of mud. Many sick prisoners collapsed and simply could not stand up again. Their weak but healthier buddies helped them along. After what seemed like hours of this slow march, our guards called a halt as we passed a school building. They instructed us in broken English to find shelter, then slipped off to do the same.

A hopeful POW tried the door of the school to see if we could escape the downpour, but it was locked and there were no other structures in sight. Prisoners meandered in different directions, searching for a relatively dry place to sit out the storm. Joe and I, along with probably a hundred others, crept underneath the school building itself. It was built on planks about three feet off the ground—the heavy tempests of the tropics made flooding common. Joe and I put up our half-tents under there and stayed relatively dry, though water trickled underneath us.

Morning brought an end to the rain, which meant we would have to walk under a hot sun again. We were herded into line with no breakfast. Joe and I had eaten no dinner or lunch the day before—our last meal had been some rice soup the previous morning. We learned there had been a large pot of rice for the POWs the night before, but many of us had not known of it, and its contents were long gone by morning. So we marched along on empty stomachs for about three hours until we finally arrived at Cabanatuan Prison Camp Number One.

We were not the first prisoners to arrive. Many survivors of the Bataan Death March had recently been transferred there from O'Donnell Prison Camp. They were a frightfully thin bunch, pale and weak—they had been POWs only a month longer than we, yet they looked as if they had been imprisoned for years. They told us the camps had been a training area for the Filipino army and said there were two other camps down the road, each full of U.S. POWs, and called, appropriately enough, Cabanatuan Camp Two and Camp Three. With the thousands of prisoners already there, we totaled nine thousand POWs at Cabanatuan Number One.

In Camp One, Lt. Col. Shigeji Mori, the Japanese commander, segregated us by rank: the captains, the lieutenants, and the enlisted men.[1] The Japanese believed that splitting us up would help foster discord among the POWs and stratify us into groups, the officers versus the enlisted men. They did not want us to become unified as one set of Americans who shared a common enemy in the Japanese.

There were about ninety captains in the camp. For the first month, we were housed in the regimental headquarters building, which, like all the other buildings, was made of *siwali*—a woven reed found in the Philippines. The building had hardwood floors, a real expense in the camp, but the luxury proved our misfortune—sleeping on those hard floors was like dozing on concrete. The packs that Joe and I had been lugging from camp to camp proved well worth our efforts—we at least had improvised bed rolls in our tarps, something many others in our section did not have. Still, we were happy to transfer out of the headquarters to an actual barracks four weeks later.

We learned in those first few weeks what the Japanese term *Bushido* meant for their POWs. Bushido is an ancient Japanese concept, one that is integral to their social hierarchy. The word translates roughly as "code of the warrior"; that code requires unquestioning obedience and loyalty of the soldier, and it also requires that he be ever attentive to his honor. For the Japanese, war was a sacred event, one performed honorably and religiously for their emperor, who was believed to be descended from the gods. During World War II, Japanese military leaders used this traditional war concept to hone their army. Their troops learned that according to Bushido, surrender was not an option. If not victorious, a warrior was to die in battle and should attempt to kill as many of the enemy as he could while dying; to surrender in order to preserve one's life, even when presented with unsurmountable odds, was dishonorable, cowardly, and unconscionable.

Our captors considered us cowards. And there was nothing worse than for an honorable Japanese warrior to be insulted by a cowardly POW. So any prisoner who appeared to slight a guard was punished severely for it. Downcast eyes when one should be staring straight ahead was enough to draw a kick or a slap. Gazing straight ahead when one should be bowing could also provoke a blow, as could an answer without the requisite "honorable sir" attached to it. Our guards who spoke English told us that we were inferior, a loathsome mass of failures who didn't deserve to live, and that as a fighting force we had been negligible at best. They told us that the Allied soldiers who weren't their prisoners were losing on all fronts. We learned how to bow, to ignore insults, to respond promptly and impassively whenever addressed by a guard, no matter how abusively. We were forced to salute the Japanese flag that flew over camp, and we did. But we loathed that flag —someone somewhere nicknamed it "the flaming asshole" because of its bright red center circle, and the name stuck. With that nickname, the mandatory salutes were bearable, for our respectful public gestures were private obscenities, expressions of our hatred of our captors.

The Cabanatuan camps were crowded, hot, and filthy. At Camp One, there were only several pipes that issued unpurified water for us to drink, which added to our digestive problems. There were no toilets, only ditches that prisoners dug for that purpose. The stench from these maggot-filled ditch-latrines was everywhere, and the air was thick with millions of flies and mosquitoes. If we wanted to bathe, we did so in the rain or by using the pipes with their pathetic trickle of water. Nobody was clean or healthy, and nobody slept well. Any virus was quickly an epidemic, and a cold could kill. Malaria or dengue fever wreaked havoc on many POWs because few had mosquito bars to protect them while they slept, and it was a given that we all had "the trots"—dysentery or acute diarrhea. Diphtheria was also a threat. And as we lived on a diet of rice and little more, we were all malnourished; some developed beriberi because of the lack of vitamins and minerals. The death rate was abominably high—dozens of men died each day in June.

The camp's "hospital" consisted of several thatched roof structures that were across the compound from the other buildings. Thousands of men were housed there. The hospital was, if possible, filthier than the rest of the camp. Our few prisoner-doctors did the best they could with what little supplies they had, but it was a losing battle. They could not even provide bedpans; prisoners defecated or vomited where they lay. The doctors had few medicines to offer the ailing—they were usually only able to diagnose the prisoners and then wait for them to get better on their own or die. Once in the hospital, a sick POW received half-rations, which further narrowed his chances of recovery. This reduction in food was on the order of the camp commander. Mori claimed that sick prisoners were not working and thus needed less food. As a result of all this, about one-third of the prisoners who were in the hospital that summer died there.[2]

Nestled among those hospital buildings was a notorious section that we called the Zero Ward. That number represented one's condition if taken there, as well as his chances of leaving the place on his feet. By the end of June some five hundred POWs had died in the Cabanatuan hospital; it was from the pathetic huts of the Zero Ward that most of the bodies were carried to the mass graves outside the camp every day.[3]

While I was there, Cabanatuan Camp Number One was neither fully fenced nor heavily guarded, and in the early days some men managed to escape into the surrounding countryside. The escapes were not immediately noticeable because Mori left roll call to us. He required the officers to account for the POWs twice a day, and we were in no hurry to report that someone had slipped away in the night. But the Japanese were aware of just how porous our camp's "walls" were, and about a month after our arrival, they acted to stop the escapes. They devised a scheme that would leave the work of camp security to us. They organized us into groups of ten and told us that if any one man out of a group escaped, the nine he left behind—men who had become his friends in those tight quarters—would all be executed.

The new system worked well. Before the plan was adopted, several men per week were slipping away at night into the dense trees around the camp, and from there they would perhaps join Filipino guerrilla bands who were fighting the Japanese or buy food and come back into the camp to sell it. Joe and I had considered attempting an escape before the grouping system was initiated, but we shelved it upon hearing of the new rule. There was too much at risk—we ourselves would be killed if caught, and the friends we left behind would be shot.

This banding into ten made each group fiercely dependent on one another, and very close, but at the same time we became suspicious of each other. We kept tabs on everyone in our group while repeatedly questioning and doubting each other. The general refrain in regard to escape was the same: "If you go, take me with you." No one went. His buddies watched him too closely, and the chances of ten men escaping undetected were not good. We stayed where we were.

At Cabanatuan, no guard was kind—they were the most abusive guards of any I encountered while a POW. Many prisoners were beaten; some men were beaten to death. And the verbal abuse was constant. Several of the guards were insane with hatred as they screamed insults while striking out at a hapless POW with their fists. We learned in those early days that the best way to survive a Japanese POW camp was by simple avoidance—a prisoner who never stepped close to a guard was one who wouldn't be beaten. We couldn't all avoid all of them, of course, but most of us tried to keep out of their reach. We also discovered that violence is rarely a cathartic outburst— it only begets more violence. This lesson our guards at Cabanatuan Camp Number One taught us well.

OUR MEALS CONSISTED primarily of a watery rice soup called *lugao;* this was sometimes mixed with a miso paste. We were rarely given vegetables. The Japanese had found that there were certain edible plants around the camp and added these weeds to our diet—they were our "greens." They ordered work details from among the enlisted prisoners to search the nearby fields every day for "weeds you can eat," as Mori referred to them. I have no idea what these plants were, but if mixed with miso, they went down easily enough. We received the weeds once a day, at our midday meal, along with the rice soup. The rice quickly became monotonous, so our cooks, who were also POWs, tried to add some variety to our lives in the way they cooked it. They discovered that the burned rice on the bottom of the large kettles was a chewy, more satisfying way to eat the grain than the mushy lugao that was dished out in the morning. So they scraped the pots each afternoon and gave a small hunk of the charred rice to each prisoner at dinner. Any nonworking prisoner received less food than the paltry amounts a working POW was given, so we officers (most of us didn't work at Cabanatuan) had less food than the enlisted men.

A black market sprang up among the POWs almost immediately after our surrender. American prisoners slipped out of the camp at night to meet Filipino contacts, or Filipinos slipped in to us, and they bartered for basic foodstuffs and cigarettes. Those who had money—and most of us had a few pesos—would "shop" at highly inflated prices. A can of evaporated milk went for 5 pesos, or about $2.50, which would be expensive now and was outrageous then. A can of beef cost about 10 pesos, or $5.00, and a carton of cigarettes had almost as much value as the silver ingots rumored to be at the bottom of Manila Bay.

Any nonsmoker was dealing from a point of strength in the POW camps. He could use his weekly allotment of cigarettes as a monetary unit (we usually received three cigarettes a week—these came from Red Cross packages and Filipino markets). Neither Joe nor I smoked, thus we were able to get more goods out of the black market. We supplemented our rice diet with our vitamins and would share a can of bully beef or evaporated milk twice a week. A trade system also sprang up in which a prisoner would promise a service to another for a few pesos or a cigarette. Such services included doing laundry, keeping watch over gear, taking over work details, and so on.

The Japanese were not happy with the black market activity and did their best to destroy it. They first announced they would kill anyone trading for products from outside the camp. They weren't bluffing. Several prisoners who had left camp one night for a supply run were caught by a Japanese patrol while meeting their contacts. The next day they were beaten and publicly berated for their actions. A detail of Japanese guards then raised their rifles and the POWs crumpled to the ground after a volley of shots. Hundreds of prisoners were witnesses to their murders—Commander Mori had in fact ordered us to watch. These deaths dried up the black market for a while, but it was back within weeks. With so many starving prisoners, there was too much need and too much potential for gain, and the trading continued.

Whenever cans of food came into camp, we immediately checked the backs of the labels. The Filipinos had set up an elaborate underground system through which they were able to convey word of outside events to us, and they sent news through on these labels. Messages intended for specific prisoners usually arrived on the back of labels of evaporated milk. If there was a message, we would pass it on, and through the camp grapevine, it would eventually reach the intended prisoner.

It was in this way that I learned that Virginia was still in the Philippines —she was in the civilian prison camp that had been set up at Santo Tomas. Santo Tomas had been a university that spread over several acres outside Manila. Because it had been a school, it was a nicer prison than Cabanatuan, but there were rumors that the Japanese were doing nothing for the American and European civilians there. The Filipinos were providing them with water and food. My message said that Virginia was healthy enough, but that the situation wasn't good, as many of them were suffering from the same diseases and malnutrition that afflicted us. We later learned that Joe's wife, Phyllis, was in Santo Tomas as well. Joe and I worried about our wives together for a few weeks until we realized the danger in that. There was no helping them from the Cabanatuan prison camp, and they could not help us. Worry only sapped precious energy.

Though the Japanese made the enlisted men work (searching for edible plants, preparing food, working burial details, or repairing battle damage), most of the officers were idle. Among us captains, there were several who felt a zealous urge to keep spirits up in the camp. They thought the officers should set an example for the enlisted men, thus they were constantly exhorting us to keep busy and somehow use our minds. Joe and I ridiculed the go-getters when we first encountered them, but their projects did help time go by, so after a while we joined some of their activities. For example, many of us had managed to bring a book or two with us, and with the go-getters' encouragement, we set up a small library. They also established a lecture series. They invited anyone who had any special knowledge to share it with the rest of us. These lectures took place as often as there were speakers. Of course, many of the lectures were lousy and poorly attended. Few prisoners were interested in hearing of, say, coin collecting or the nature of spiders, but one fellow, after a lecture or two, began to draw large audiences.

Captain Christensen had a particularly popular talk that was based on his knowledge of San Francisco—he had lived there before coming to the Philippines and had come to know the restaurants of the city like the back of his hand, or so he said. His lecture series, entitled "The Eating Establishments of San Francisco," was the most intriguing I've ever heard. Christensen had a descriptive flow of speech that made our mouths water as we listened to him; the man could paint pictures with his words and expressions. Though it was rather torturous to talk of food when we had so little of it, POWs frequently talked of meals, and Christensen was the master of food oratory, a verbal magician. "Gentlemen," he would tell us, "there's a certain restaurant not far from Fisherman's Wharf. It's a small place, secluded and not well known, but the cooks there have the ability to take an unimpressive bit of salmon and redesign it into a divine masterpiece that somehow requires no effort to chew, yet at the same time makes for the most filling meal you will ever partake of. The texture, gentlemen, the texture of that salmon."

And on and on. Of course, Christensen exaggerated as he described the restaurants, and he spoke with words coated with nostalgia and homesickness, for if such heavenly restaurants ever existed, they would have been known the world over as paradises on earth. Yet no one among us had heard of them, not even natives of San Francisco. But no one cared. While sitting there in those bleak surroundings, Christensen helped me imagine that I was in San Francisco on a misty night, with a foghorn's echo drifting across the bay that I had never seen, gobbling up fresh salmon and just-baked sourdough bread. With this speaking ability, it wasn't long before Christensen was the most popular man in the captains' area.

Christensen's talents were not limited to his knowledge of eating establishments. While in Manila before the war, he had also taught bridge. Joe and I became friends with Christensen, for he was in our ten-man group. When we heard he played bridge, we suggested he teach us the game to help while away the long hours between meals. We found a fourth, scrounged up some cards, and set out to become bridge players.

Christensen was a crack bridge player, and he did his best to teach us all he knew. After each hand, he would analyze what we had played, tell us whether it was good strategy, and lightheartedly insult us for our more foolish mistakes. To add some zest to our games, we made a bet that was to be paid off when we returned to the States. We kept track of our scores, and the team that ended with the higher score would be treated to a night out on the town in San Francisco by the losers. Of course, Christensen would advise us as to the place to go. Our card games went on for weeks, filling our days, until the summer was nearly over.

Christensen made those days more endurable, for he was ever an optimist. He had survived Bataan and had endured the Death March and the vicious conditions at Camp O'Donnell; he seemed to be the one man the Japanese couldn't vanquish. He paid little attention to their beatings and tirades—he simply avoided them. Whenever a friend of his fell into despair, he was quick to assure him that it was simply a matter of time before the United States would win the war and we would be released. And he always had a good story to tell. We knew that at least half of what he said was an exaggeration or an outright lie, but none of us cared. We just played cards and listened to the man talk.

Christensen rarely talked of his personal life and had no really close friend—no "buddy." We discovered later that much of Christensen's strength came from his relationship with his wife, whom he adored. She was his "buddy," and no one could replace her. She and Christensen had come to the Philippines just before the war, when he got a job in Manila as a civilian communications specialist. But soon after they arrived, Pearl Harbor was bombed and Christensen joined the army. Because Christensen was an expert in communications, he was immediately made a captain. When Corregidor fell, Christensen's wife became one of the many civilian internees in Santo Tomas; Christensen was determined to live so they could have a life together again after the war.

As it turned out, Christensen's love of his wife was also his Achilles' heel. The Filipino underground sent a message through to him that his wife had had some sort of breakdown and was no longer in Santo Tomas but was in a mental ward somewhere in Manila. On hearing the news, Christensen told us his wife had had some emotional problems while in the States and this was one of the reasons they had left San Francisco—to find a warm place in the sun for her to heal. It was an ill-fated decision, as soon after their arrival Manila was transformed in one night from an idyllic tropical city to a major theater of war.

With that single message about his wife, Christensen began to crumble. The note did not speak of his wife's prospects, but as an enemy civilian suffering mental problems in an occupied city, they seemed bleak. He was certain she would not survive the war. And if she died, he said, he himself would no longer have a reason to live. He withdrew to his corner in the barracks after telling us about the message and would speak to no one. The next day, he was openly weeping, and we couldn't help him. We tried to make him listen to the same optimistic words he had said to others just a few days before, but nothing helped.

The thought of his wife's collapse left Christensen desperate, and at Cabanatuan such anguish was deadly. Like all of us, Christensen had the trots, and was painfully thin, but he seemed healthy enough before the news about his wife arrived. Within a few days of receiving that note, his dysentery worsened and weakened him, leaving him prey to all the other diseases running through the camp. He contracted beriberi, or it flared up, and four days later, he couldn't stand up. But neither Joe nor I wanted to take him to the hospital, for we knew where the doctors would put him.

Two mornings later, we had no choice. The other captains were complaining about Christensen. They were not cruel, only realistic. However popular he had been, a dying man in our midst was demoralizing—he also was a threat to the others because his ailing body harbored contagious diseases. He belonged in the hospital, they said. Joe and I tried to help Christensen stand that morning to prove the others wrong, but he collapsed in our arms. There was no avoiding it after that. Joe and I and two other captains took Christensen to the hospital.

Just as we feared, when the doctors examined Christensen they said there was nothing they could do for him. They told us to take him to the Zero Ward. We entered that pathetic hut and put Christensen down on a straw mat on the floor. The ward was crowded, as usual. The burial detail was just going to work, shaking each unconscious body, checking for life.

Christensen was oddly grateful to us for bringing him to this godforsaken place, and a bit of his former optimism returned. "Fellas," he told us, "I'm so appreciative. I'll sure make it up to you. This is a dinner for every one of you. It's a dinner on me for the four of you when we get back to San Francisco."

Joe and I couldn't look at each other when Christensen said that; while avoiding each other's eyes, we murmured encouraging words to our friend. We stayed with him a little while, but it wasn't a pleasant place, and Christensen soon became incoherent again. Joe and I walked to the door and called goodbye from across the room. Christensen waved back. And then we left him there to face the Zero Ward alone.

We tried to see Christensen that afternoon, but he was asleep or unconscious when we looked in on him—we couldn't tell which, and the doctor was far too busy to help us with him. Another time we saw him, and he didn't know who we were. We didn't try to see him again, not because we didn't care, but because we didn't want to remember him that way.

Two days later, some ten days after first receiving news of his wife, Christensen's body was among those removed by the burial detail. A few weeks after his death, we received a message meant for him, saying that his wife had died of unknown causes in an unnamed mental hospital in Manila.

Although there were others who played bridge in our barracks, Joe and I didn't play the game again. Our mentor was gone. And we never mentioned the bet. In retrospect, it seems odd that when we confidently made that bet, we did not seriously consider that none of us might make it to San Francisco for a night out on the town. After Christensen's death, though, Joe and I tried to think more consciously about survival strategies. Christensen's death furnished a vital lesson: however strong we seemed in comparison to the sick in the Zero Ward, the two of us and every other "healthy" man in Cabanatuan were only ten days from being removed by a burial detail. Learning that so early in my imprisonment helped keep me alive, I think. I only wish I had not learned it by witnessing the demise of the best bridge player and most magical speaker I have ever known.

6 . Betrayal

WHAT BECAME CLEAR at Cabanatuan was that a person had to be determined to live. Those who were not determined to live simply died. I do not exaggerate. Anyone who was unwilling to bend his needs to meet the paucity of camp conditions took ill and soon was dead. A young enlisted man comes to mind who irrationally refused to eat rice. He hated the stuff, had hated it since he was a child. "I'd rather die than eat that shit," he said. He did—some two months after arriving in Cabanatuan, his body was removed from the Zero Ward by a burial detail. Volatile emotions—be they intense fear, hatred of the Japanese, or antagonisms between POWs—could be deadly because they were an energy drain. Many prisoners who indulged such emotions dwindled and died.

Those of us at Cabanatuan discovered there are two approaches one can take when facing horrendous living conditions such as those found in our POW camp. One can either become selfishly devoted to one's own self-interests—an approach that has obvious advantages—or one can pool one's resources with those of a group and share whatever is available, which also has its advantages. A partnership uses both survival strategies. Though Joe and I never actually talked of a partnership, like hundreds of other pairs in the Cabanatuan camps, we were partners. We were not exactly against the other prisoners in the camp, but there was a recognizable competition among the POWs, a determined commitment in most of us to survive, whatever the cost. This competitive attitude was expressed most often in the theft of food or valuables from a neighbor. But it also displayed itself in fiercely loyal partnerships between prisoners. Joe and I were that; we were tacitly devoted to surviving our imprisonment together.

Especially in those early days at Cabanatuan, there was a tense competition for survival. Your belongings were not safe, and any food had to be closely guarded. With everyone else in the camp, Joe and I were always protective of our own interests as a unit. With each other, however, we shared everything and helped each other through dangerous emotional states. Christensen hadn't had this support. His independence worked well enough when his spirits were even, but when he faced an emotional crisis, he had no partner to buoy him up. He must have been worried about his wife before receiving news of her breakdown, but he never said a word of it. A partner, of course, would have known that story. But Christensen carried his worries locked up within him, and when he met a real crisis, no one knew him well enough to help him through it.

Joe and I knew all this, and after Christensen's death, again by unspoken agreement, we became all the more determined to survive. We had learned by then not to think of the future. Every day it was enough to keep ahead of the psychological and physical barrage imposed on us by the Japanese, and that was all we would allow ourselves to think about. Thoughts of Virginia or Phyllis in Santo Tomas or of the more pleasant past in Manila were self-defeating, so we purposefully did not think of such matters. We would not allow ourselves to dwell on the beatings and deaths of yesterday or the gruesome possibilities of the day to come. Nor did we plan for the future after our release because that too required valuable energy. We survived the day, one day at a time.

Our daily concerns were simple: how much longer before the next meal, how could we get hold of some protein, how many vitamin pills did we have left, and how could we get some more? We awoke at 6:00 A.M., tramped with thousands of others to the ditch-latrines and with them relieved ourselves there in the open, then returned for a watery breakfast of rice. After that meager meal we talked, played cards, or read whatever books were available. Sometimes we engaged in some mild fitness routine; other times we checked out what was available on the black market. Lunch and its rice with weeds came at noon, and half the day was over. The afternoons were the worst, for the heat became nearly unbearable, a real enemy. It left us weak and languid, unable to do much but read or sit thinking vacant thoughts while swatting at insects. But that was relieved by dinner at six o'clock—the best time of day, for with it came food and the promise of darkness and cooler temperatures. With night, a soothing blanket covered the camp, shielding us from the heat and shadowing the stark outlines of our lives as POWs. And in spite of our hungry bellies and the hard floors, we could sleep.

It was a dull life. This, perhaps, was the harshest reality of our prisoner status: the bland nature of each day. Our lives seemed to lose all singularity. Our personalities blurred into a single mass, that of Prisoner, and we moved and existed and suffered as one, in spite of the competition between the thousands of us. One hot day followed another, with flies and stench and meager, unappetizing rations.

Then, in the fall of 1942, there was finally something new to contemplate. The Japanese planned to move some POWs to several camps in Mindanao to relieve the crowded conditions in the Cabanatuan camps.[1] Immediately we all began to wonder how the departing POWs would be chosen, for all of us wanted to be shipped away from the filth and starvation of Cabanatuan.

At about this same time, in mid-October, I encountered Major Hart, whom I had known on Corregidor. He had done cryptanalysis work in the Manila area; when we moved operations to Malinta Tunnel, he worked near us in the communications lateral. I met Hart when I was summoned to the little office that Mori had set aside for the senior POW officer-in-charge. Mori had appointed Lt. Col. D. J. Rutherford to do much of the running of the camp for him out of this office.[2] I did not know Rutherford, but I was not happy to see Hart. I had never liked him—among other things, Hart was responsible for the demotion of one of the enlisted men in our section. The man had failed to consult with Hart before carrying out some trivial task. Joe and I both thought the demotion petty and mean-spirited. In my opinion, Hart was a small-minded, overly ambitious officer who carried a rule book with him everywhere he went, even inside a POW camp.

Rutherford had sent for me that day because he had bad news: the Japanese wanted the names of all officers and enlisted men who had worked with codes and ciphers. Hart had told the Japanese about me, Joe, Pfaff, and

James, but Hart could not remember the names of the enlisted men in our section. Rutherford said the Japanese wanted those names.

A long silent moment passed before I fully understood what Rutherford had said. I stared at Hart incredulously. Of course the Japanese knew we had worked in the communications section, but Joe and I were confident we had convinced the Japanese during our interrogations that we had done nothing but deliver messages. I was furious. I told Rutherford we did not have to supply the Japanese with such information and that I resented Hart's having given my officers' names to the Japanese. Rutherford accepted my answer, but Hart argued with me.

"Who are you kidding, Grady? The Japanese will get any information they want. If we don't tell them what they want to know, they'll start with the torture and cut our rations. They'll always get what they want."

I still refused to cooperate.

Hart changed his tone. "Frank, I'm out on a limb here. The Japs want answers." He lowered his voice. "If they find out I broke that code, I stand to be executed." With the help of two Japanese Americans who worked under him, Hart had managed to break a Japanese field code before our surrender; that success had earned him his present rank.

I was still angry. "I don't care if they execute you. You didn't have to tell them you worked codes in the first place. How did they find out? They didn't know we did, not until you told them. We told them we were couriers. I don't know where the other guys are, and even if I did, I wouldn't tell you." I caught myself before letting loose with a string of profanities. He did outrank me, even in this godforsaken place, and however distant the U.S. Army's hierarchy was, it had taught me well. "I think you've made a stupid mistake, Major, and placed us in unnecessary danger." I asked Rutherford for permission to leave, which he granted.

I fairly sprinted across the compound to find Joe and tell him of Hart's treachery. He was as angry as I was, and together we vented our fury against Hart for some time.

"I wonder if he'll find them," mused Joe finally.

"I hope not," I answered. Hart was trying to find Harold Pohl, Sam Blank, and Frank Goss, and I was thankful he had forgotten their names, for the three of them were near, very near, in one of the Cabanatuan camps. We had not seen them, but we assumed they were still alive in one of the camps down the road or perhaps among the thousands of faces in this very camp with us. Pohl, Blank, and Goss had all worked with codes, though they never did the final decoding and encoding of documents—Joe and I did that. I hoped that Pohl, Blank, and Goss had followed our instructions and told the Japanese they were message clerks and nothing more, for as enlisted men they were more vulnerable than officers. With their respect for hierarchy, the Japanese might forgo the torture of officers, but they felt few reservations about torturing enlisted men.

We felt especially angry with Hart because Sam Blank was the sergeant Hart had demoted in the Tunnel. Blank was a dedicated and diligent worker, yet Hart had broken him to a private in spite of the protests Joe and I lodged. It didn't surprise me that Hart had forgotten Blank's name. It was like Hart to ruin another man's standing and then forget his existence. If we survived, Joe and I resolved to tell our superiors of Hart's betrayal and to help Blank get his rank back.

If we survived. Now our future looked even bleaker. Once the Japanese knew we had actually worked with codes, they would want to interrogate us again. And if they looked at our interrogations of the previous May, they might see the discrepancies between what we had said we did and what Hart had told them we did. Images of the golf club–wielding Japanese officer loomed in my head. By the autumn of 1942, Japanese forces in the Philippines were far more organized than they had been in May, and they now knew that we were more than couriers.

Joe and I talked for a long time that night. Neither of us slept much.

The next morning, Joe and I went in search of Pfaff and James. They were in our camp also, but as lieutenants they were segregated from us and we didn't see them every day. The two of them were in relatively good spirits, though, like us, they were thin and wan.

After exchanging camp news, Joe brought up the reason we had found them. "Do you fellows remember Major Hart?"

James nodded. "The SOB who broke Blank? Sure." Hart had not been popular with any of us.

"He's been talking to the Japs. Now they know all of the officers' names who worked crypto in the Tunnel, and they know all of us handled codes."

There was a stunned silence as they absorbed this. James and Pfaff exchanged alarmed glances before James spoke. "Why? Why'd he tell them that?"

"Who the hell knows," I said. We then told them all we knew of Hart's betrayal. The four of us attacked his character for a while, then Joe and I brought up our second reason for seeking out Pfaff and James: we had a plan as to how to respond during interrogation.

Pfaff and James listened to our strategy and added their own ideas. When Joe and I returned to our barracks later, we were satisfied that at least none of us would be caught off guard. Now we could do nothing but wait for the Japanese to find us and hope that they would not find Pohl, Blank, or Goss. We couldn't establish our narrative with them—if they told stories that didn't match ours, we were all in trouble.

We did not wait long. Several days later, Joe and I were summoned by Colonel Rutherford, and in his office we met Pfaff and James again. Also in the room were three other POWs, two of them enlisted men and one an officer. None of them had worked in the Tunnel with us.

One of the enlisted men was tall and very young; he seemed unconcerned that he was soon to be interrogated by the Japanese, probably because he was so bad off. He looked as if he had once been a husky fellow by the size of his frame, but now he was horribly thin and drawn, more so than most of us, and his skin was ashen. His sunken eyes had no luster and were ringed with dark circles. I wondered if the guards had pulled him from the hospital to bring him here.

The other two men in the room were like us, malnourished and weak but relatively healthy. One of them, Corporal Rosenberg, talked with us a bit. The man who looked so ghastly only listened apathetically to us after saying his name was Cpl. Walter Maddock. The other officer was quiet; he remained apart from us. None of them knew why they had been summoned. Colonel Rutherford told us soon enough. Commander Mori had told him to tell us that we were all to be interrogated because of our jobs before the surrender. He said we would soon be leaving for Manila, where our interrogations would take place. Rutherford knew nothing more than that, so we left his office.

Once outside, James, Pfaff, Joe, and I mused for a few minutes about the other POWs, for we had never seen them before. We were relieved by this—

Hart apparently still had not remembered the crypto section crew's names. The conversation turned again to Major Hart. None of us could understand why he had given the Japanese our names so readily. When we had seen him, he had shown no signs of abuse and had said nothing about being coerced. His fear that they might discover he had broken a code was a feeble excuse for releasing our names—the Japanese couldn't know that kind of information without an informant. And why had he waited so long to divulge his information? It had been months since they had asked us about our former jobs. Hart's actions made no sense.

The next morning, Joe and I discovered why Hart had been so eager to help. Five hundred prisoners who were bound for Mindanao were lining up on the road outside our camp for their march to the train station. Many of the POWs who had to stay behind milled about, watching enviously as the group prepared to leave this death trap. Those of us watching assumed these departing men had been chosen indiscriminately, and I still believe that the majority of them were picked that way. But one prisoner preparing to march away was more than just lucky.

Joe saw him first. "Frank, isn't that Hart? There, in the front?" He pointed at an officer at the front of the line who was just then hoisting a pack on his shoulder.

I felt a rush of fury. "It damned sure is." Without another word between us, Joe and I moved quickly toward where Hart stood. The group was just beginning to march, led by Hart and their Japanese escorts. Joe and I drew as near as we were allowed.

"Hart!" I yelled. He swung around to look at me. He looked surprised, then defensive. "Damn you, Hart, is that why you told them?" Hart quickly looked away, which answered my question. "Goddamn you, Hart, you told them about us so you could go to Mindanao! You son of a bitch! You stinking traitor! You sold us out!" Joe started yelling at Hart, too.

Hart kept his face averted and began to march. Joe and I shouted a string of obscenities at him. "We'll get you, Hart," I yelled as he drew away. "I'm gonna report you when we get out of here! We're gonna prefer charges against you! You're gonna get a court-martial for this, you bastard!"

Joe and I continued to shout after him until he was long out of earshot. The other prisoners gazed at us curiously, wondering why we were threatening another officer. After several minutes more of unleashed fury, Joe and

I finally fell quiet when two guards with raised guns moved toward us. Hart was out of sight. I don't believe he felt threatened by us, and he hadn't seemed ashamed of his actions, just irritated by our discovery. He hadn't looked back at us once as he marched away. Joe and I stood there in silence for a few minutes after the other prisoners dispersed. I felt angry, afraid, defeated, and very, very tired. I wondered how much Hart had told the Japanese in exchange for his exit visa from Cabanatuan. He knew quite a bit—he could have chatted about U.S. code-breaking abilities, cryptographic technology, and more for several weeks at least. Or maybe he told them that we worked with codes while claiming that he did not, which left us with the messy business of answering an interrogator's questions as he took up a new routine in a Mindanao POW camp.

As I stood there, Hart became as repugnant and hateful to me as any POW-abusing guard. Some forty-five years later, I still feel his betrayal.

ABOUT TWO WEEKS later, on 31 October 1942, Joe and I walked away from Cabanatuan Camp Number One with the five other POWs who had been called to Rutherford's office. Two guards marched us the five miles to the train station and then ordered us into a wooden boxcar. We climbed in and the doors were locked behind us. Fortunately, there were slats missing in the boxcar walls that let in some light and fresh air. With only seven of us in the car, this trip promised to be more endurable than the ride up from Manila had been.

It was obvious why we four officers from MacArthur's and Wainwright's cryptographic staffs were to be interrogated, but we still didn't know why the Japanese wanted to talk to the others in our group. We asked them why they thought they were to be interrogated. Corporal Maddock said he had been a code clerk at the battalion headquarters of the 31st Infantry. He had written this down on the form that the Japanese had had us fill out upon becoming POWs. I was relieved to hear this, for I knew that Maddock never would have worked with any high-security devices at a battalion headquarters. Their code security never lasted longer than twenty-four hours after transmission. I checked Maddock off my mental list.

Corporal Rosenberg's presence was not so easy to explain because he had never worked with a cryptographic device. Our only clue was the fact that a Japanese soldier had recently shown Rosenberg some papers and asked him to identify them. Rosenberg had recognized the papers as part of a workbook that he studied from while taking a correspondence course in cryptography at Fort Stotsenburg, which was some fifty miles north of Manila. Each page of the workbook had his name, rank, and serial number on it. We could only assume that the Japanese had searched through U.S. Army records and found Rosenberg's course assignments. We guessed that they decided the person who could solve such problems must be an expert on codes, thus Rosenberg's transfer to Manila. We laughed about that, and I marked Rosenberg off my list. The other officer offered little information, only saying he had worked with battalion ciphers. So he too had little of importance to say to an interrogator.

Pfaff, James, Joe, and I were determined not to help the Japanese and yet avoid torture or beatings. Our biggest problem was that we didn't know how much Hart had told them. We were gambling that he had only given our names and not our specific duties. After all, he knew little about our end of the communications lateral. Hart had no idea what Pfaff and James actually did—he could not have told the Japanese that they worked with codes, only that they worked in the cryptographic section. He did know that Joe was the co-commander of the crypto section, though, and this we would have to take into account. Hart knew the most about what I did, as I was the one he most often worked with. If he had told the Japanese anything, he would have told them about my duties. With this in mind, we put our stories together.

We decided that we would acknowledge that I, Captain Grady, was the officer-in-charge in the cryptographic section. Joe, we would all verify, was immediately under me, while Pfaff and James, as lieutenants, were simply couriers. I would say that I was basically a courier as well, but that I had encoded and decoded less-important messages from time to time, which I passed on to either Pfaff or James, who delivered them. Captain Iacobucci was in charge of the operations of the section and had no real knowledge of the machines, we would say, and we would add that he hadn't been in the Philippines long before the war started (which was true) and had few responsibilities (which was not true). That would leave the Japanese expecting answers only from me, or so we hoped.

I should add here that only Pfaff, James, and I would relate this story—as a graduate of West Point, Joe was adamant that he would tell the Japanese nothing besides his name, rank, and serial number.

In my interrogations, I would recite from a book on basic cryptography that I had read after I received my assignment to the code room. The book was simplistic and at the time could be found in any U.S. public library. Our hope was that by reciting the book's contents, I would be giving the Japanese answers while not compromising U.S. communications security. We also hoped that they might do with us what we had heard they had done with some U.S. POW telephone technicians. According to Christensen, the Japanese had put them up in a Manila hotel, fed them decently, and told them to fix the telephone system that had been damaged in battle. We knew that our codes couldn't be broken, not even by us, but the Japanese didn't know that. We hoped they would tell us to break unbreakable codes, and we'd get several weeks of decent room and board.[3]

I wasn't happy about being the one to blab, for although I would say little, my interrogators might become intrigued and force me to say more. I am not now and was not then an especially brave man—I wasn't sure I could take torture for even a moment. And I didn't like being singled out from my friends. We had performed similar duties, but to the Japanese I was to represent myself as someone who knew something more. It was, however, the best defense we could come up with, and as I had been the officer-in-charge in the section, it was a role for me to bear.[4]

The four of us discussed all this quietly in a corner of the boxcar, as the less our fellow prisoners knew about our duties the better. After going over our responses, we joined the others and advised them to go ahead and give the Japanese any information they had so as to avoid possibly being tortured.

I sat down on the floor of the rickety boxcar next to Maddock. Maddock was very young to be struggling for his life at a POW camp—he couldn't have been more than twenty. While walking to the train station, I had noticed how thirsty Maddock was. The five-mile march had been hard on him because of his condition, and he had finished off his own canteen. I offered him water from my half-full canteen. He took several swallows, then politely handed it back. I offered him another drink, but he refused and said he was OK.

But he wasn't OK. It amazed me that he was still alive. His eyes were red-rimmed and starved; with the dark black circles under them, he looked ghoulish.

Maddock noticed me staring at him. "I guess I look pretty bad, huh. I haven't seen myself in a long time, but I saw sick guys all around me in the Zero Ward and they looked terrible. I must look the same."

"You were in the Zero Ward?" I asked incredulously.

"Yeah. That place was bad. I had to get outta there."

In a style that I was to discover was characteristic of him, Maddock told us his story as we shared water and a bit of black market food with him.

"It all began a few weeks ago," Maddock said. "I was like everybody else, but one day I got sick. I figure it musta been something I ate, something gone bad. Maybe some meat I bought from a guy. Well, you know what happens when you get sick there," he gestured vaguely in the direction of Cabanatuan. "I just got sicker. I had a fever—one guy keeps saying I have malaria, but I keep saying I don't. I was hot and cold and hungry and tired but I couldn't eat, or make food stay down anyway. One day I got so weak that I can't get off my bunk. That day my buddies carried me to the hospital, and the doctors put me in the Zero Ward.

"Well, I'd been there a couple of days, not getting any worse, but not getting any better, neither. One night I fall asleep, but I wake up in the middle of the night. The man next to me had been thrashing around somethin' fierce, and I guess that's what woke me up. He quit thrashing. The quiet wakes me up. The orderlies wake up, too. They come over and shake him, asking him to speak but he doesn't. They check him and the guy's dead! I'd been talking to him just that day and there he was, dead! They pick him up and carry him outside in the dark. I didn't sleep for a while after that.

"Well, I slept finally and the next morning I woke up and I looked over at the empty cot and remembered what had happened. I turn to the guy on the other side of me. 'Geez,' I said, 'Did you see that last night? They took that guy away, dead. What do you think of that?' And I get no answer. So I ask him again what he thinks of it. The guy still doesn't answer me so I get mad and reach over to shake him. He doesn't wake up. That guy was dead too!" Maddock looked annoyed at the thought of the two dead men. "I called the orderlies over and they said, 'Yep, he's dead,' and they carried him outside for the burial detail to pick up. Well damn, I wasn't about to wait around for someone to find me dead one morning. I got up and kinda stood there wobbling but I stopped after a minute and started walking. This one doctor shouted after me 'Where you going?' but I just kept walking. I was dizzy, but I went back to the regular hospital and just sort of hung around, avoiding work details and sleeping. Then a couple days later this Jap comes up to me and says the commander wants to see me." Maddock fell silent while we marveled over his survival.

"You know," Maddock said after a while, "if they would just give me some food, I'd be OK. None of this watery goo, some food. God, if my ma was here she'd fix us some food." We all then turned to what had become our favorite conversation as POWs: Great Meals We Had Eaten. We whiled away a large portion of our trip talking of that.

The train made many stops on the way to Manila. We could hear Filipinos milling about outside our car whenever we halted. At one stop, Maddock and Joe were standing with their heads and shoulders hanging out of the car where a couple of slats were missing.

"Hey," I heard Maddock exclaim, "those people have food with them!" He raised his voice. "Hey, you! Do you have any food for us? Hey, we need food! Do you have any food?"

I got up to see if he was able to get a reaction. At first the Filipinos who milled about the car ignored him. We were traveling in a train controlled by the Japanese military, whom the Filipinos hated. But after a few moments an old woman sitting on a bench must have realized that we weren't Japanese, because she pulled a package from her bag, gave it to a little girl, and whispered to her. The girl cautiously approached the train, handed the parcel to Maddock, and then scampered away before a Japanese soldier could yell at her.

Maddock ripped open the package excitedly. Inside were several types of tropical fruits and a small loaf of bread. We all gathered round and shared in the feast.

At each of the stops after that, we all yelled at the civilians, shouting and gesturing to let them know that we were Americans and not the Japanese they so hated. And at every stop, with Maddock's surprisingly strong voice leading us, we received food, usually fresh fruit but sometimes bread or sweets. Before long, we were almost full, as our stomachs had shrunk to the size of walnuts by then. Only Maddock wasn't encumbered with this problem, for he vomited numerous times on the trip, reminding us that he was still a sick man. Nonetheless, he kept shouting to the people outside the train for food, and he kept gobbling it down long after the rest of us were leaning up against the walls of the car, exhausted and as full as our stomachs would let us be. When it came to food, the man who had survived the Zero Ward had more energy than the rest of us.

And all the while, the train kept on moving southward toward Manila and the fate that awaited us there.

7. Manila: November–December 1942

W E ARRIVED IN Manila late that night and were led by a guard along the darkened streets to Bilibid Prison. He escorted us to an empty cell—we were to be segregated from the other POWs. The guard then left, but he reappeared with another Japanese soldier; each of them carried a bucket of food, which they placed on the floor. Our guard's companion said in English, "We finish. You eat." The two of them then left. Apparently we were to eat the guards' leftovers.

The aromatic leftovers were our first clue that our interrogators were not going to beat us into cooperating; they were going to try using privilege instead—no one else in Bilibid that night got leftovers for dinner.

Though he was a very sick man, Maddock was somehow the first to reach the buckets and lift off a lid. He made a low, purring sound as the smell of a meat sauce filled the room. It was covered with some two inches of grease, but it was a meat sauce. In the other bucket we found rice, but for once there was a considerable amount of it—both containers were about half full. All of us by this time were unfastening our mess kits. Maddock was already digging into the greasy broth with his cup. He jubilantly announced a few seconds later that the sauce had actual chunks of meat in it—lamb, as it turned out. In moments each of us sat down with our lamb and rice. The broth was cold by then, and the congealed grease might have struck less-hungry folks as unappetizing, but for us it was a feast. And there was so much of it! For the first time in months, we were having a meal that was more than just an appetizer.

But we ended up eating less than we thought we would—none of us could eat more than a cup or so of the greasy meat and rice. None of us but Maddock, that is; he vomited once, but, as on the train, this didn't faze him in the least. He kept eating. An hour later, before he ate every scrap of food in the two pots, we stopped him so we could have some left over for breakfast. Maddock's appetite was truly impressive.

When our cell was opened the next morning, I went out to see what was new in Bilibid. The POW camp was more organized than it had been five months before. It was not nearly so crowded now—there appeared to be fewer than five hundred prisoners there in early November 1942, whereas in May the prison had housed thousands of us.[1]

After a few minutes of wandering around the compound, I was surprised to hear my name called. I turned to see a doctor I had known in the Tunnel approach me. We greeted each other, and I told the doctor why we were here. He told me of the news at Bilibid. By then, they actually had medicines available. He asked if I needed help with anything.

I was all right, but I thought of Maddock. The doctor had access to sulpha drugs, quinine, and vitamins. I told him about Maddock, and he told me to send him around. I went and got Maddock and led him to the hospital.

When I returned to our cell, a Japanese lieutenant was there. He was wearing a uniform with a four-star insignia across the front pocket—this meant he was a member of the Japanese army interpreter corps. He told us we would soon be interrogated, took our names and ranks, then left the room.

We all assumed the interpreter meant we would wait only a short while before our interrogators summoned us. But no one came. We were left alone all afternoon and into the evening; we finally realized that our interrogations wouldn't take place that day. Nor did they the next day, or the next. Every morning we awoke full of a dread that our interrogations would begin that day, while at the same time hoping they would so we could get them over with. But nothing happened. Several weeks went by, and still we had not been interrogated. We had arrived in Bilibid 31 October; it was now early December—one tremendously long year after Pearl Harbor, and a month after our arrival in Manila.

But at least we were eating better, for every night the camp guards gave us the lamb and rice leftovers. We received no lunch or morning meal, as the other prisoners in camp did—the nightly leftovers were to tide us over for each twenty-four hour period. We didn't complain. The bits of greasy, cold lamb were worth it.

With some decent food and medical care, Maddock filled out a bit. The doctors gave him shots of B vitamins to clear up his beriberi and sulpha drugs to cure him of the worst of his dysentery. His fever was gone, and he quit vomiting. This left him irrationally grateful to me—Maddock could never get it into his head that I had not saved his life, the doctors and their drugs had. I had let Maddock borrow my blanket the first night in Bilibid because I was hot and he was cold, and I happened to be the one who led him to the hospital in Bilibid the day after we got there. Based on these two acts, Maddock became convinced that I had personally saved him from an early death. Maddock, a happy-go-lucky kid—he seemed a kid to me, though at twenty he was only eight years younger than I—had come to idolize me.

We all grew closer in Bilibid. Pfaff, James, Joe, and I had been close in the Tunnel, but now, as we were constantly together again as POWs and felt a shared stress over our impending interrogations, we grew even closer. Rosenberg and Maddock became part of our group. We played poker together for hours and filled up our days by talking and rehearsing our lines for our interrogations. We all hoped to spend the rest of our POW days as a team with three subgroups: Pfaff and James, Maddock and Rosenberg, and Joe and me. We were certain we could survive anything with our six-man team.[2]

Joe and I shared an unfamiliar optimism in Bilibid, for we were both closer to our wives. Phyllis and Virginia were not far from us; in fact, from one corner of Bilibid's compound, we could see the tower of Santo Tomas, where they were incarcerated. It was comforting to see that tower. While we were there, we got hold of a little bit of money and sent it to them with several letters. We didn't allow ourselves to think of our wives too much; after all, we were still prisoners of war awaiting interrogations, but it was nice to quietly be aware that they were nearby.

We were into the second half of December before the Japanese were ready to talk to us. Two guards arrived one morning and led Rosenberg and Maddock out first. The two of them returned about an hour later with no horror stories. The Japanese asked them where they had been before their surrender, what they had done, and whom they had worked with. They answered all of their questions—there was no reason not to. The other officer reported the same experience.

We four from the Tunnel were next. The guard escorted James away first, and all went according to plan. He told his interrogator that he was only a code clerk and that all he had ever done was to take sealed messages from me or from a slot on the code room door and deliver them to the proper personnel. Pfaff told the same story.

Joe left the room next with a bulldog expression on his face, determined to say as little as possible—I believe he actually looked forward to reciting only his name, rank, and serial number to his interrogators. His session was the shortest one—he returned to the room about half an hour later, looking rather proud of himself. I could imagine him sitting there, repeating in a quiet but firm voice that he was a professional soldier, and that by the Geneva Convention, which he professed to know by heart, he did not have to tell his captors anything.

The guard led me across the compound and into a room that had once been a cell but was now an office. There was a U.S. Army–issue desk and four chairs in the room, along with three Japanese officers. One sat behind the desk. From his elaborate uniform, I guessed him to be of high rank, the equivalent of a major at least. His expression remained impassive as I entered the room. Behind him stood a lieutenant wearing the four-star insignia of the interpreter corps. And to the side of the desk stood a young Japanese officer who also appeared to be a major or higher, but among the insignia on his uniform were the familiar four stars, which made him an interpreter as well.

On the corner of the desk was a tray with an ornate silver teapot, matching silver cups, and a platter carrying delicious-looking bar cookies. The higher-ranking interpreter nodded, this time in the direction of the tea service. Certainly this wasn't the interrogation scene I had envisioned. I was relieved and suspicious at the same time.

The higher-ranking interpreter spoke. "Will you have some tea, Captain Grady?" I started to reach for a cookie, then stopped with my arm in midair. The interpreter, I suddenly realized, spoke English perfectly; if I had not watched him form the words, I might have thought an American had invited me to partake of tea. I stared bewilderedly at him.

The interpreter cleared his throat. "I earned my bachelor's and law degrees from Yale," he said. He looked ill at ease for a moment, then came around the desk. "Go on. Have a cookie. They're very good." He turned to the seated officer and said something in Japanese. That officer in turn spoke to the lieutenant behind him. The lieutenant promptly left the room after saluting the two officers.

The interpreter again encouraged me to have a cookie, then began to pour the tea. My amazement at his impeccable English quickly gave way to a desire to stuff as many of the cookies into my mouth as possible. None of the other guys had said anything about treats—I wondered if they had been offered them.

"Have a seat, Captain," he said while nodding toward a seat on my side of the desk. I sat. "Do you take sugar in your tea?" he asked.

I nodded emphatically. The idea of all those calories in my body at once almost left me giddy. The interpreter poured a cup of tea, no sugar, for the other officer, whom he served first; then he poured a cup for me, then one for himself. Throughout all this, the higher-ranking officer silently watched me.

After handing me my tea, the Yale graduate began. "We understand that you were the officer-in-charge in the cryptography section under MacArthur and Wainwright. Is that correct?" He spoke in a respectful manner.

I nodded while eying the cookie in my hand. I then recited my serial number and prisoner number.

The interpreter glanced at the cookie I held in my hand. "Go ahead and eat it, Captain." He turned to the officer and presumably translated our exchange to him.

That sweet, sticky cookie was the best thing that had happened to me in months. I savored the first bite slowly, washing it down with a sip of tea. One taste of my drink informed me that the interpreter had dumped at least three teaspoons of sugar into the hot liquid. I thanked him for it. It was delicious. I hadn't had any sugar since long before Corregidor's fall.

My interrogator had finished talking with the officer and turned back to me. He politely asked me what my duties were in the Tunnel.

I chewed carefully, gathered myself together, and answered. "I supervised the delivery of messages. Sometimes when it was very busy, I decoded and encoded messages also."

The interpreter relayed this to the officer. I grabbed some more cookies.

The next questions were about my rank, whom I had worked with, who did most of the encoding and decoding when I didn't, and so on. I tried to fatten each one of my answers and talk as much as possible. I tossed in some cryptographic jargon to see if the interpreter recognized it, which he did not. He did know something about cryptography but his background was in law; I didn't think he knew enough to disrupt our plan.

"Captain," the interpreter finally said, "we have come from Tokyo to talk to U.S. cryptographic personnel. We want to learn more about your codes. You are out of the war and will be until our victory. You cannot do anything about the war now. Have you thought of this?" The interpreter then recited some propaganda against America to persuade me that I might just as well help the Japanese defeat the scoundrels in Washington. I expected to hear such propaganda—we always did as prisoners—though not from an enemy soldier who spoke fluent American English and who had received several college degrees from an American university.

The interpreter continued. "Upon our victory, we will need people with your skills to help modernize and develop communications in Japan. If you help us now, this will be remembered. Get your foot in the door while you can."

His English really was amazing.

I stood up quietly. I hoped I looked as though I were considering his words about the imminent Japanese victory in a new light. I hoped I looked confused, but torn. I wondered when I should throw out to them my first tantalizing tidbit about basic codes.

But the interpreter was not finished. "Sit down, Captain. You must know that the Americans are losing everywhere. Do you hear the news in the camps? We drove you out of the Philippines and any day now we will invade Australia. It is inevitable. But remember, you did not start this war with us. Your government did."

My interrogator was finished for the time being. A silence settled over the room for a few minutes, during which both of the officers watched me. It was time. But I had to do this carefully. I began to speak, but cut myself off and let the silence rest over us. My nervousness was not a show. I was uneasy with this intelligent Japanese interpreter.

I finally cleared my throat. "What exactly do you want to know?"

The interpreter cocked his head to one side and considered me for a moment before carefully answering, "We would like to know about the ciphers you used, how they worked, what your machines were like."

I suddenly felt panicky. This Yale graduate might not be a specialist in codes and ciphers, but he was obviously a smart man who knew something about Americans. And he wasn't necessarily as considerate as he appeared, either.

The officer behind the desk spoke for the first time; as he did so his eyes were focused on me. The Yale graduate answered him, then turned to me. "What type machines did you use in the Tunnel, Captain?"

I named a simple cryptographic machine. He didn't seem to recognize the name. He said something to the officer, then returned to me. "Would you tell us how it works?"

I nodded nervously, and began to talk, haltingly at first, but then warming to my subject as I tried to make the interpreter understand how a simple field code machine worked. As I spoke, the interpreter made notations and small drawings on a pad. I made a mental note of this; I would have to be careful that I always made matching statements. I went on with this for some time, then stopped. My first solo, I thought, had gone well.

My interrogators asked me a few more questions, but I refused to answer. I did not want to appear too eager. After a short discussion between the officers, I was dismissed.

I returned to our cell. The others there looked up, curious to hear my report. I dug into my pocket and pulled out three cookies. They were a bit dirty, but I didn't think the guys would mind. "You'll have to split them," I said. "Did you guys get cookies while in there? And tea?"

Maddock's eyes nearly popped out of his head as he shook his head in answer to my question. He quickly split a cookie, handed half to Rosenberg, then stuffed his portion into his mouth. Joe said they had offered him cookies, but that he had only got one. After he recited his name, rank, and serial number, the cookie platter and tea service were removed. There were advantages to being a songbird.

James took up a cookie, broke it in two and gave half to Pfaff. The two of them stood and walked toward the door. Joe and I followed them outside. Once we had withdrawn into a corner of the compound, I told them about my interrogation, and the four of us made plans for the next day's interviews.

We eventually learned that our interrogators were of high rank. The silent one was a colonel and the interpreter a lieutenant colonel. The interrogations went on for about two weeks, basically in the same manner. Rosenberg and Maddock were interviewed first, then the other officer, then Pfaff, James, and Joe. (Joe never did say anything more than that he was a professional soldier who refused to cooperate.) I was always last, and there were always cookies for my interrogations. I slowly revealed to my interrogators a good portion of that elementary book on codes and ciphers, plus whatever other trivia about crypto machines I could remember. We were always treated humanely. The torture and endless questioning that we had all feared did not occur.

Had the Japanese sent someone to interview us who had expert knowledge of codes and ciphers, we probably would not have succeeded in our ploy during the interrogations. But as it was, we were speaking to men who had only basic knowledge of cryptography, so we apparently convinced them that the interviews were worthwhile. I was rather surprised by this—did they really think that Joe and I were able to handle all the communications going through USAFFE headquarters without any other officer's or enlisted man's help? We decided that the heightened Japanese sense of hierarchy worked in our favor in this instance—in the Japanese system, enlisted men and lieutenants probably wouldn't have handled sensitive information or worked on highly intricate machines, so our stories made sense to them.

The Yale graduate was an enigma. He was educated in a country that was far different from his own, but he must have come to like America at least a bit. He did spend at least seven years there, which he would not likely have done if he had detested the place. We assumed that sometime after earning his law degree, he had returned to his own nation—just in time, perhaps, for the war to begin with the people he had lived among for at least seven years. I remember his impassive manner as he recited his anti-America speeches. He seemed detached from his words as he spoke. He performed admirably as an interpreter—he caught every word and demanded explanations for every incongruity. But I wondered whether he didn't see himself as caught in a mire that, to paraphrase him, was not of his making. Whatever his thoughts about the United States, he had to act as if he felt no attachment to that country at all. And he did—he was stiff and inscrutable during every interrogation he performed.

Such is war. Everyone it touches—we become automatons all.

In early January 1943 I went for my final interrogation at Bilibid. The high-ranking officers were not there that day; two camp interpreters asked me a few questions, then they talked between themselves as I sat, wondering if the interrogations were over. Finally one of them turned to me.

"You go to Japan," he said with a gesture toward the north. "You go Tokyo by ship. More questions."

I was stunned. This was not part of the plan.

He stood up. "You go with him now," he gestured toward the other interpreter, who also stood up.

I continued to sit there, frozen. I did not sense that they were using the word "you" in its plural sense. "All seven of us will go to Japan?" I asked.

The interpreter shook his head. "You only."

I still could not move. I was to go to Japan alone? Up north, I would be distant from the people who had become so dear to me. My friends were here, men I had come to depend on and trust. And Virginia was in the Philippines —though I couldn't see her, I at least felt close to her, especially in Manila. I knew nothing of Japan. I had only heard rumors of great horrors taking place there. According to scuttlebutt, Japan was the worst place on earth to be as a POW. I wanted to kick myself. I had sung too damned well.

The second interpreter motioned for me to follow him. I stood slowly. My mind was tumbling—perhaps they had known all along of our strategy and were sending me off to face a real interrogation in the capital of the Japanese empire where they could get answers more efficiently, without other Americans around. Perhaps they would punish me for our attempts to satisfy them while in fact saying little. I thought of all this as I followed the interpreter to a storeroom. In it were boxes of uniforms, coats, and blankets that I recognized as U.S. Army and Navy issue. I was to choose outer wear for the trip up north; it would be frigid in Japan. I grabbed a coat and a blanket and some warm woolen shirts. The interpreter picked up another coat and said it was for my orderly; I was to pick an orderly to go with me to Japan.

An orderly?

I later deduced that the Japanese, with their respect for hierarchy, could not send an officer to Japan without an orderly. The Yale-trained interpreter's strategy was to convince me that the Japanese were decent people and that I should cooperate with them. Offering me an orderly was yet another decent

Japanese gesture. I immediately thought of Joe, but soon discarded that thought. They wouldn't allow Joe to go—they knew he wasn't of "orderly" status, as he and I were the same rank; they had told me to pick an enlisted man. The interpreter handed me the coat he had picked up and instructed me to give it to my "orderly." He told me I would leave in two days. I was dismissed.

I slowly walked across the compound and entered our cell. Maddock looked up expectantly. "No cookies today, Maddock," I said. Joe asked how my interrogations went. I told him I hadn't been interrogated at all. And then I told them all that I was being sent alone to Japan.

A chorus of incredulous and alarmed voices answered me: "Japan?! Why?"

I shrugged. I did not know why they were sending me to Japan. I repeated everything the interpreter had said, but for the bit about the orderly.

Joe nervously began shuffling our deck of cards. "Jesus Christ," he murmured. "Jesus Christ. Japan."

Someone wanted to know whether any other POWs were going with me. I didn't know that, either. "None of you will go with me, anyway," I said.

We all were quiet after that. There was nothing more to say. I was going to Japan; they weren't; and there was nothing my companions or I could do or say to prevent that from happening. They couldn't stop the war for me, nor I for them; whatever fates awaited us, we would face them apart. Joe was still shuffling cards while cursing mildly to himself. He kept his head averted, and I knew why. There were tears in my eyes, too.

I sank against the cool stone wall behind me, next to Joe, and let my tears fall.

Some while later, I told them that I was to choose an enlisted man to be my orderly. I turned toward the young man who had recently decided, however incorrectly, that I had saved his life. "What about it, Maddock? Are you willing to go to Japan?"

Maddock looked surprised. "Japan?" He thought for about half a minute, then shrugged. "Sure. Why not? Better than going back to Cabanatuan."

I was hoping he would be willing to go, but I thought that someone should be cautious for him. "Don't decide yet, Maddock. Think about it. You might be making a mistake." I paused. "We don't know why they're sending me there. Maybe it will be rough. And it'll be cold. It's winter in Japan. Maybe you don't want to be there."

James spoke up. "We've all heard they torture people in Japan, Maddock." He looked at me, then quickly away. "Put some more thought into it."

Our warnings seemed to make Maddock all the more set on going. "Doesn't matter, Lieutenant." He turned to me. "Captain, anywhere you go, I'm gonna go." He repeated several times the story that I had saved his life, then said again that anywhere I went, he would go. His decision was made.

It was probably selfish of me, but I was glad Maddock was going with me. I told him we would leave soon, and gave him the coat, a warm shirt, and a blanket for the trip north.

I remember that night we played bridge for the first time since Christensen's death. Joe wanted to teach Pfaff and James and Rosenberg how to play. We played until late and did not speak of Japan again that night. We made no bets to be collected after our release, for we would not be released together—that is, if any of us survived to be released. The Japanese military were breaking up our team, and several times during that game of bridge, I wept silent tears of fear, rage, and remorse.

THREE MORNINGS LATER, in mid-January 1943, Maddock and I stood outside our cell with our friends, silently waiting for a guard who was to escort us to our ship bound for Japan. It was Joe who finally spoke. "Well, Frank, see you after the war. In San Francisco. And I'll buy. I'm a better card player than you, but I'll still buy." At that, we both began to weep openly.

I remember repeating myself many times that morning, saying the same trite things over and over again as I said goodbye to the best friend I had ever had. "You take care of yourself, Joe. You take damned good care of yourself."

Joe had taken up my hand and stood mechanically shaking it up and down.

Pfaff put his arm around my shoulders. "You take care of *yourself*, Frank. You hold on. We'll all meet up in the States after the war and talk over steaks about the rice balls at Cabanatuan. You be there, right?"

"We'll all meet in San Francisco, at the army base," James said. He stopped a minute. "Is there an army base in San Francisco?"

"Damn, who's been to San Francisco," answered Pfaff.

We all laughed, the tension momentarily broken, then fell silent again. Joe was still shaking my hand. I released myself and took him aside. I didn't know how to say it, but I had to try. It was too important. "You find your-self a buddy, Joe, right?" I whispered. It was the first time one of us had openly talked of the "buddies" we were—I felt foolish saying it, but I was afraid for him. It was too dangerous to live without one. Too many things could go wrong, drag him down, if he was alone.

"Don't worry about me, Frank," he said. "I'll be here where it's warm and where they leave me alone. You take care of yourself. Don't let them torture you. Tell them something important if you have to. But don't give up." We stepped away from each other as our guard approached. Joe continued, "I'll be waiting there in San Francisco. If you get sent back to Manila after the war, count on it, I'll be here. Or in San Francisco. Look for me." He wiped his eyes and watched me as I gathered up my gear. He then lowered his voice. "You find a buddy too, right?"

It was time to go, the guard informed us when he arrived. James, Pfaff, and Rosenberg in turn solemnly shook my hand. After I put on my pack, Joe handed me one of the flight bags Phyllis had given us and hugged me.

I wiped away a tear with my free hand, then clapped Joe on the back. Neither one of us could speak. The guard gestured at me, and I fell in be-hind the guard with Maddock at my side. When I was about twenty paces from my fellow officers, I turned and waved. They waved back.

I looked in the bag then. Inside was some Japanese money—I did not know how much it was worth, nor had I any idea how Joe had managed to get it. There were also two small cans, one containing spiced beef and the other condensed milk. I wondered at Joe's resourcefulness and turned to wave my thanks and another goodbye. They still stood there. Joe waved again.

We reached Bilibid's main gate. A Japanese soldier opened it, and Mad-dock and I walked out behind our guard. I resisted the urge to look once more at my friends. I think I was afraid they would not still be standing there, and I wanted to remember Joe and Pfaff and James together, united and supportive, as they blessed me on to my fate in Japan.

The Japanese soldier slammed the gate shut behind us and we headed to-ward the Manila docks.

8. Transport North

WHEN WE ARRIVED at the dockyard, we boarded a transport ship and met the third of our group, Lieutenant Finn of the U.S. Navy. He had been taken prisoner in the southern islands—he too had worked with codes, on a ship, thus his trip to Tokyo. Our guard told us that Maddock was to act as orderly for both of us. We discovered that this same guard would escort us to Tokyo. He seemed a decent man, meek even; he seemed frightened, not of us, but of the responsibility of escorting three POWs to Japan. He spoke some English, but had to supplement each command with hand signals.

The ship we boarded surprised us. It was not laden with U.S. POWs, as we expected, but with Japanese soldiers; we were to make the voyage north on a troop transport ship bound for home with its war-weary human cargo. This worried me—U.S. ships would attack a Japanese troop transport, but not a ship marked as a POW ship. If the U.S. Navy was finally regrouping in the Pacific, I did not want to die because of it.[1]

As we walked past a group of Japanese soldiers, they gazed at us without animosity. They looked rather like the U.S. troops I had seen while on Bataan, resigned, hungry, tired. I noticed that the troops were quartered in the hold beneath the horses (some of the Japanese cavalry were aboard); the animals got the upper deck, leaving the loyal fighters for the Japanese emperor to endure the stench of the equine cargo from below. When we saw the shabby quarters that the Japanese soldiers were given, we wondered what sort of berths prisoners of war could expect.

Our guard led us through a maze of passages until we reached a crowded little room. As we stepped in the door, all conversation in the room ceased, and twelve Japanese heads swiveled toward us. We were to bunk with some of the war-weary soldiers, it appeared. As our escort nervously motioned us toward our bunks, Maddock asked him in halting Japanese (Maddock was quickly picking up the language) if we were to stay there. The guard, who was by then noticeably anxious, nodded impatiently. We three prisoners exchanged looks of fearful disbelief, then moved toward our bunks. The small room was hardly first class, but it was ranks above the conditions we were accustomed to as POWs. The three of us approached our bunks cautiously, as if they might be booby-trapped, but they were innocuous enough. As we did so, the Japanese soldiers in the room slowly dropped their eyes from us and took up their conversations again.

We soon discovered that we three Americans were the only POWs on board, and we also found that we could trust our roommates. We slept with them and shared one meal a day with them (as at Bilibid, we got what they didn't eat at dinner), while they ignored us. We learned from our guard that they were all master sergeants, going home after a long assignment in China. (He never explained why they had been sent home via the Philippines.) Perhaps the fact that they had been fighting in China explained their lack of hostility toward us Americans. Anglo faces had not been killing their buddies, other Asians had. As it was, the sergeants simply ignored us. When they resumed their own conversations that day, we ceased to exist for them. With one notable exception, they left us alone for the entire trip north.

After a day's travel, we reached the open sea and passed unmolested across it toward Formosa. This made me wonder about the "enemy"—just where was the U.S. Navy in January 1943? I was of course happy not to go down in a sinking Japanese ship, but were U.S. submarines no threat at all to the Japanese? While on deck for our daily exercise, I found myself searching the waters with contradictory feelings. I dreaded spotting a U.S. vessel, for it would certainly fire upon us, but the patriot in me mourned the fact that the Japanese seemed to have complete control over this part of the Pacific.

We stopped only once on our trip northward, at Formosa; we stayed there several days. One afternoon we POWs and our guard were up on deck for fresh air and exercise. I had my navy overcoat on as I stood there and was glad of it. We were no longer in the tropics, and a cool mist that never could have formed in Manila covered the water, leaving a damp chill in the air. Finn joined me at the rail while Maddock ran up and down the deck. The lieutenant and I stood quietly for a few moments, staring out at the city.

"Wainwright's supposed to be here in Formosa," Finn said after a few moments. "I've heard the Japs make him come out and greet Allied POW ships bound for Japan here."[2]

The rumor made sense to me. The Japanese would probably think it another way to demonstrate their victory if the vanquished general waved to defeated Allied soldiers. They would have thought it a way to dishonor the former commander. I myself would have been proud to see Wainwright. But of course Wainwright was not on the dock, though I wistfully looked for him. I suddenly felt terribly alone as I gazed at the mist-shrouded city.

I think Finn felt the same sense of desolation that I did while gazing at those empty docks under oppressive clouds, for neither of us said anything after his comment about Wainwright. A few minutes later, I moved away from the rail, leaving Finn to his thoughts, and joined Maddock in his runs along the deck. Leave it to Maddock to know better than to indulge melancholy while a prisoner of war.

SEVERAL DAYS LATER, when the ship was far out to sea again, I was alone in our quarters with one of the sergeants. Maddock, Finn, and our guard were on deck for their exercise period, and I had chosen not to go. It was a dreary day; through the porthole in the room I could see the discouraging gray water stretch away toward some indiscernible point where ocean met sky. I did not want to go out into the gray day, so I skipped exercise and lay morosely on my bunk.

All at once I heard a clearing of a throat, which startled me; I thought I was alone in the room. I turned to see one of the Japanese sergeants sitting on his upper bunk, looking at me. He smiled, then turned away and, grabbing his duffle bag, began to rummage through it. There was something faintly irreverent about his expression, which put me on guard—I thought I would be the target of some attack.

After a few moments of searching, the sergeant jumped down from his bunk and came toward me. I warily sat up. But the sergeant's eyes were friendly as he approached me, albeit somewhat mischievous. He stopped next to my bunk, grinned at me, then went quickly to the door. After peering out in both directions, he hurried to his bunk again and pulled down his bag. He gestured me toward him. I hesitated. He again motioned, this time more excitedly. I went to his bunk, fearful that I would make him mad if I didn't.

The sergeant grinned at me triumphantly, reached into his bag and brought out two bottles of beer. He turned once more to the door with beers in hand to make certain no one was coming, then returned to me and handed me a beer, only to grab it back immediately. I was confused and afraid as he brought out a small knife, but he only took the top of the beer off with it and thrust the bottle back to me. I took it reluctantly. Was it a test? An insidious form of torture—offer a man a beer with poison in it? I sniffed at it suspiciously as the sergeant opened his own bottle and took a swig. He saw I was hesitant, so he snapped my bottle away again, took a swallow, then handed it back. I was incredulous. This Japanese sergeant was offering me, a prisoner of war, a beer?

The man was still grinning as he raised his own beer in a salute of some sort, then took a long drink from it. He lowered his bottle, watching me expectantly, so I raised the bottle slowly to my lips and took a small sip. Beer it was. In fact, it was my favorite brew of the Philippines, San Miguel. I had not had one since before Pearl Harbor. I took another swallow, and the sergeant laughed aloud. He raised his bottle and waited for me to do the same. After our toast, which we uttered in both Japanese and English, we took long swallows and then both burst out laughing. And so we enjoyed our beers, laughing and talking in our separate languages, neither one of us understanding a word the other said.

We made several toasts that day. I do not know what the sergeant was saluting, but I do know that my last toast was to him, to the soldier who was consorting with his enemy, and laughing while he did so. I toast you, young Japanese sergeant, tired, disgusted, and war-weary after battling in China and who knows where else; I drink to you and your humanity and generosity in the face of propaganda and paranoia from your peers and mine. To you.

Five days later, on 29 January, we arrived in the port city of Moji on Kyushu, the southernmost island of Japan, where the sergeants, due to their rank, were the first to disembark, leaving us POWs and the other Japanese troops behind. The beer-smuggling sergeant was the last to exit the room. At the door, after he had pulled on his pack, he turned back to me and grinned, then hurried forward to catch up with his comrades.

I toast that nameless Japanese sergeant to this day.

WE THREE POWs and our guard boarded the deck later, after all the horses and the Japanese troops had disembarked. Once we were on the dock, we stood at the end of a long line of soldiers. I had no idea what we were waiting for; I only knew that it was too cold to be standing on that exposed dock. A damp wind blew in off the ocean, making me clutch my overcoat together. But Maddock seemed unaffected by the cold; he was actually whistling. He seemed used to this cold climate.

"Where are you from, Maddock?" I asked as another wet gust swept across the dock.

"Southern California, near Los Angeles," he said nonchalantly. "Do you think it snows up here? I've only seen snow once before. I liked it." Maddock hadn't even buttoned his coat up. Walter Maddock was in a class by himself.

By the time we made it to the front of the line, I was thoroughly chilled. When I saw what we were standing in line for, I grew even colder: several Japanese nurses stood in front of a table, all busily wiping at glass rods with cotton swabs. Next to the table stood more nurses, who were methodically approaching a line of bared bottoms in front of them with glass wands in hand; they were checking for dysentery. The thought of the cold glass intruding on a very warm and personal part of my body left me mighty uneasy. I still had a mild case of dysentery, but were they actually going to treat me for it? I doubted it. Our turn came in line, and Maddock and I doffed our trousers, Maddock making crude comments the entire time. I survived the humiliating cold probe, then quickly bundled up. And as I expected, if they found I had dysentery, they gave me no treatment for it.

Our escort led us off the ship and away from the dock area to the train station. It was midafternoon, and the streets were crowded. People were everywhere. Each and every one of the hurrying civilians we saw carried a cloth bundle—sometimes they had two or more of the bundles, and they carried them carefully, even jealously. On bicycles, behind carts, under great loads, guiding small children—in 1943, Japan was people-propelled because most of their petrol stores were being used for their war effort. The few cars we saw were running on coke, we later found out; coke was cheaper and more plentiful in Japan than gasoline. Coke did not burn as efficiently as gasoline—the cars were slow and moved haltingly at times. Few of the people rushing past paid any attention to us, for they kept their heads lowered or turned away from us. This surprised me; I thought we would be a novelty in Japan, and an unwelcome one. But no one seemed interested in three Caucasians who walked among them.

Once we were in the train station, our guard led us to a bench and told us to remain there. He then wheeled around and disappeared. Maddock, Finn, and I looked at each other apprehensively. The Japanese masses left us alone when we had a soldier with a sword to protect us, but how would they react if there was no one to defend us? We gathered close together, kept our heads averted, and tried to look inconspicuous.

But our fears were for naught—nobody bothered us. After fifteen minutes of scrunching together and examining our shoelaces, we realized we were still being ignored. We relaxed a bit and looked around. The station seemed to be efficiently run. There were no long lines or impatient people about—rail transportation appeared to be a smooth operation in Japan, even with fuel shortages and a war going on.

Our guard finally came back. He had been taking care of our tickets. Sometime later in the early evening, a train pulled into the station. The guard pointed to the sign on the front of it as it approached. "Twenty-seven hours," he said haltingly. We looked at him uncomprehendingly. "Twenty-seven hours," he repeated while again pointing at the sign on the train. We still did not understand. The guard suddenly grinned. I think he realized just then that we could not read the Japanese script. "Tokyo," he translated. We finally understood. This train was to take us to our final destination— in twenty-seven hours, we would be in Tokyo.

There were many Japanese travelers waiting for the train, and our guard was determined to get a seat. He signaled to us to pick up our bags and rush forward as soon as the train came to a stop. We did so, but the Japanese masses were obviously accustomed to boarding trains this way. Our guard and strange appearances were of no advantage—the train was already packed by the time we squeezed aboard.

"Squeezed" is not an exaggeration—the train was packed to the walls with people and their bundles, small and large, all bound for points north. The seats had been grabbed by more aggressive travelers. Maddock, Finn, and the guard were in the same car with me, but there was no way to sit together. As it was each for himself, I found myself some space to stand along the wall. A few minutes later, the train lurched and began to move while people were still trying to board it. Japanese trains obviously did not wait for latecomers.

The car was stuffy, for there were too many people aboard, but in spite of their discomfort, the passengers were still polite. They murmured niceties in Japanese to one another that I recognized as "excuse me" and "thank you." And none of them looked at me directly. I wearily closed my eyes and leaned against the wall. I was tired and I suspected there was more interest in me than the politely averted eyes portrayed—I had detected their furtive but inquisitive eyes darting in my direction whenever they thought such glances would go unnoticed. The people around me would find it easier to study me if my eyes were closed.

A little while after we left Moji, I opened my eyes when I heard a rise in conversation on all sides of me. The ride so far had been a quiet affair, with only the sounds of the electrically powered cars running along the track and slight jostlings of passengers. But now everyone was whispering excitedly and gesturing toward the front of the train in anticipation of something. A few moments later, the train rushed into a tunnel, which seemed anticlimactic after all the excitement, but the people around me became all the more animated once we were in the tunnel. They kept looking at their watches. I was beginning to think the Japanese an easily excitable crowd when I realized that the train had not emerged from the tunnel. We had been in it for some time, rushing along at high speed. I understood their wonder—this was some achievement, this long tunnel. I discovered later that it had just been completed—it linked Kyushu and Honshu Islands. The tunnel underneath the sea was a brand-new time-saver to these passengers, thus their excited whispers as they checked their watches.

But the train was no express train. Once back on land, it started making frequent stops. I decided about four hours later that it must be stopping at every hamlet and village along the way. The reward for all the stops was that many people were getting off the train, and eventually I got a seat. A tiny middle-aged woman dressed in a simple kimono took the seat next to me, after bowing to the three men opposite us and the man on the other side of her. From this, I supposed that they were all traveling together. She gave me a slight nod too as she settled in, which was my first acknowledgment from a Japanese civilian.

It was late and I was exhausted. We had not eaten since the night before, and I was hungry. But I was used to hunger and fell asleep in spite of my empty belly. Some time later I awoke. The train, I vaguely remembered, had stopped several times while I dozed, leaving fewer people in the car. Most people slept, but a few stared pensively out into the rushing darkness. An old man stood in front of me, grimly clutching a live chicken to his chest that surprisingly did not struggle much. An old woman stood next to him, holding a large cloth bundle, and though there were several empty chairs, neither took one. It must have been two or three in the morning. As I shifted my head, I noticed it was cushioned by something dark and wispy—the woman next to me had fallen asleep and dropped her head onto my shoulder, and I in response had fallen asleep with my head atop hers. Across from us, the woman's companions slept in the same fashion. Being careful not to awaken her, I raised my head and searched the car for Maddock. I found him three seats ahead of me. He had somehow managed to commandeer two seats, and was sprawled across them, sound asleep; I heard a deep snoring and fancied it was he. I did not see Finn or our guard.

That night on the train seemed serenely unreal after the harshness of the war and our imprisonment in the Philippines. I had dreaded being among these people who were said to be so hostile toward Americans, and yet there I sat, sleepily contemplating the peaceful faces around me with an enemy head resting on my shoulder. I closed my eyes and sank my head onto the woman's head again, wondering if she had a son out on a battlefield somewhere.

I SLEPT FOR several more hours, then awoke to a misty light outside the windows. I sensed a movement from the woman on whose head mine rested. I raised my head slowly and rubbed my eyes, then mumbled "excuse me" in Japanese to the woman.

The men across from us began to stir while the woman next to me straightened her hair and kimono. She then reached for one of her cloth bundles and rummaged through it. A moment later, she carefully pulled smaller bundles from the larger one, all neatly wrapped in paper. These she carefully arranged on her lap. On seeing the men opposite her awake, she unwrapped two of the packages and my stomach began to growl. Inside each package were dainty-looking rice balls and small cakes. I looked away. She and her friends were to have breakfast now, I assumed, and I was to witness it as my stomach yelled for a share.

The woman turned to the man next to her, bowed her head to him politely, then offered him a rice ball. He took one, bowing his head as he did so, and said thank you. The woman then presented the food to the man nearest the window across from us, who politely accepted one. The performance was repeated with the other passengers across from us, all smiles and consideration as they addressed one another. It was a lovely outing for all, I thought bitterly as I concentrated on the scenes rushing by outside the opposite window. I wondered resentfully if any of them had noticed how thin I was.

I then felt a hesitant tap on my elbow and turned to see the woman's shy face. She bowed her head to me with the same respectful air with which she had approached the other men and offered me a rice ball. I was surprised, but nodded back as the other men had done, expressing my thanks as best I could in Japanese. "Arigato," I said several times, and bowed again. She inclined her head once, then turned away while I took a small bite of the morsel as the other men had, reining an impulse to swallow it whole. It was rice once again, but far better fare than what I was accustomed to—I wondered if the woman had made it herself. "Arigato," I announced again when the woman looked in my direction. She beamed back at me, then lowered her eyes.

Happily, the meal wasn't over. Our next course consisted of seaweed-wrapped rice with fish in the center—I had never seen this before (there weren't any sushi restaurants in Chicago when I was growing up), but I enjoyed it. Once we were all finished with those, she passed around gooey and delicious little rice cakes. The small meal took some time to complete, for with each course, she used the same ceremonious style, and each of us had to bow once or twice in return. I felt like a dignified human being again as I ate that meal.

About an hour later, I was sorry to see the woman stand with the man next to her and prepare to leave—she said something to me that I didn't understand; I said thank you again. The three men opposite stood and bowed, but did not follow them. They weren't traveling together after all. The two of them then left the train, but she left her bundles behind. This perplexed and alarmed me—the woman had lost interest in her precious bundles? Should I chase her down and give them to her? A moment later one of the travelers opposite me stood again and shoved open the window. His companion grabbed one of the bundles and shoved it out, and I thought for a confused moment that they must be a gang of ungrateful thieves (and she had given them such a nice breakfast). Then I saw the woman and her companion outside the train below us, taking each bundle as it was handed out. It was their way of coping with impatient train conductors who were determined to keep their trains on time; this was a quicker way to get oneself and those cumbersome bundles off the train before it left the station. I tried to help, anxious to show my appreciation to the woman for her kindness, then waved to her as the train left the station a short and very punctual minute later. She waved back and bowed.

I turned away from the window slowly, then jumped to my seat just in time to save it from a middle-aged Japanese man. I fully expected him to hit me for my impertinent repossession of my seat, but he merely bowed and turned away while I gave thanks to God that these people were as polite as they were. I wondered what the chances were that three Japanese citizens in the United States could ride unmolested on a public train during this war. Not good, I decided.

As I was musing about the difference between these decent people and the typical Japanese POW camp guard, a group of four Japanese soldiers climbed on the train, which immediately made me nervous. None of them looked in my direction though, and when one did, he was as unalarmed by the American faces on the train as everyone else. The soldiers were in jovial spirits, laughing and talking loudly among themselves.

They found four seats together and were soon shouting with laughter two seats away from me. At one stop, two of them stood, threw open the window, and scrambled out of the car. But they weren't going AWOL, as I at first suspected; instead, they approached the vendors and food machines that lined the tracks. But they didn't buy anything—apparently not just any food would do. As the train was leaving the station, they raced back to the train and climbed in through the window with their two buddies' help. I realized then that they went out the window because it was quicker than going through the crowded doors. And of course it was more fun to jump out the window. They repeated this sequence at the next couple of stops. At the third stop they finally found a vendor who sold the item they wanted: ice cream.

I watched the four of them unwrap their ice cream bars as an idea took hold of me. (If the staff sergeant on the ship had not shared a beer with me, I'm certain I would never have thought of this.) They seemed to be friendly enough, and besides, they enjoyed taking turns hopping out of the train. All they could do was hit me for asking, and I had been hit before by a Japanese soldier. I stood and dug in my pocket for the few yen I had there, compliments of Capt. Joe Iacobucci, then approached the friendliest-looking of the four soldiers. I conveyed to him that I wanted him to buy me some ice cream, then said "please" in Japanese.

The soldier didn't speak English, but as ice cream holds a unique universal appeal, he got the idea. I was very happy to see him grin and nod his head. He put his hand out for the money and I gave it to him while suddenly filled with second thoughts. If he should decide to keep it, there was no getting it back, and I had so little Japanese money.

But at the next stop, the Japanese soldier with my money jumped out of the train to find a vendor selling ice cream. He didn't find one, and made his mad sprint back to the train. He babbled something to me as he climbed back in the window that I imagine was, "I couldn't find any, but I'll try again next time," for that is exactly what he did. Before he jumped off at the next stop, I thought of my friends and held up three fingers while pointing to Finn and Maddock. The soldier understood with a nod and once again leaped from the train, only to fail once more. A few stops later, however, he succeeded and bounded back to the train with three vanilla ice cream bars. He gave them to me with a triumphant grin and then handed me my change. His challenge met, he returned to his seat and began to chatter with his comrades again.

That ice cream was without a doubt the best I have ever tasted in my entire life.

The soldiers stayed on the train for about two more hours and then disembarked. The soldier who had bought me my ice cream did not acknowledge me. Our truce on the train was over, I supposed. He was a soldier again.

Some hours later, after dark, the train slowed on entering what appeared to be a large city. I say "what appeared to be" because it was difficult to discern whether the city was there or not—all was black outside, and only with effort could I descry the shrouded shapes of buildings. I was sitting next to Maddock by then. He asked our guard, in Japanese, if the city was Tokyo, and the guard nodded.

How different it was from what I had expected! Tokyo seemed frightened and vulnerable—it looked as Manila had looked before the U.S. forces pulled out in late 1941. For the first time since just after Pearl Harbor, I felt real hope that the Allies might win the war, for the Japanese were obviously wary of Allied bombers.[3] Our guards and camp commanders informed us daily that the Japanese and Nazis were winning on all fronts and that it was only a matter of time before they had unchallenged control over Asia and the Pacific. But the blackout conditions in Tokyo belied such blustering; the Allies were still in this war after all. This was a new thought as we slid along the tracks in that darkened city-in-hiding. A cog must have fallen into the mighty Japanese war machine, and I suspected the cog was American-made. As we arrived in Tokyo, I felt more optimistic than I had in months.

9. Yokohama Camp Number One

As we stood outside the train station waiting for a transport truck, we discovered that Tokyo was much like Moji. It was a city crawling slowly along on coke, and it was cold. A light snow fell, but it was not accumulating; the few flakes were swept away by a sharp wind that whistled down the street. After a long ride in a lumbering coke-fed truck, we arrived at Shinagawa Camp, which sat in an industrial section of Tokyo.[1] There we parted from Finn—as a naval POW, he would go to a different camp. We never saw him again.

Nor did we see our guard again, but before he left us to our new guards, he gave me a letter. He had been told by his superiors to give it to me upon arriving in Tokyo. It was from Virginia. I read it under a streetlight while we waited for transportation to our camp. She was all right, she said, and had received the money and letter that I had sent her from Bilibid. She couldn't say much more than that, but it was enough to make me feel close to her again, in spite of the weeks that had passed since she had written the letter.

A taxi took Maddock and me and our guard to an industrial area of Yokohama.[2] Our new home sat in a cluster of run-down warehouses. In the dark, we could see that the warehouses were fenced in and dimly illuminated by hooded lights on each corner. By the smell of the air and the sound of water slapping against wood, we knew we were close to the waterfront. I hoped that by day the area would not look so dreary; I realized then that in spite of the deprivation within the fences, the POW camps in the Philippines had a certain aesthetic character to them—Bilibid in beautiful Manila and Cabanatuan in the lush north. This new camp simply looked cold, damp, barren, and miserable.

We were left in a small, chilly room. Unaccustomed to the cold as we were, neither Maddock nor I slept much that night; we had only our thin blankets to cover us and the room had no heat. The next morning a guard took us to the camp commander. We discovered then that we had spent the night in the guardhouse.

The camp, we saw in the light, consisted of two large warehouses, some smaller shacks, and a newer building in front of us to which we were being led. It looked no better by daylight than it had the night before. The grim cluster of buildings was surrounded by a single wooden fence topped sporadically with barbed wire. There was no large compound area, only a dirt track all around, with the fence about ten feet from the walls of the warehouses. But for a few POWs who were dressed in odd-looking uniforms and working menial jobs, the camp appeared to be empty.

We arrived at the commander's office. The room was warm—a wood stove glowed in the corner. A Japanese lieutenant gazed up at us as we entered. Maddock and I both saluted him, then bowed.

The man directed his comments toward me. "I am Lieutenant Nichizawa, commander Number One Camp, Yokohama. You?"[3]

Maddock and I in turn rattled off name, rank, serial number. Nichizawa again spoke to me; he demanded Maddock's uniform after giving him one of the odd uniforms we had seen the other POWs in. Per Nichizawa's orders, only officers were allowed to keep their uniforms. Maddock quickly changed. Nichizawa also declared that as an enlisted man, Maddock would work. Just then a POW slipped into the room, dressed as Maddock now was. He politely greeted Nichizawa and then spoke to him in rapid Japanese—he spoke fluently, with no stumbling as Maddock still did. Nichizawa answered him, then dismissed all of us. We left with the POW; a Japanese guard walked close behind us.

Once outside, the man introduced himself in a hurried whisper. "My name's Sherman. The bloke following us is Shishido. He doesn't speak much

English so you can talk around him, only make sure you always smile and talk fast. Try to keep him happy—he'll slap you when he's angry." Sherman smiled and nodded at Shishido. Then he turned back to us. "Most of us here are British—I'm from England. Captured at Singapore. I was a gunner. Where are you from?"

We answered him and introduced ourselves.

Sherman continued. "That bastard you just met is Lt. Masao Nichizawa, the camp commander. I'm his orderly. I do some interpreting too. His interpreters speak miserable English. If you need to talk to a Jap, come to me first." He waved toward the building we had just left and raised his voice. "That's the Japanese quarters, where the gunzokos and the soldiers assigned to the camp sleep. That over there," he pointed to the smaller warehouse, "is the bathhouse and kitchen. You get a bath once every two weeks, on rest days. Those are the latrines next to the main barracks. And this grand palace," he made a sweeping gesture to the largest warehouse, "is our home. Welcome." With a deep bow, whether to us or Shishido I did not know, he started to leave us.

"What's a gunzoko?" Maddock hastily asked before Sherman stepped away.

"*He's* a gunzoko," Sherman whispered, nodding toward Shishido. "A civilian actually—they aren't really in the army. Be careful with them, because they don't transfer out. The army guards, they change every two weeks, but the gunzokos are permanent. Remember that." Sherman then left us.

Shishido led us into the dim building—there was no light but for the rays that slipped in through the windows. The room was huge and barren, constructed of wood and cement; it was an uncomfortable and drafty hall meant to store objects, not house men. A wooden platform was built up off the ground on which we saw Japanese mats, tatamis, carefully lined up. A wood stove sat in the corner, but it was unlit and so did nothing to warm the chilly room. Shishido led us to a ladder used to get to the beds above. He pointed to Maddock, then said something in Japanese that I didn't understand, but Maddock did. He was to sleep up there.

Shishido then led us to the camp hospital area. The room was literally overflowing with men lying close together. The hospital inmates were in varying states of health. A few looked as if they had only a few days of life

left in them; others looked less ill but utterly exhausted. All were under-
nourished. Several POWs were acting as medics. One was a tall man in a
British officer's uniform—he looked amazingly sharp and nicely dressed
among the motley group of sick prisoners. He looked casually at Shishido
and us, then returned to his work. Another officer of about fifty or so was
also attending to the ill. He took one look at Shishido, became flustered,
and dropped something.

Shishido told Maddock to stay in the hospital area and help the doctors,
then led me into the next area of the partitioned warehouse. In this area
were more sick prisoners, about twenty of them, and some thirty-five officers. Shishido led me to a man in a British lieutenant colonel's uniform. The
colonel bowed to the gunzoko and said something in Japanese; Shishido answered and left me with him.

The man extended his hand. We shook hands and introduced ourselves.
The lieutenant colonel's name was Thomas Lindesay; he was the prisoner-
in-charge. We exchanged surrender stories, then Lindesay gave me some
information on camp life. He pointed to the sick men in the room and explained that they were in the officers' area because there were so many ill
POWs that the doctors needed help watching over them. Most of the enlisted men who were able worked at Mitsubishi Shipyards, which was three
miles away—a six-mile commute by foot each day. The majority of the
officers were British; only four were American. Some one hundred of the
enlisted men were Americans along with a few Australians and Canadians;
there were also about seventy-five Dutch POWs. The rest were British, to-
taling about five hundred POWs in the camp. The officers were separated
from the enlisted men, but conditions were the same in both sections of the
warehouse; both areas stank of the latrines just outside the door. Each POW
was allowed two blankets and I was glad, for the room would be frigid at
night. There was a single wood stove at the far end of the room, but it, like
the one in the larger room, was not in use on this wintry day, the last day of
January 1943. With that brief introduction, I was left to find myself a tatami
and a square of free space on the shelf that was our sleeping area.

Some thirty-five prisoners were in the hospital area, I learned; along with
the sixteen in the officers' area, more than fifty men were too ill to work. As
in the Philippines, there was little medicine for the ailing POWs. Due to

the lack of space, there was no segregation of the prisoners by illness, so those with pneumonia slept next to those with infectious diseases. Colonel Lindesay said things were not good. Eleven men had already died since the year began, most of them of pneumonia. But Lindesay reported that it had been much worse in December, for many of the prisoners had just arrived from the southern latitudes, and hard labor in the cold air left them vulnerable to any new virus.

I met the doctors of the camp far sooner than I thought I would. As I set about familiarizing myself with the place and my fellow prisoners, I noted that I had a nagging earache that soon grew worse and spread into both ears. By my third day there, I was in constant pain, half deaf, and I had lost my sense of equilibrium. I was stumbling around, yelling at my new roommates to speak up, and generally not making myself very popular. I went into the hospital area for help.

On entering the hospital area, I met the tall man I had seen tending to patients a few days before. He too was British. I again noted his neat appearance. His uniform was clean and carefully arranged, and he worked methodically, even rhythmically. He seemed unruffled by his status as a POW. When my turn came to speak with him, he introduced himself as Lt. John Brackstone and asked me how he could help me.

When I asked him to repeat himself three times, he seemed to get the idea as to what was wrong.

"Ah, something wrong with your ears, is it? Let's have a look." He peered into one of my ears.

"Thank you, Doctor," I yelled at him.

"I'm not a doctor," Brackstone shouted back. "I'm an engineer. Price is the man you'll see about this, he's the doctor. I just help him out a bit. And you don't have to yell. I can hear fine."

Later, when I could hear better, Brackstone explained why an engineer was probing about my ear. He had trained to be a doctor while at university, but after becoming an intern, he decided he liked engineering better. So he changed to engineering, eventually became part of the Royal Corps of Engineers, and was stationed in Singapore. When that area fell to the Japanese, a large portion of the Corps—the twenty-five British officers—ended up in our camp.

Brackstone tried to explain to me that day that earaches such as mine were common. He shouted a question: "Did you only just arrive in Japan?" I yelled that yes, I had.

"You don't need to shout," Brackstone yelled again. "I'm the one who has to shout!" But he did not continue to do so. He dropped back into a normal voice, and I could only watch him mouth the words. "You see, the change in climate will do this. Did you spend much time in the tropics?"

I stared at him blankly.

Brackstone frowned, unwilling to yell anymore. He went to find Dr. Price. A few minutes later, Price diagnosed me as having an acute ear infection. He yelled into my ear: "We need a syringe of some sort. We need to burst your eardrums." (I wished I had not heard that.) "Then they will heal properly. We need only the syringe. Bracky will ask Nichizawa for one." Price gave me a towel and told me to soak it in hot water from the kitchen and hold it next to my ear.

I later understood why Brackstone asked for the syringe rather than Price. I discovered over the next month that Price was as nervous as he looked, and he was terrified of the Japanese, especially Nichizawa. He would always send the cooler Bracky—as Brackstone was nicknamed—to deal with the camp commander.

Nichizawa refused to give Bracky the syringe. As it happened, there was a feud going on just then between Nichizawa and the officers, specifically the engineers. As I saw Bracky frequently in those first few days, we became friends. When I was finally able to hear again, he told me the story behind Nichizawa's refusal.

Any healthy POWs were expected to work. The enlisted men put in ten hours of labor seven days a week. (They were given every second Sunday off.) Most of the officers, however, did not work—only those officers who volunteered for the lunch, burial, and hospital details were busy every day, which left some thirty officers idle. I soon found that this caused much animosity between the enlisted men and officers. Though the enlisted men were respectful enough in an officer's presence, there was a considerable rift between the two groups that only a few officers bothered to bridge, most notably Bracky.

Nichizawa was furious over the idle officers. He saw in the Royal Corps of Engineers great work potential, and his daily laborer numbers were low.

Just before I arrived, Nichizawa had approached Colonel Lindesay and demanded that the engineers go to work tracing plans for Japanese ships and equipment. Lindesay had put the matter to a vote, and the engineers had unanimously voted not to help the Japanese war effort by tracing plans. When Lindesay reported to Nichizawa that the officers refused the work, Nichizawa hit him. But Lindesay and the engineers didn't back down. They refused to help the Japanese with any of their blueprints.

Bracky told me that when I had arrived Nichizawa was at the height of his fury with the officers. "That's why he wouldn't give us a syringe for your ears," Bracky explained. "He said he wouldn't help any POWs who would not work. You're an officer, presumably you will not work, so no syringe."

It was a week before Price got a device that would burst my eardrums. It wasn't a syringe, but a sponge ball attached to a slender stick. Price saturated the sponge with hot water, slid the contraption into my ear, and forced it against my eardrum. I felt a painful burst when he did so, but it was worth it the following day when the pain began to disappear and I could hear again. We didn't get the sponge from Nichizawa. Bracky got it through the black market.

This stalemate between the officers and Nichizawa continued. Nichizawa beat Lindesay several more times, but this only made the officers all the more determined. Nichizawa cut the officers' rations by a third, declaring that since the officers were not cooperating they deserved even less food. (As in the Philippines, any working prisoner received more food than a non-working one.) The officers only shrugged en masse and still refused to trace the blueprints.

Nichizawa was not willing to concede defeat, however. His honor had been sullied, and he was determined to somehow humiliate the stubborn engineers. After I had been in the camp about ten days, he marched into the officers' area with some wire and black rice paper. He stood on a small tub above the prisoners and began to bellow.

"You do not do simple trace work, so I find other work for officers." He reached down and picked up some of the paper. "This black paper. It is for lamps. Blackout lamps. You officers, you make lamp shades. Woman's work. Woman's work for officers who will not trace plans." The commander was smiling in an ugly manner, assuming himself triumphant. "This is not for war, but for civilians. You must do this woman's work. All officers will do woman's work." Nichizawa was almost aglow in anticipation of the Brits' outrage.

But Nichizawa didn't understand the British character. Lindesay was not the least bit angry, nor were the other officers. They immediately saw an opportunity in the situation. Lindesay bowed respectfully to Nichizawa. "That will be fine, honorable sir. We would be happy to make blackout lamp shades for the civilians."

A lieutenant spoke up from behind him. "I just love working with my hands, sir. This will be perfect."

There were snickers around the room. Lindesay gazed blandly at the commander and asked when they could start.

Nichizawa, who had fancied himself so close to victory over the officers, grew absolutely livid. "It is woman's work!! You work paper, you work cut, cut, it is woman's work! Men do not do this!"

The officers gazed back at him, silent and undeterred.

Nichizawa went into a frenzy. "You are women, all of you, women!" he screeched, stamping his feet. "Women!" He jumped down from his tub, striking any POW within his reach with the back of his hand. In his rage, he began sputtering in a mixture of Japanese and English and burst from the room, with his guards trailing behind him.

The officers chuckled quietly at first, then more loudly until the room was a roar of laughter and crude comments about Nichizawa. For once, the difference between Japanese and Anglo cultures worked in our favor. Nichizawa could not shame the officers into doing "men's" blueprint work by making them do "women's" lamp shade work. The Western sense of honor and proper male work wasn't as deeply ingrained as that of the Japanese.

But Nichizawa wasn't finished. He returned the next day with a young Japanese woman from a local factory. The woman mutely demonstrated how to make the lamp shades, then was escorted from the room. Nichizawa screamed at us again to make our lamp shades, then left. One of the gunzokos remained in the room with us to make certain we would perform the "humiliating" women's work.

We officers went at the work with gleeful vengeance—a few of us even became rather proficient at it. We constructed lamp shade after lamp shade until there seemed enough to provide a blackout lamp shade for every home in Tokyo. It became a challenge to see just how many lamp shades one could finish in a single day. One of the officers, who was a self-proclaimed expert in the art of lamp shade–making, stood up one day to announce that he was offering a course in proper methods of cutting and pasting.

"I've noticed several of you putting together some sloppy shades, which just won't do. I recommend that all of you attend my class and learn how to do it properly. Our reputations as engineers are at stake here, you know."

This same fellow always made a point of showing his pieces to Lindesay when a gunzoko was nearby. "What do you think of this one, sir?" he asked loudly one day, pointing inside the shade. "I tried a new cutting style here, and went lightly here with the glue. I think it's rather distinctive."

Lindesay went along with him. "Oh, that really is lovely, Captain. You do fine work," he concurred.

The captain dropped his eyes and smiled shyly. "Why, thank you, sir." He dropped a curtsy and went back to work.

Such episodes as these went on for several weeks, always in front of a scowling Japanese gunzoko. More than a few officers received blows from the guards because of their comic displays, but no one was hurt badly enough to stop the pranks. They were enjoying the situation too much.

Nichizawa did not supervise the lamp shade production again after the young woman's visit. If he could have shot every one of us officers without repercussion, I'm sure he would have. After a few more weeks, though, he broke; Nichizawa had had all he could take of the Jolly Lamp Shade Makers. He ordered the gunzokos to confiscate the paper and glue after a last tirade against the effeminate officers and their utter lack of male dignity. The officers only smirked. We knew who had won this battle.

EACH GUNZOKO IN our camp had a personality of his own, but they all had one thing in common: without exception, they abused the POWs under their control. As Sherman had explained, a gunzoko was a civilian, either a former soldier who had been ousted from the regular army for some reason or someone who was not soldier material in the first place because of some emotional or physical problem. If a man had a tendency to steal, quarrel, and beat upon the defenseless, the Japanese military had good reason to keep him out of their ranks—I only wish they had had the decency to keep him from ours. I realize that every society has its maniacal fringe, but there must be a better place for such people than in a POW camp where they may express their violent urges with impunity.

The slightest provocation sent the gunzokos into excited and violent frenzies. I hadn't been there long before two Americans, Private McQueeny and Private Mannix, were severely beaten for having dirty pillowcases and then sent to the guardhouse to hold buckets full of water in front of them for several hours. (This was a favorite form of punishment on the part of our gunzokos.) It was impossible for the pillowcases to stay clean in our filthy warehouse-barrack, but this made little difference to the gunzokos. The pillowcases were Japanese issue, the emperor's property, and the prisoners had dirtied them. One evening, Shishido severely beat a British lieutenant, Michael Wright. His offense? His shoes were scuffed. It made no difference that none of us had access to shoe-cleaning materials; the untidy shoes were an insult to Shishido, and thus he attacked Wright. But the gunzokos didn't have to have a reason for beating defenseless men. Two of the gunzokos beat Private Davis, an American, nearly to death one evening in the compound for no given reason. He suffered several broken bones and a concussion.[4]

A gunzoko was at his worst when he was made officer-in-charge for a day, a job that the gunzokos rotated among themselves when Nichizawa left the camp at night and on his weekend rest day. Much of the gunzokos' abuse of POWs occurred when Nichizawa was out of camp because when a gunzoko wore the red-and-white officer's sash and carried an officer's sword, he would have no one to answer to; he was top dog. Many POWs were slapped, slugged, and screamed at on such days to prove the omnipotence of our temporary camp commander.

Along with the gunzokos, a contingent of some twenty soldiers from the regular Japanese army were assigned to our camp at any given time. These units came and went, staying only a few weeks at most. In general, the soldiers acted more decently toward the POWs than did the gunzokos, but they were terrified of Nichizawa, who, as a second lieutenant in the army, had as much right to beat them as he did the POWs. The soldiers were subject to the orders of both the camp commander and gunzokos; if they were told to beat a prisoner without cause, they did so without question. If they weren't ordered to join a beating, the soldiers became silent sentinels with guns who made certain that the other POWs would not protest the bloodshed.

Of the five gunzokos permanently assigned to the camp, one seemed friendly and approachable. Kambe, or as we called him "One Eye," talked and joked with POWs and exchanged cigarettes or candy with them. But the first week I was in Yokohama, Bracky warned me to avoid Kambe no matter how chummy he appeared. The advice confused me, for Kambe seemed genuinely friendly.

Bracky's warning proved true. Kambe did have his favorites for whom he would sometimes do special favors, but his favorites all wished they had never seen the man when Kambe fell into a bad temper, for Kambe was, either congenitally or because of his war experience, schizophrenic. According to the story, Kambe had fought in the regular army in China for years; he had only recently become a gunzoko when he was wounded and was deemed by his superiors no longer fit for active duty. Thus he ended up in our camp. The wound that Kambe had suffered had been a brutal one, one that none of us fully understood how he survived. He had been shot in the head, thereby losing his eye, and the bullet, he boastfully told us when in good spirits, was still lodged in his head. He often showed us the lumpy scar in his better moods, talking proudly of the Chinese metal that was in his head but could not kill him.

But the wound apparently was not entirely healed. The pain returned sporadically, sometimes once a week, sometimes once a month, and during those times Kambe cried out in pain, and then we who knew better avoided him at all costs. At first he only moaned as the pain commenced; several hours later he became poisonous, taking out his suffering on anyone within reach. Those who had been his favorites a few short hours earlier fell soundly from favor if he recognized them in his rage. He might make his former friends do calisthenics by the hour in the cold, or hold a bucket outstretched in the guardhouse while he bellowed at them for hours, or he might simply beat them with his fists.

Another face we saw regularly in the camp blustered about, trying to appear a tough number, but he didn't fool many people. Okimoto, an interpreter, arrived in the camp six weeks after I did, in the middle of March 1943. We first saw him on a rest day in the enlisted men's area where I had gone to chat with Maddock after the officers' roll call. While we talked, a gunzoko entered the room. With him was a Japanese man of fifty or so with silver hair. When he stood before us, he drew himself up tall, but it was clear that he was ill-at-ease and unaccustomed to ordering people about. He was also noticeably wary of the gunzoko with him.

After collecting himself, he bellowed, "All right, youse guys, fall in for roll call!"

There was a momentary silence in the room as we all realized that this Japanese guard did not stumble around with the English language or mix it with Japanese. He spoke it perfectly, even colloquially, with an accent that all the Americans in the room immediately recognized.

An American standing a few feet away from me collected himself in a hurry. "Holy mackerel, get a load of Brooklyn!" he called loudly, then emitted a loud whistle. A light ripple of laughter flowed over the room.

Okimoto attempted to draw himself up taller and called out over the titters, "I said it's time for roll call! Fall in, youse guys!" The Americans laughed out loud over this, but everyone separated into their assigned groups.

Okimoto, it turned out, had spent the last thirty-six years in Brooklyn, New York. He had gone there as an adolescent, found a job, and stayed, so his English was that of a person born and bred in Brooklyn. His years in New York made no difference when the war came, however; he had been put into an internment camp in the United States immediately after Pearl Harbor and had stayed there some six months before he and several hundred other Japanese nationals were exchanged for U.S. prisoners being held in Japan. When Okimoto arrived back in the country he had not returned to in thirty-six years, the Japanese authorities were at a loss as to what to do with him. At his age he was not a candidate for active duty, and although he spoke English fluently, he could not be trusted as an interpreter performing interrogations; he had, after all, spent more time in the United States than in Japan, and naturally the Japanese suspected his sympathies might lie elsewhere. Thus, Okimoto was made an interpreter in our POW camp, where any pro-American feelings would do little harm.

But Okimoto was not exactly free to be friendly with the POWs. When he knew us better, he told several of us that he believed that he and his family were being watched. That was why he tried to act the tough Japanese guard. But Okimoto was not an unyielding gunzoko, and we POWs knew it. We played along with his tough guy image when there were other Japanese personnel present, but we knew we could trust Okimoto. If ever one of us needed a favor or some sort of a break from the harsh conditions, we approached Okimoto. More often than not, Okimoto couldn't do much, not without making himself look too friendly with the prisoners, but he always tried to help if he could. He gave us cigarettes, food, newspapers, and other goods. Okimoto even tried to improve conditions in camp; several times he approached the camp commanders with ideas for remodeling the barracks or ways of supplementing our food allotment. Most of these proposals were refused, but at least Okimoto recognized we were suffering and spoke up.

In Kambe and Okimoto, we saw the worst and the best of Japanese nature.

IN MY FIRST month in Yokohama Camp Number One, I had many times heard the camp commander referred to as "the Murderer" by other POWs. It wasn't long before I discovered how Nichizawa had earned the nickname. His most obvious offense was in the way he ran the camp: he was so frugal with food and medicines that men were dying of malnutrition and disease. He ran the camp as cheaply as possible—the POWs would not receive one grain of rice more than what was necessary to sustain them; every POW who was able to stand would work; and there would be no money expended on frivolous items such as medicines for the prisoners.

The camp was very cold that winter, with temperatures below freezing throughout the month of February, yet we were allowed only two hours of heat in the drafty warehouse each day—one hour in the morning and one hour in the evening. The two small wood-burning stoves never would have raised the temperature to the comfort zone on those frigid nights, but they would at least have made the warehouse more bearable had they been burning constantly. As it was, half-starved men struggled to keep warm; their immune defenses dropped; and our sick rate soared. For POWs who had grown accustomed to the warmer climes where their armies had surrendered, the cold was all the more deadly. They brought their tropical diseases north with them. Malaria, beriberi, dysentery, and deadly fevers were almost as common in Tokyo as they had been at Bilibid and Cabanatuan.

But Nichizawa didn't believe that POWs were ever really sick, thus in our camp we had a daily "sick parade." Sick parade was a roll call of those men whom Price and Bracky deemed too ill to work, but the patients weren't allowed to lie on their tatamis during roll call; they were forced to stand in the hospital area each morning after the other men had left for work. Nichizawa and his gunzokos would then "inspect" each prisoner, assessing his ability to work, and then judge whether they would go to the shipyards the following day. Men who were reeling from recurring malarial fever, men who were weak from a bad outbreak of dysentery were forced to stand, sometimes for two hours, while Nichizawa and his thugs examined them. An ailing POW was in a bad predicament when Nichizawa confronted him. If he managed not to flinch under Nichizawa's examination, he would be declared healthy and sent to perform hard labor in the bitter cold the next day, and if he wavered the tiniest bit, Nichizawa or the gunzokos might beat him for being disrespectful.

Not long after my arrival, an American named Peterson complained of a sore back. When Nichizawa heard of this, he asked Peterson where it hurt, then kicked the man several times in that spot. The man fell to the ground and Nichizawa continued to kick him. There were uglier episodes. During sick parade several weeks before my arrival, Nichizawa had beaten a man to death. When Lindesay, Bracky, and several other officers complained to Nichizawa about the murder, he declared that the prisoner had died of his illness, not of the beating. He also said the abuse was only a test, an attempt to find the "malingerers" who were not actually sick. According to Nichizawa's logic, POWs who knew they might be beaten before they could miss a day's work were more likely to continue working in spite of their ailments. But that winter the numbers at the sick parade did not diminish, they increased, and fewer men went to work each day. Nichizawa deserved his nickname, and I too began referring to him as "the Murderer."

During my first weeks in the camp, I helped Bracky in the hospital. I liked Bracky and found him to be the best source of information around. He could separate scuttlebutt from fact and did not seem as embittered as many POWs were. Bracky was also brave. It was he who bought our black market medical supplies, which was an offense punishable by death. He always made a point of dressing as well as possible, for it unnerved the Japanese, this tall, calm officer in semidecent attire. Bracky simply refused to let the Japanese get to him.

Bracky was deeply concerned about the enlisted men, for they suffered more than the officers. They had no choice but to work for the Japanese; because of their respect for hierarchy, Nichizawa and his gunzokos refrained from forcing officers to work, but nothing restrained their actions toward enlisted men. They would work or be beaten up. The work at the shipyards was demanding. They awoke each day at 5:45 A.M., ate a meager breakfast, and marched off to work by 6:30. Once at the shipyards, they were released to the custody of civilian work bosses who separated them into groups to do riveting work, roll steel, cut plates, do electrical work, and so on, on various types of ships. Their work was strenuous and cold—most worked outside all day and then returned with numb fingers and feet to a chilly warehouse.

The POW uniforms provided by the Japanese were drab and filthy affairs: khaki trousers and flannel shirts under a Japanese army tunic. They were given overcoats (courtesy of the British and U.S. military supply houses that the Japanese took over in the Pacific), but they were only allowed to wear them on especially cold and snowy days—thirty degrees was not deemed cold enough to wear the wool coats to the shipyards. They were given no gloves or socks, and often made their own out of their blankets. If a gunzoko discovered this, it made little difference that the blanket was U.S. or British issue—a cannibalized blanket was reason enough for a beating. Their things were never safe, for a gunzoko or two searched through the barracks daily, and they pilfered whatever they found of value, be it food, a cigarette, a watch, or photographs of loved ones.

Red Cross packages were sent from America, Australia, Britain, and Canada, but Nichizawa and his gunzokos got most of the goods in them. As Nichizawa's orderly, Sherman was able to report that much of the camp commander's diet came out of packages and cans with English labels (chocolate, canned meat, sugar, etc.). Complaints from Lindesay did no good—Nichizawa simply denied any Red Cross packages had arrived. The POWs had received half a Red Cross package each at Christmas and another on the emperor's birthday (that was the first one I ever received). But there was no way for the enlisted men to make the treats last any length of time, for the gunzokos helped themselves to any boxes in the barracks when the men left in the morning for the shipyards.

The first few weeks I was in the camp, two hospitalized enlisted men who were lying near me died of pneumonia, both on the same night. The two had slept side by side, and apparently were good friends, having become buddies before the war. They had worked at the shipyards together on the same work details. They had even become sick together and coughed together all day and all night. I have often wondered if one discovered that his echo was no longer coughing next to him and then decided simply to quit coughing also. I had trouble sleeping the next few nights after their deaths, for I think the warehouse was haunted for a couple of days. But the phantoms seemed to leave after a week or so. Yokohama Camp Number One drove even the ghosts away.

In consideration of the way the enlisted men suffered, I decided that the smartest thing I had ever done in my life was to take some correspondence courses some four years earlier and receive my officer's commission. At least officers were present to protect our goods. At least officers did not have to labor for hours in the cold. At least officers were less likely to be beaten upon. I say it now with a shameful sense of relief mixed with deep sympathy: the enlisted men suffered the most as POWs under the Japanese.

Frank Grady at home, December 1940. *Courtesy Elizabeth Grady*

Joseph V. Iacobucci.
Courtesy Frank A. Iacobucci

Lt. Makoto Inaki, commanding
officer of Sendai POW Camp
Number Five, Kamaishi.
Grady collection

Sgt. Masaru Mikawa, second-in-
command at Sendai POW Camp
Number Five, Kamaishi.
Grady collection

A portion of the site of Sendai POW Camp Number Five, Kamaishi, looking approximately northwest. The photograph of the Kamaishi Harbor area (*opposite page*) was taken from the tower shown at rear of site, left center. The fences and building were constructed after the POWs were evacuated; the new fence on the south was about fifteen feet closer to the riverbank than the original. Frank Grady is standing about where the original fence line was. *Grady collection*

(*Opposite page*) Kamaishi Harbor area, looking east. A portion of the Kamaishi POW camp is visible in the foreground of the photo, with an antiaircraft battery just beyond. This and subsequent photographs were part of the affidavit that Colonel Grady prepared for the Japanese War Crimes Trials of 1946–1947. *Grady collection*

One of the tunnels that POWs withdrew to during the shelling of 14 July 1945. The tunnel collapsed during the attack, trapping many of the POWs. *Grady collection*

Interior of the tunnel where five POWs died when they were buried under debris. *Grady collection*

Site of the locomotive repair shop and steel mill in Kamaishi where many POWs worked. *Grady collection*

The interior of the steel mill. POWs worked in the furnace pit area. *Grady collection*

A slit trench in the Kamaishi POW camp. POWs withdrew to trenches such as this one during air raids and shellings. *Grady collection*

The larger building (*center, right*) was an abandoned schoolhouse where POWs were housed after the Kamaishi POW camp was destroyed in the 9 August 1945 shelling. The smaller building on the left served as a hospital for POWs. *Grady collection*

The hospital area of the makeshift POW camp. Hospitals in many Japanese POW camps offered nothing more than this one; they provided a roof overhead but little else. *Grady collection*

10. Bearing the Dead

ALTHOUGH NOT ALL officers worked, Nichizawa expected some officers to attend to several duties around the camp. Because I wanted to keep busy, and because there was no sign that my interrogations would be taking place soon, I asked Colonel Lindesay to be assigned to a work detail as soon as there was an opening, and soon after Nichizawa put a stop to the lamp shade manufacture, I got on the burial detail, or rather, the cremation detail. Hauling a corpse along the crowded streets of Yokohama was exhausting and somewhat gruesome, but it got me out of the camp, so I was satisfied. Our work was simple enough. Every morning after a man died, another officer and I collected the corpse from the hospital area and placed it in a plain pine box that Nichizawa provided. We loaded the coffin onto a cart, took our places in a harness (the cart normally attached to a bicycle), and walked to the crematorium, some two miles from the camp; we were accompanied by a guard with a gun. Twenty-nine men died in February—we were going to the crematorium nearly every day that month.

On those trips to the crematorium, I learned a bit about Yokohama. It was a busy city, with people rushing everywhere on foot, on bicycles, by bus. I noticed the civilians gave our guard with his rifle a wide berth; few of them came near us and they seldom looked in our direction. It became obvious that the Japanese were terrified of their military; it was also clear that most of them were not much better off than we were. They were certainly in no position to support a costly war. Most people dressed simply and seemed poor; Okimoto confirmed that most Japanese were struggling economically. I am convinced that many Japanese citizens did not understand why their country was at war, but that made little difference, given the control the military had over their lives.

An old man, grizzled and weary but usually friendly, worked at the crematorium. He met us in that hot building every day, dressed in the same ill-fitting overalls and scuffed sandals. He would lead us to one of the hot ovens and we would line our coffin up just outside the oven door for the attendant to attend to later. In exchange for the corpse we brought, the old man would give us a small box containing the remains of the most recently cremated POW. He handed it to the guard with a bow, who handed it to one of us. We all then filed out of the crematorium and from there we made our way home with the empty cart between the other officer and me.

On one trip to the crematorium, the operation did not run as smoothly as it usually did. For some reason, the crematorium attendant was not ready for us yet. Our guard argued with the old man, but to no avail. The attendant only shuffled away with a shrug, leaving us alone in the room. The exasperated guard told us in Japanese, which I was beginning to understand, that we would have to wait for the corpse we had left the day before. Our guard sat down against the wall.

The British lieutenant assigned to the detail with me had been doing this work for some time. He too sank down against the wall. "Damn. Forgot our corpse yesterday, I suppose. You might as well sit down. We could be here a while."

The idea of waiting in a hot crematorium for an hour or more did not appeal to me. After sitting idly for awhile, I stood up. Our guard had fallen asleep with his head cradled against his rifle; he didn't awaken when I stood. The building was quiet, with only the sound of the ovens' muffled roar to disturb the silence. I moved a few paces down the hall, hoping to get a breath of fresher air. I found myself looking into a small room decorated with subtle watercolor figures. In it a group of people stood mutely and expectantly; they glanced toward the door from time to time. They must have seen me, but no one seemed to care that I was there. There were five women—all of them dressed in formal dark kimonos, with hands folded in front of them and their eyes downcast when they weren't looking toward the door. Four men were also formally dressed, standing quietly.

A moment later a man carrying a small, decorated urn brushed by me with a murmur and entered the room. He too was wearing a kimono, but his was of a richer material; he also wore an elaborate headdress. One of the women, her eyes swollen and red, bowed formally to the man, and her companions quickly followed suit. The man bowed back to all, then stood gazing at the woman with swollen eyes while speaking to her quietly. Just then the old attendant came in, pushing a heavy metal cart covered by a large, shallow lid. He positioned the cart in the middle of the room, then removed the top. Underneath were light gray ashes in the shape of a human form; encircling this was a darker color of ash, the remains of the wooden coffin the person had been incinerated in. After a poignant pause, the group stepped closer to the table.

The man in the kimono began to speak in hushed tones, almost a chant, addressing in turn each of the people in the room. He was especially attentive to the woman on his right, the woman he had first spoken to—she had obviously lost someone dear to her. After a few minutes of speech, the man in the kimono paused and stood silently for a moment, then slipped his hand into a fold of his kimono and pulled out a pair of ornate chopsticks. These he held lightly in his hand while chanting again, then, with a bow, he turned toward the woman on his right and handed the utensils to her. She bowed back and took them as he spoke. Tears began streaming down her face as she approached the table. Using the chopsticks, she sifted through the ashes until she came upon a small hunk of bone that had not been entirely reduced to ash, lifted it from the light dust and gently placed it in the empty urn that the speaker held out to her. She then turned to the person on her right, bowed, and passed the chopsticks on. That person also picked out a piece of bone and put it into the urn. Each person repeated this process until they had been around the room. Then the speaker used the chopsticks to pick out a bit of charred bone and place it in the urn. He then sealed the urn while chanting a gentle dirge. He held it close a moment, then handed it to the woman on his right. She took it with a formal bow, her chin quivering. The speaker and mourners stood silently for several minutes, then the speaker addressed the group again. After a short speech, he moved to the door, with the mourners behind him, and all of them left the room.

A few moments later I saw the old attendant return to the room with what looked like a sieve in his hand. He brushed the ashes on the cart into a pile, then shoved them through the sieve that he held over a large box already full of ashes. He picked out several small bits from the sieve, studied them a moment, then slipped them into a pocket of his overalls. He then closed up the box and left the room with it.

So ended that final ceremony in honor of a human life.

We waited a while longer before the attendant finally brought us the remains of our comrade. Our guard handed them to me, and we left the crematorium. I remember that a heavy fog had moved in from the sea, distorting and muffling the shapes of the buildings. I asked my British companion if he had seen a ceremony like the one I had seen. He had; he said it was the Shinto funeral ceremony. We stepped into our harness and started pulling the empty cart back to camp.

"Just what do we do with these, anyway?" I asked, gently tapping the box in my hand that held a POW's remains.

"The colonel is saving them, putting them aside to take home after the war," the lieutenant answered. He seemed to recognize my somber mood. "They'll get back to the proper hands. Family and that," he said quietly.

I only nodded and held the box close, trying not to jostle it as I tugged at the cart behind me, and we headed toward camp through the thick mist.

It was on those trips to the crematorium that I realized how frightened the Japanese were of the soldiers in their midst. They avoided all uniformed men, including the police guards who kept order on Yokohama's streets— the police guards were recognizable by their uniforms and armbands. They carried no guns, only clubs of some type; from what I could discern, they were a sort of glorified traffic cop, and some abused their power over the people.

One afternoon our detail was headed back toward the camp with our empty cart between us. It was a bright March day, the first warm promise of the season, and the streets were more crowded than usual, full of people out running errands or just enjoying the sun. Across the street from us a young woman was stopped, as we were, waiting for the light to change. The woman was pregnant, and though I knew little of such matters, I could see she was drawing close to term. She also had a toddler on her back.

The woman looked irritated and in a hurry, for her young son was crying loudly. When the cars cleared, she did not wait for the signal to change but stepped into the street. Just then a loud bellow made the crowd jump, and the woman stopped short, startled; a police guard just behind her was yelling at her, apparently for crossing the street against the signal. She turned to him, then stepped back on the sidewalk as he berated her. She bowed her head, dropped her son to the ground, and pulled him close to her. The soldier yelled at her unrelentingly for a full minute, and although I didn't understand everything he said, I knew it was harsh. The woman only raised her head once to say something, but as she began to speak, the police guard struck her across the face. She uttered a short cry and then cowered there with her son, humiliated and terrified. After the police guard finished his tirade and dismissed her, she slunk away from him cautiously. As she did so, he yelled some final epithet at her and gave her a hard shove on the shoulder that almost knocked her down; had it not been for a sympathetic man next to her, she would have fallen.

We passed the woman a moment later in the middle of the street. Her son was silent now, staring at passersby with frightened eyes. His mother kept her head averted when she saw us, pulling as far away from our guard as she could. In a moment she was past, and quickly became another bobbing head in the crowd.

For a moment, I wanted to cry. I wanted to cry for the young woman and her son; I wanted to cry for her nation and mine, two countries at war with each other. On that spring day, the prisoners of war on one side of the street and the young pregnant mother on the other side were of one status. Battered and alone, we were all victims in a world full of bullies.

As APRIL BEGAN and warmer weather set in, the death rate mercifully dropped off, which left me without a job. I was glad there was no longer a need for a cremation detail, but I wanted to keep occupied. I requested more work, and soon Nichizawa assigned me as POW supervisor in the kitchen; I was to help Arai, the kitchen gunzoko, oversee the eleven POW cooks. Too much food was being wasted, Nichizawa said. Arai supervised the food allotments, but still rice seemed to disappear; I was to make certain that did not happen anymore.

The kitchen work wasn't difficult, but it was tedious and time-consuming. There were two work shifts, each consisting of five men, which covered nearly a twenty-four-hour period. One shift came on at 4:00 A.M. and worked until 2:00 P.M.; the second shift worked from 3:00 P.M. until 1:00 A.M. The breakfast meal, which consisted of five hundred small dishes of watery rice, had to be ready by 6:00 A.M. Once breakfast was over, we prepared and boxed up lunch for the prisoners at the shipyard. The second group of cooks then prepared for the evening meal and cleaned up after it. Nichizawa required me to be in the kitchen for at least half of each shift, which kept me cooking and cleaning some ten hours a day.

Though we received slightly more food at Yokohama than I had at Cabanatuan (because the Mitsubishi company helped pay for our rice), our diet was still monotonous and meager. Working POWs were to receive 750 grams of cooked rice a day, officers 500 grams, and sick POWs 250 grams. Our meals were sometimes supplemented with sardine-size fish and soy sauce. We also occasionally were given fifteen kilos of pork, which didn't go far with five hundred men, but at least it flavored our rice. The food was allotted to us by Arai. Every morning I would barter with him for our rice allowances—these were based on how many men were working. The more men who were working, the more food we got. But we didn't distribute the food based on whether a man was working or not; if a sick man received only 250 grams of rice a day, he might die, so we POWs agreed that we would all get equal amounts of food, whether one was ill, an idle officer, or working at the shipyards.

The long hours in the kitchen made me rethink my request for work, especially when I considered that most of the other officers were idle. But soon I changed my mind—though I was very busy, the job was one of the best ones in camp. The cooks had been working in the kitchen for some time—it was the one work detail that experienced little turnover due to illness or death—and they required no real supervision to get the job done. And though still thin, the cooks were the healthiest prisoners in camp. This was because no matter how closely Arai watched, they could easily gobble up sneaked handfuls of rice and stolen spoonfuls of soup before the allotments were measured out. Because of this, we had a rule that cooks did not eat at mealtimes. Their snacks were larger than allotted rations.

The cooks were privileged in other ways also—one of the greatest of these privileges was bath rights. Once a fortnight, the gunzokos fired up the coal stoves to heat the water in the bathhouse and issued a sliver of soap to every two POWs. The cooks and camp orderlies, for some reason, were the first into the hot water. It proved a scorching bath for us, as we climbed into the water just after the stoves had been turned off, but the clean water was worth the heat. After five hundred dirty men had washed, the water was filthy and lukewarm for the last bathers. Cooks also were allowed to walk freely about the kitchen and barracks when other prisoners were confined to the sleeping and latrine area; the odd hours of their work shifts gave them this right.

After I had been working in the kitchen awhile, I saw that the cooks were ingenious as well as lucky. They took full advantage of their position as cooks in order to bargain with other POWs. For a cigarette or sweets, they would smuggle food to other prisoners. They could do this because they had more access to food than the Japanese personnel realized. They were raiding the supposedly secure food storeroom by night.

One of the cooks had to have been a thief's apprentice before the war, for, given time, he could unlatch any door's lock. Next to the kitchen were several storerooms of varying size; in one of them rice, flour, and sugar were stored. Arai was in charge of the food supplies, which he carefully locked up every night. But one of the cooks had long before fashioned a key from some wiring that fit the lock almost as well as the original did. The kitchen crew kept quiet about their passport to the food stores, swearing any new cook to secrecy about it only after he had been in the kitchen for several weeks. They couldn't let all the prisoners know about their access to food stores—big thefts would have been noticeable, and Nichizawa would have a new lock installed and put the storeroom under guard after punishing the wily cooks. Although I suspect that a new lock would have proved only a minor hindrance to our able thief, a guard with a gun would be a problem, and then no one would benefit from the extra food.

The cooks were ever discreet in their thefts—they never stole more than a relatively small amount any week, and they manufactured ingenious ways to hide the food once it was in the kitchen. They dumped flour into empty canteens, tablespoons of sugar into extra mess kits, and small bags of rice into obscure corners all over the galley. In the wee hours of the morning, when the gunzokos had retired, leaving only the soldiers to pace the camp, the cooks pulled out their goods to make little cakes and bits of bread. They placed the rolls of dough into their mess kits and buried them in the ashes beneath the great stoves. In a short ninety minutes, they had what they called a duffy, a scone of sorts, and though they were not exactly what one finds at an English tea, they were better than the rice and soup rations. Arai occasionally complained to the cooks about the losses of food, but the men blamed the shortages on mice and rats. The storeroom door seemed such a solid one, and a makeshift key in the hands of the prisoners was inconceivable. Arai believed them.

It was just this sort of action that I was supposed to put a stop to; Nichizawa obviously suspected the cooks were up to something, but he never stayed in the camp at night to pursue his suspicion. Nichizawa wanted me to do his detective work for him, but I had no intention of helping him. When I learned they were breaking into the food stores, I took on the job as lookout as they slipped into the storeroom or mixed together their precious morsels.

I saw Maddock every day. Maddock and I had become close on the voyage northward; he was not my orderly, he had become my partner in survival. Maddock and I shared everything, just as Joe and I had. Both of us would eventually become close to other POWs in the camp (partially because we were quartered in separate areas), but throughout our imprisoned years together we were closest with each other. I learned that Maddock had been what we used to call a hell-raiser; before enlisting in the army, he had run with a motorcycle gang and gotten into some trouble with the police. I suspect his devil-may-care attitude toward authority served us well in a prisoner of war camp—Maddock knew how to break our camp rules without getting caught, which often resulted in extra food for us.

Maddock and Sherman had become good friends, perhaps because they had similar personalities and attitudes toward the Japanese. Sherman had recommended Maddock to Nichizawa, and Maddock was removed from the shipbuilding detail in March. He became one of the camp orderlies, which pleased him no end; an orderly's job was less grueling than shipyard work. With this new job, Maddock tagged along with Sherman as much as possible, helping him wait upon Nichizawa. He was improving his Japanese this way and also learning some survival strategies from Sherman. Maddock and Sherman were soon good friends and cunning conspirators.

Sherman, I learned soon after joining the camp, was the most resourceful POW in camp. He had been a cobbler before the war and was putting this talent to use. The POWs quickly wore through their shoes while at the shipyards, and so Sherman had volunteered to construct new shoes for the men. Nichizawa agreed to the idea and allowed Sherman to set up a small workshop in a storeroom just off the kitchen. Nichizawa sent one of the gunzokos for leather, nails, and other materials for the work as needed. Maddock became Sherman's apprentice. Sherman's work on shoes combined with his orderly duties kept him very busy every day, but it was worth it, for he had enhanced his position in camp all the more. He was Nichizawa's orderly (which gave him access to useful information about Japanese personnel), an able interpreter, and the man to see for shoes. He had made himself indispensable, and an indispensable POW was less likely to be abused and more likely to gain certain favors. Sherman also played a role of which neither Nichizawa nor any of his gunzokos were aware. He was acting as cobbler for the Japanese soldiers stationed temporarily at the camp, and for them his work was not free of charge.

The Japanese guard details assigned to our camp for three-week periods were not Japan's top soldiers. Japan's best fighting representatives were battling in other parts of Asia or on the islands of the Pacific. The units that were assigned to POWs were made up of farm boys who had little understanding of why they had been conscripted and put into uniform. Many of them were illiterate. I believe the majority of them were confused and afraid; the war had transformed their worlds just as much as it had ours. These were the sort who ended up in our camp, assigned the task of guarding the foreign devils of which they had heard much but few had ever actually encountered. We prisoners gave thanks for their lack of sophistication, for confused and unworldly guards could be manipulated.

Sherman was perhaps the POW most aware of this. Sherman spoke a colloquial version of Japanese very well, and after Okimoto's arrival, he began to improve his formal Japanese. With the uneducated soldiers, he always used the more familiar version of the language and chatted amicably with them about their lives before the war, their families, their hometowns. The soldiers, of course, would never have responded if a gunzoko or Nichizawa were around, but Sherman knew better than to approach them then. He was their friend in private, late at night when the gunzokos were off duty and Nichizawa had left the camp. The soldiers were happy for a bit of friendship —it helped while away the long night hours, and Sherman was so pleasant. He had a personality that could charm a striking snake into submission.

In the two-plus years I knew him, I never once saw Sherman make the mistake of being friendly with the wrong guard—he seemed to know who was mean or untrustworthy, and he wouldn't go near such a man. He would instead concentrate all his efforts on those he sensed were vulnerable: the confused but decent guard who didn't understand the war. His performance was simple, but beautiful. The first time I saw it, I nearly applauded.

I was sitting talking with Maddock one night in the cobbler's small workshop when we heard Sherman call to a Japanese guard who was walking by. Maddock told me to listen up, for the guard and his unit were new to the camp and Sherman was going to try to find some new customers.

"Excuse me!" Sherman called out in Japanese to the nervous-looking young soldier. The guard stopped. "Do you know what time it is?" he asked.

The guard looked at him suspiciously. He was not accustomed to an Anglo speaking his language so smoothly.

Sherman smiled and asked the question again, this time with an "honorable sir" attached. The guard answered. Sherman then motioned the man over with such an air of confidence in the guard's compliance that the poor man had to move in his direction.

Sherman reached inside his tunic pocket to pull out a candy bar. "Have you been a guard long?" he asked the guard pleasantly. Sherman broke the candy bar in two and offered the soldier half.

The guard, still wary of this friendly and fluent foreigner, continued to stare at Sherman apprehensively, but he couldn't help but eye the candy hungrily. Guards in prison camps weren't eating many more candy bars than we were.

"Go ahead, take it. It's all right. I got it from a guard who was here last week."

Once aware that another soldier had been sociable with the prisoners, the guard took the candy.

"You must be new—I haven't seen you before. Are you from the country?"

And on the conversation went from there, halting at first, but slowly warming up as Sherman politely talked about Nichizawa, the gunzokos, and procedures in the camp, all idle talk, nothing threatening or too friendly. Sherman spoke in a respectful tone, but not obsequiously—he was a new friend, his words lightly conveyed, a person this misplaced and confused farmer could trust. This conversation went on for about thirty minutes before Sherman went into his spiel about shoes. It began innocently enough: "Some guards make the circuit of Tokyo camps—maybe you'll be back here in a couple of months," Sherman said. He then dropped his eyes to the guard's feet, and gazed at them solemnly. After a few moments he said, "What happened to your boots?"

The guard asked Sherman what he meant.

In response, Sherman launched into a series of lies. "There was a soldier here, a guard like you a couple months it must be now. Nice guy. Very careful, you know. But he had boots that looked like yours—soles worn, scuffed up.

"An officer on inspection of the camp caught him with his boots looking like that and began yelling at him in front of Nichizawa and the gunzokos, everybody. He was sent away somewhere, China or the South, I think. A real disgrace."

The guard, somewhat alarmed, asked if the offense could have been as simple as worn boots.

"It appears so. Something about destroying the goods of the emperor." Sherman lowered his voice. "I'm Lieutenant Nichizawa's orderly—he calls men into his office all the time and screams at them for the appearance of their uniforms. That's what he yells—'The uniforms belong to the emperor. He's lending them to you until the war's over. You must take care of them!' " This lone truth—that Sherman was Nichizawa's orderly—lent a sheen of authenticity to the entire story, and the guard swallowed it. After all, guards were inspected all the time, and a sloppy uniform did bring them a slap from time to time. Sherman ended by saying that the Japanese army was always looking for men to go to China to fight, and they probably saw scuffed boots as a good enough reason to send a man there.

The guard's face clouded over while staring at his boots. "We can't help how they look. We march a lot. All of our boots look this way."

"All of them? All of you have boots like that?" Sherman shook his head but said no more about boots. He just picked up a shoe he was working on for one of the POWs and began to tap away at it. The alarmed guard wasn't willing to stop talking about shoes, though. He asked Sherman whether he ever worked on Japanese boots.

Sherman smiled. He knew he had him now, this confused and frightened guard, and would probably have all the man's friends visiting him soon with their worn shoes. In return for his leather-working skills, Sherman could expect extra food, cigarettes, candy, and other special favors—he might even earn a few yen.

But Sherman let none of this expectation show on his face. "Yes. Yes, I've repaired shoes for a few guards before. I guess I could do it again—I'm not too busy right now. Maybe I could help you."

After seeing such a performance, I fully understood why Sherman was considered the most resourceful prisoner in camp.

Sherman helped Maddock learn Japanese, and though Maddock never did speak Japanese as well as his teacher, between the tutoring of Okimoto and Sherman he became proficient in the language. It was Maddock who later translated the parts of Sherman's performance that I hadn't understood.

Sherman and Maddock worked hard—they often put in sixteen-hour days fulfilling their orderly duties and working on shoes. But there were returns for their hard work. Like the cooks, they walked the kitchen and barracks unquestioned at odd hours, for they always had shoes to work on. Although one army unit might be more strict than others, all invariably were somewhat lenient with the camp cobblers. The soldiers certainly never reported them—Sherman was seen too often in the company of Nichizawa, and Nichizawa seemed genuinely fond of his orderly. The guards didn't dare trespass on that fondness. And they could never be sure they wouldn't need Sherman's services one day.

It was late in April when I finally had to reckon with the reason I had been sent to Japan. For almost three months I had worried about my interrogations, until Nichizawa called me into his office one afternoon to tell me that the next day I was to dress in my better uniform and be in his office by nine o'clock; my interrogators would be here then. What was of note during all this was that Nichizawa was different as he talked to me. The belligerent man who ruled over the camp with an iron fist seemed positively meek; he sat behind his desk and nervously watched me. But he was also notably curious about what I could have to say that would interest several interrogators. He was actually polite to me that day.

All of which made me nervous. If these interrogators were powerful enough to impress Nichizawa, maybe I should be alarmed. I was also uneasy because in Japan I was without my Signal Corps friends, and Joe, Pfaff, and James could not help me rehearse my lines. But I did have a plan. The last ploy that my Signal Corps buddies and I had put together was simple. I was to talk of the basics of cryptography again—but I would add a few juicy tidbits that I had omitted in Manila. I would describe a simple field cryptographic machine—one that the Japanese had likely confiscated after the fall of Bataan. They would know how that machine worked by now, and even if they didn't, information on the field device would not help them—the machines had only a twenty-four hour security guarantee on the encoded messages emitting from them. I would also offer to explain any U.S. coding device they might have in their possession, if they would show it to me. If they showed me one, I would memorize its serial number, then claim that I had never seen the machine before, so I couldn't help them. Once the war was over, I would tell someone in Washington that the security of that specific machine had been compromised. It was a minuscule contribution to the war effort, and by the time I would be able to give such information to someone, it would probably be old news. But I at least felt I still had something to offer to the U.S. fighting forces with this plan—it was a scenario I enjoyed turning over in my mind late at night. It lightened the impotent, sidelined feeling all of us suffered as POWs.

The next morning I arrived at the commander's office dressed in my lessworn uniform. Nichizawa stood outside, staring at a staff car that stood in the drive. It was a smooth-looking vehicle, low to the ground, and it ran on gasoline, not coke; a driver sat inside it. Nichizawa had a profound respect for rank—he would have been impressed by a first lieutenant from a neighboring POW camp. He seemed almost overcome by the high-ranking officers who had arrived in this car. He looked pale and excited. I bowed. "Good morning, honorable sir," I said. Nichizawa nervously told me that the officers were waiting for me in his office. Apparently Nichizawa would not be a part of the interrogations. Much to his dismay, I was certain.

In the room were two Japanese officers. The higher-ranking officer I had not seen before; he sat at Nichizawa's desk. The other officer, who was standing, I immediately recognized—it was the Yale-trained officer who had interrogated me in Manila. I bowed to and saluted them.

The interpreter motioned me toward a chair, then uncovered a tray with small cakes, a teapot, and three cups. I was glad to see that certain aspects of the interrogations in Japan were to be as they had been in Manila.

My interrogation went much as the earlier ones had. There was no torture, no harsh language, or heavy threats. As before, I only had to carefully answer an intelligent interpreter's questions while consuming sweet tea and cakes. The Yale man wrote in and read from a small notebook. He frequently began a question with, "When we spoke before" or "While in Manila, you said." I was glad I had opted to tell only the truth to this sharp officer. Had I lied, even once, I believe he would have caught me. After about an hour of review of previous interrogations, I was dismissed with an order to return the following week at the same time.

From a few paces across the compound, I turned to watch as the two officers emerged from the building. Nichizawa, who had been standing outside his office, followed the two of them to their beautiful staff car. Once there, he bowed deeply to the two officers, then gave another slavish bow to the car as it left the camp gates. Once the car was gone, he cast a curious glance in my direction, then returned to his office.

I turned and headed toward the galley and work, stopping first at Sherman's small workshop.

"Some visitors," Sherman said. "One of the guards tells me they're from the Japanese Imperial Staff. The one with the extra polish is a full colonel. The other officer, he's a lieutenant colonel," continued Sherman. "You know, Captain Grady, it never hurts to have friends in high places."

"They aren't friends," I said. "They're interrogating me, for God's sake. They want me to tell them everything I know about crypto machines."

"Doesn't matter, Captain, sir. You're an officer—they aren't so likely to knock you about as they would one of us." Sherman suddenly looked concerned. "They treated you all right, didn't they, sir?" he asked.

I didn't answer, only pulled out two slightly squashed cakes that I had slipped in my pocket. I had one more—that one was for Bracky.

"It doesn't look like it was too bad," said Sherman with a grin, reaching for a cake. "Like I said, friends in high places. That might be useful."

Maddock grabbed up a cake and took a huge bite. "Did you hear that staff car, how smooth it was?"

Sherman made a smacking sound. "Petrol. Real petrol," he said with his mouth full.

I leaned against the wall and wished I never had to see those "friends" ever again.

THERE WAS ONE key difference between my interrogations in Japan and those in Manila. The Yale-trained interpreter had done some more research into cryptography—I realized this during the first interrogation in Yokohama. I could no longer use elaborate explanations to make my answers seem more interesting; he readily understood every basic concept.

Nichizawa dogged after the two officers before and after every interrogation, ever the sycophant—the staff car had left an indelible impression on him. They were indeed from the Imperial Staff, as he made clear when he addressed them. He bowed to them repeatedly and volunteered the latest events of the camp while the officers regarded him grimly. It was a disgusting sight. Neither of my interrogators ever talked much with Nichizawa before stepping into their car and motioning the driver to leave. This was satisfying somehow.

I always smuggled away sweets to give to Bracky, Maddock, and Sherman. I'm certain the interpreter knew that I was hiding extra cakes, but as in Manila, he didn't seem to care. The lieutenant colonel was different in Tokyo than he had been before, though. He seemed more determined, and his questions were more direct. Though always a formal man, he had seemed less tense in Manila; in Japan I didn't see him bend once. I wondered whether the Japanese were watching him. Okimoto was certain his family was being watched; if Japanese authorities would keep tabs on an aging civilian POW camp interpreter, would they not be rather concerned about a young, intelligent lieutenant colonel and lawyer who had spent at least seven years in an enemy nation? I believe the interpreter was under pressure to get some results from me; his determination to do so emerged during our third session.

"Captain Grady," the lieutenant colonel said after a long description on my part, "there was more to your duties as a cryptographer than using these simple machines, there must have been. You're repeating yourself."

I did not say anything while I considered the fact that I had run out of basics to tell him.

The lieutenant colonel continued in a tired voice. "You were the custodian of codes and ciphers for MacArthur and Wainwright; you handled messages from Marshall, perhaps even the president. I cannot believe you used only those basic machines. I also cannot believe that you seldom worked with codes yourself, and that when you did, you used such simple devices." He gestured toward a primitive drawing of a field machine I had sketched the week before.

I nervously watched him a moment, still considering the situation, then decided it was time. "Yes," I said slowly. I had to appear hesitant. "Yes, there were other machines."

The interpreter looked surprised, but nodded. "More powerful machines, more complicated. These devices you have talked about are for simple codes. They are used when in a hurry, on the battlefield. We can break those codes without much trouble. But you have some codes we cannot break. You will tell us about the machines that encode those?"

I was suddenly afraid. It was a question, not a demand, but there was a sharpness behind his words. It appeared the lieutenant colonel expected something in return for all the tea and cakes, and he knew more than I had realized. I remained silent, calming myself and renewing my resolve to go on with our plan. It still seemed the best path of action.

"The machines were more complicated, yes." I was hesitant, and it was no act. "They were very complicated, actually. They had to be. They're difficult to explain. I don't really understand how they worked." This last was a lie. I had taken those machines apart to clean them more times than I cared to remember.

"Perhaps you could draw us a picture again," the interpreter said.

I took up a pencil, thought a moment more, then accentuated my rather complete lack of drawing ability and sketched a boxy-looking object that could have been a radio, a typewriter, or one of our crypto machines.

The lieutenant colonel studied my drawing briefly, then looked up at me skeptically. I half-expected to see anger, but there was none. After a full two minutes of silence, during which he studied me quietly, he finally nodded. "I see," he murmured.

It was time. I rushed into it. "They're difficult to describe—I'm no artist. It would be easier for me to show you one and then you could see how it works. If you have one. Maybe you confiscated one in the Philippines?"

The interpreter was still watching me closely. He did this for several more long minutes, nodded again, then turned from me and spoke to the colonel in a low voice. Their conversation went on for a few minutes while I sat tensely wondering what they were saying—I could only catch a few words here and there. What was clear was that the interpreter was unenthusiastic about my offer. After discussing matters for some time, the lieutenant colonel turned back to me and switched to English. "We will consider your offer, Captain Grady," he said in a formal tone. His lips were tightly pursed, his voice cold, but not threatening. The colonel began to collect his papers while the interpreter rose to his feet.

I said nothing.

After a silence, the interpreter spoke again. "You may leave, Captain Grady."

I stood, bowed and saluted, then left the room.

I did not see the Imperial Staff officers again, nor did anyone ever bring me a machine to identify. My interrogations did continue, but they were obviously mere formalities after that final day with the Imperial Staff officers.

I have thought often about the Yale-trained lieutenant colonel and his interrogation strategy. He used decency in an effort to get answers from me and our crypto gang, but he seemed to realize in Tokyo—I believe it was when I volunteered to examine a machine—that decency had only yielded carefully rehearsed and empty answers. He could have abused me because of that or told Nichizawa to pressure me as only a prison camp commander can pressure a POW under his control. Many other Japanese interrogators of POWs certainly would have acted this way had they faced the disappointment and loss of face that I represented to the lieutenant colonel. Yet there was never any suggestion that the Imperial Staff officers might resort to torture; I believe the idea would have appalled those two men.

Another thought haunts me when I think of this young Japanese officer. His interrogations had removed me from disease-ridden Cabanatuan. The lieutenant colonel, a man whose name I never learned, probably saved my life when he arranged for my transfer to Tokyo for further interrogations.

And I have always wondered if perhaps he knew what was going on in the POW camps in the Philippines and was determined, as a kind gesture toward the nation he had lived in, to save a few U.S. POWs from hunger, disease, or death. He was a smart man. It seems possible that he knew from the start that our interrogations would lead to naught. Might he have decided to play them out with cookies, cakes, and tea because it was harmless activity when there was so much harm in the world? I do not mean that the Yale graduate aided and abetted the enemy, but he could have closed his eyes to the obvious and gotten two skinny Americans—Maddock and me—out of the worst of the POW camps in the Philippines. It was about all an interpreter could hope to do to redress the malevolence of the Japanese military during the 1930s and 1940s.

I will never know the truth of that interrogator. All I can say is that almost fifty years later I still wonder what became of that young officer, what he did with his sharp mind. To this day he represents to me the rational Japan, the Japan that did not want to go to war, the Japan that was shocked by its own barbarity. The lieutenant colonel helped fight a war against a country he knew well and probably respected at least a little bit. He had an unbending, confident demeanor on the outside—I have always suspected that through it all he was torn and full of doubt on the inside.

As SPRING ARRIVED, the deaths stopped, but the hospital area was still full. In early May, Nichizawa suddenly went on the rampage over our ill POWs. Perhaps the cold attitudes of the Imperial Staff officers toward him set him off, or maybe he was still furious because the POW officers had refused to trace blueprints four months before. Whatever, Nichizawa cracked the whip to show us just who was in control of the camp, and the results were ugly.

Although any tour through the hospital would prove that the POWs there were indeed ill, Nichizawa refused to believe this was actually the case. It was spring, he shrieked, and it was warm—why were so many men claiming to be sick? Malaria, he repeatedly claimed in a shrill voice, did not exist in Japan, ignoring the ample evidence in the hospital that malaria did not simply go away once one arrived in Tokyo.

Nichizawa ordered the hospital emptied of all who claimed to have tropical diseases—they were to go back to work, in spite of Price, Bracky, and

Lindesay's objections. After two days of simply yelling and getting no cooperation from the doctors or Lindesay, who refused to remove or order
POWs from the hospital, Nichizawa began to beat the prisoners suffering
from malaria, sometimes personally, other times vicariously through his
gunzokos. He ordered them to their feet, and if they could stand, he struck
them with a short stick, the back of his hand, or the flat of his sword. Other
men were actually lying on their makeshift cots in the hospital while they
were slapped and kicked because they could not get up. The other prisoners, the stronger ones, could only watch helplessly; cries for decency were
often answered with a blow.

The general Japanese policy was to cut a sick prisoner's rations to one-
third the working man's one; Nichizawa took this a step further and cut
those rations by half again for those complaining of malaria, leaving them
with one-sixth what they would receive if they were working. Because we
didn't divvy food according to whether a man was working or not, we all got
less food.

The man most enraged by Nichizawa's actions was Bracky. Bracky was a
friend to all. The enlisted men in camp addressed the officers by their titles
—all but Bracky. He was Bracky to everyone, whether the speaker was a private or Lieutenant Colonel Lindesay himself. He was truly a compassionate
man. Watching ill prisoners who had come to the hospital for help receive
beatings tore him up. Bracky and Lindesay went to the commander's office
daily to plead with him to stop the beatings and reinstate the rations, but
Nichizawa refused to see them most of the time.

One morning a few days before my last interrogation with the lieutenant
colonel, I was helping with sick parade. Nichizawa entered the hospital with
Kambe, another gunzoko named Kawamura, and Okimoto. Nichizawa said
something in Japanese, which Okimoto translated.

"Lieutenant Brackstone and Colonel Lindesay have explained that malaria
is a disease that will not go away. It returns to the victim the rest of his life.
With this in mind, will each of you with malaria step forward?"

Bracky had been watching Nichizawa suspiciously; with the announcement to step forward, he became alarmed. "We told him that two weeks ago,"
he whispered to me and tried to speak to Nichizawa. He was silenced. Bracky
shook his head at the men, trying to warn them, but few understood. Some

ten men believed the lieutenant's words meant they would be excused from work, so they stepped forward. As they did so, Nichizawa began to yell without an interpreter.

"You lazy malingerers! You will work! You no sick, no sick! Malingerers!" With this, he began to beat upon one of the men who had stepped forward just in front of him, slapping him across the face with the back of his hand. Kambe and Kawamura began to beat two others. As Bracky and I watched, Nichizawa drew out his sword and bashed a sick man across the shoulder with the flat of it, then he began swinging upon any sick POW with his sword. It was one of the most vicious scenes I ever saw as a POW.

Bracky shouted at Nichizawa to stop, that he would kill someone. I shouted. Several of the sick POWs shouted—to no avail. Nichizawa continued to attack the ill prisoners with his sword, Kawamura and Kambe with their fists. When it was finally over, some ten minutes later, Bracky left the hospital immediately after Nichizawa did and ran to the latrine; he later told me he had vomited up his meager breakfast. After he returned, we tried to help the men who had been beaten by bathing their wounds. Aside from that, there was nothing we could do to alleviate the pain and humiliation of the beatings. I don't think I ever felt more powerless in my life than I did that day. There was never anything we could do to stop such atrocities from happening.

We weren't the only ones who felt powerless. Throughout the beating, Okimoto had not moved; he had stood silently with his head bowed.

Later that day, Bracky asked me to come to the hospital. When I arrived, he led me to a blanket where a man was lying without a shirt. There were vivid bruises and slash marks all over his chest and face. He was asleep or unconscious.

Bracky stared down at him. "Do you know he doesn't even have malaria? Nichizawa beat him for having malaria a few days ago, but it's pneumonia." He shrugged. "Oh, he might have malaria as well, probably does. But he's in here just now with pneumonia." Bracky's voice dropped. "I don't think he's going to make it, Frank." Bracky was silent for several minutes. He wiped his eyes before he continued. "Lindesay and I have just seen Nichizawa again. We asked him to stop the beatings. We brought up the Geneva Convention; we told him the beatings were illegal and barbaric. He just dismissed us again. He never pays any attention to any of us." He paused. "But you know, Frank," he said wearily, "he might listen to you."

I was surprised and asked what he meant.

"The man's a panderer," Bracky said. "You say he dogs after those Imperial Staff officers and slobbers over their car. He'd do anything for them. He'd jump in front of their damned car if he thought that would impress them. He might even be decent for them. You say he doesn't know what's going on in your interrogations. You could use that to your advantage."

The thought of trying to talk to Nichizawa about his indecent behavior left me mighty uneasy, but that day's visit to the hospital was beyond tolerance; I was willing to try anything to stop the tirades. And Bracky was right. All Nichizawa knew about my interrogations was what he saw: two high-ranking officers arriving in a smooth-running car to interrogate me. Nichizawa had little respect for civilized entreaties or human kindness—perhaps it was time for a mild threat. He couldn't maltreat prisoners any more than he already was, though he might beat me. It was this that frightened me.

Bracky and I talked for a long time that afternoon, then met with Colonel Lindesay and talked some more.

The next morning, Bracky told me that the prisoner Nichizawa had beaten two days before had died during the night, and another prisoner he had beaten with his sword the day before had also died. I let the deaths fuel my resolve to speak with Nichizawa. After I finished my duties in the kitchen, I approached Okimoto and asked him to come with me to speak to Nichizawa.

We crossed over to Nichizawa's office. Initially, Nichizawa did not want to see me, but I insisted that it was important and connected to the interrogations. When Okimoto relayed this, Nichizawa admitted us.

Nichizawa glared at us, but with a hint of curiosity in his eyes, that same curiosity that I had seen in him after my first interrogation. But his staring eyes unnerved me.

"Tell him," I paused, suddenly panicky. Tell him what, for God's sake? I had forgotten the lines I had put together with Bracky and Lindesay. "Tell him that I expect to be interrogated many more times." It sounded foolish.

Okimoto nodded, though he looked slightly perplexed, and translated my words in an impartial-sounding voice.

Nichizawa said nothing, only stared at me, unimpressed.

Okimoto looked at me expectantly.

"Tell him that until now, the interrogations have gone well. They've been important. Make him understand that."

Okimoto translated this, but still the commander sat staring at me expressionlessly.

"The interrogations have gone smoothly," I floundered. "The Imperial Staff officers who talk to me will be back to talk again. The colonel will be interrogating me many more times." I was repeating myself, but Okimoto translated it.

At the mention of the Imperial Staff officers, Nichizawa blinked and dropped his eyes. I felt a wave of relief flood over me. And I remembered a few of my lines that I had rehearsed with Bracky and Lindesay.

"We still have much to talk about, the officers and I," I announced more confidently, talking directly to Nichizawa. "But I may talk no more. I may talk no more, Lieutenant Nichizawa." I lowered my voice then, and told Okimoto he could leave. I didn't need him now—I was fairly certain that Nichizawa would understand the rest of my words. And Nichizawa would be more pliable if he didn't need to preserve his honor in front of another Japanese man.

Okimoto translated this final passage, then asked to be dismissed. Nichizawa nodded permission—Nichizawa apparently did not want a witness to this conversation, either. Okimoto cast me a warning glance once his back was to his superior, then left.

After Okimoto was gone, Nichizawa spoke for the first time, in English. "Why? Why you talk no more?"

I spoke slowly, using Japanese words when I knew them. "Because you are beating prisoners," I said, making striking movements with my hands. "You beat two prisoners to death. I saw one before he died, and I know you beat him to death."

Nichizawa looked uncomfortable. "Who prisoner dead?"

"This morning. You beat them, and they died last night." I spoke yet more slowly, pausing over each word until its meaning registered in Nichizawa's eyes. "You killed them. I will not talk to the officers anymore. I will only tell them that because you killed two prisoners, I will not talk anymore. There will be an incident, an investigation. Because of you."

When Nichizawa heard this, he looked distinctly ill at ease. "Prisoners malingerers. They no sick. I no hurt prisoners. They die other thing."

At this, I exploded inside. Did we all die of something else then; was it not the least bit our captors' fault? Was that to be their excuse after all this was over—that we were skinny and sick and dying because of some "other thing"? Would they avoid punishment for their neglect and abuse with such lies? My anger took hold of me, and I leaned forward suddenly, far more aggressively and confidently than I had planned. "If you beat any more prisoners like you did yesterday," I hissed, "I won't even see those Imperial Staff officers again. There will be an incident, Lieutenant Nichizawa. I will tell them you are a murderer and I will no longer talk. There will be an incident, Lieutenant Nichizawa, an incident."

I straightened up. I stood staring at him until he dropped his eyes again. He shuffled through some papers in front of him, then shoved them aside. It was the response I had hoped for in him, but I had gone far enough. After a long silence, I asked to be dismissed and received permission to do so. I left the room after an obligatory bow and salute. Nichizawa didn't say another word, but he looked slightly pale—I thought this a good sign.

Outside, with our gloomy warehouse camp in front of me, my audacious and unexpected courage fled. Out here I was a POW again, and I realized while crossing to our quarters that I had just threatened the camp commander. In Nichizawa's office, I had stood on even ground with that lousy little man. But as I approached our crowded barracks, I was again aware of just who held the power, who carried the guns and swords.

Okimoto stayed away from me for several weeks after the session in Nichizawa's office. He even yelled at me several times in the presence of a gunzoko to make certain that everyone knew that there was no connection between us. I didn't blame him for this. He was thinking of his family, of his own skin; I would have done the same.

Nichizawa never challenged me for my impudence—it was as if I had never visited him in his office. Life continued much as before in camp, with only one difference. Nichizawa stopped beating ill prisoners. He still railed against them as malingerers, but he restrained himself from attacking the bedridden and those who stood each day for sick parade. It was this that Bracky and the rest of us had hoped for—we knew that the senseless beatings of healthier men would continue no matter what any of us said.

Nichizawa also ordered that the rations for the POWs in the hospital be returned to the normal one-third rate for the ill. I was relieved; Nichizawa would likely have retaliated against me if I had told the Imperial Staff officers about his abuse.

I believe my threat to stop cooperating with the Imperial Staff officers helped Nichizawa act more decently toward us, but our encounter in his office that day wasn't the only thing that stayed his hand. Lindesay and the doctors had discovered that Nichizawa was most likely to listen to their requests when they informed him that after the war, win or lose, they were going to report his beatings to his superior officers. This is when Nichizawa listened, when we told him we would go over his head. When I threatened to go over his head immediately, to tell the staff officers of his vicious actions the next time I saw them, Nichizawa reacted just as Lindesay and Bracky thought he would: he quickly reformed his behavior. Not only did he not want to be punished, he also wanted to improve his own standing in the Japanese army. He wanted those Imperial Staff officers to approve of him.

Nichizawa did not stop the beatings because he was a moral man. He stopped the beatings because of his fear that his superiors might be moral men, and because of his slavish devotion to rank.

11. Summer and Fall 1943

IN LATE JUNE 1943, Lieutenant Chisuwa, a Japanese officer none of us had seen before, drove into our camp, and he had an announcement: Nichizawa had been relieved of duty. Chisuwa was the new commander of Yokohama Camp Number One, Tokyo Area. Chisuwa gave no reason for the change. All we knew was that Nichizawa, our Murderer, left the camp and didn't come back.

Everyone made guesses as to why Nichizawa had been removed. Many thought it was because of the POWs who had recently died, for Dr. Price had attributed their deaths to the beatings the men had received from Nichizawa and had reported this to Shinagawa headquarters. A more logical reason was offered by Sherman. He said Nichizawa had been under fire for months for the high sick rate that prevented so many men from working each day. Perhaps it was a combination of the above; whatever, we were happy to be rid of the vicious lieutenant, and hoped that Chisuwa might prove to be more humane.

Chisuwa was less violent than Nichizawa, but he wasn't sympathetic to POWs. He still supervised sick parade each day, though ill men were no longer beaten. We received the same food allotments and had the same work schedule. Still, we were cheered by Nichizawa's removal; we considered it a victory of sorts. With the bright skies and warm days, the camp was at its most tolerable.

Though our camp commander was less violent personally, his gunzokos were still vicious. Late one July day, I emerged from the kitchen to find a small crowd around the flagpole, watching a performance by Kambe. By the angry and disjointed shouts I heard from him, I could tell that Kambe's pain had returned. I noticed he was wearing the red-and-white sash that was representative of the camp commander. Chisuwa had already left the camp, and it was Kambe's turn to be in charge until he returned. Kambe's audience that day consisted of the officers, the off-duty cooks, and the orderlies—the rest of the POWs were at the shipyards. The men congregated in small groups; they looked uncomfortable. I asked an acquaintance what was happening.

"Kambe ordered us out to salute the flaming asshole," he said. The flaming asshole fluttered low on its halyard just then, almost touching the ground. "He wanted an audience, so he ordered us out here. You know the cat we've been feeding?"

I nodded—it was a scrawny little cat that had wandered into the camp looking for food. There wasn't much here, certainly no extra bites, but some of the men adopted her anyway. They couldn't feed her, but she was loved, and this seemed enough for her. She wandered through the various store-rooms and barracks and caught mice; because of this, Chisuwa let us keep her. Some of the prisoners wanted to eat her, but others came to her defense, saying that her state was not much different from ours. She was a neglected and starved stray who needed some affection. Besides, she was too skinny to be a good meal. Though there was much grumbling about the protein-packed dinner she would make, she was left alone. One of the cleaning orderlies had taken a special shine to her and let her share his bunk with him; he called her his girlfriend.

My acquaintance continued. "Well, she had kittens. She had four I guess, that's all I've seen. Anyway, Kambe found her today." The man paused and looked toward Kambe. "Shit, I've seen Kambe pet that cat before!"

I noticed the cats then by the flagpole, three tiny kittens—they couldn't have been four weeks old—and their scrawny tabby mother. The sergeant said she had had four—I wondered what had happened to the other one. They were scruffy looking things, but adorable, like the young of any species.

They were playing awkwardly among themselves. Their mother watched over them while she paced nervously.

My acquaintance spoke again. "I don't even like cats, but this is cruel." Somebody else in the crowd agreed.

We fell silent and watched as Kambe grabbed up two of the kittens, dumped them in a bucket attached to the ropes on the flagpole and with several yanks sent the pail upward. The kittens were curious about the ride at first, unafraid, but once they were ten feet off the ground, they began to squeal. Their cries became more frantic as they went higher and their mother began mewing loudly from below, as if offering advice and solace. She was as agitated as her babies, pacing back and forth, meowing up at her master, imploring him to save her kittens. Kambe pulled at the rope with abrupt jerks that sent the kittens smashing from side to side in the bucket, and the prisoner who called their mother his girlfriend began to cry. As Kambe hoisted the bucket higher, the Japanese flag followed the cats just below them. Finally bucket and flag were at the top, some forty feet up, with the kittens squealing uncontrollably. Kambe then began to manipulate the rope back and forth, making the pail wobble to and fro.

He stepped back to look up at the kittens while still wiggling the rope. He called to them in a soothing voice, murmuring endearments in Japanese, enticing them to come to him. The kittens' mother, seemingly aware of Kambe's ploy, cried out warnings more earnestly while sitting on her haunches and looking up at her babies.

One of the kittens managed to pull itself up on the rim of the bucket where it hung so high above us. In what appeared to be a confused attempt to reach its mother, it jumped toward her, its claws dragging along the side of the Japanese flag just below it.

A helpless murmur stirred when the kitten hit the ground a moment later with a slight thud, and we moved toward it involuntarily. Its mother reached it first, sniffing at it forlornly. Her baby fortunately had been killed instantly—I don't know whether it had died from fright or from the impact itself. The mother stood over it for a moment and mewed; she pushed at the unmoving kitten with her nose and gave it a tentative lick. The kitten remained still and she gave up after a last mewing nudge and returned her attention to the kitten above that still squealed in fright.

I saw then the fourth kitten I had wondered about. It lay in an unmoving little heap about ten feet from the kitten that had just died. It had been Kambe's first victim.

Kambe again called to the kitten above in supplicating tones. At this, one of the prisoners broke loose with a chain of profanities and yelled at Kambe to stop. Kambe seemed to have been waiting for this. Though he didn't understand the actual English words, he grasped the content. He strutted to the prisoner, a tall young Brit. He smiled nastily, then said something harsh in Japanese before striking him across the face. Kambe then commenced to beat on him in earnest.

While this was going on, the other kitten above had climbed onto the rim of the bucket. It stood there for only a second before falling, hitting the ground a few feet from its sibling, and lying still after a brief spasm of its muscles.

Kambe lost interest in the POW he was beating and turned back to the flagpole. He hauled on the halyard and lowered the bucket. Once it was down, he grabbed up the two last cats, the mother and her last kitten, and stuffed them in the bucket. They went willingly, not moving once inside it while Kambe sent them skyward with violent jerks. A few feet from the top, the mother cat peered out over the rim and pulled herself out, then fell. She hit the flagpole before the ground, which stunned her, and as a result she didn't land on her feet; the fall killed her. Her last kitten, alone and orphaned in the bucket, waited until it had been hoisted to the top, then stepped out on the rim. It sat there a moment on the motionless bucket, holding on tightly with its claws while surveying the men and murderer below. It mewed softly once, then raised a paw for an awkward lick. Kambe gave a tug to the rope then, and the kitten lost its balance and toppled over the side, hitting the ground a second later.

This last kitten wasn't killed instantly. It lay there on the ground, crying out plaintively. Kambe stared down at it while the cats' master walked, sobbing, to the suffering animal and picked it up. The kitten's head was bleeding. The prisoner held it for a moment in one hand while trying to soothe it with the other. After petting and cooing aloud to it a moment, he placed his free hand around the kitten's neck and twisted it hard to the side. The mewing ceased, and all was quiet in the compound.

A pall settled over us as we realized that the odious performance was finished. Some stood with bent heads, others stared straight ahead; one man was praying aloud in a hoarse whisper. Aside from his murmurs, no one spoke, not even Kambe. He looked at the dead cats on the ground confusedly. After a long, tense silence, Lindesay asked Kambe for permission to disperse and received it, and we all moved off. The cats' master gathered up the corpses and disappeared with them before someone realized they might make good eating yet.

As I turned toward the galley, I noticed Okimoto. He stood looking at nothing in particular. His face was pale, his lips grimly pressed together. He didn't acknowledge my nod; I don't think he saw me. I wanted to tell him it wasn't his fault, or exclusively Japanese, this torture, but I don't believe he would have heard me.

I saw many atrocities in the camps, watched close friends die, good men die, many nameless, all defenseless. But the murder of those innocent cats remains in my mind as one of the most vicious events of my imprisonment. It left me full of hatred for schizophrenic Kambe, our "One Eye." It was a malevolent eye, that; the man loved to inflict pain and dispense hatred. His sometime smiling face and manner that inspired trust in unsuspecting POWs and stray animals—all hopeful for a bit of kindness—sickened me; I had seen Kambe's opposite face too many times. Before, I had found his cheerful behavior after a fit of rage only disgusting, this time it was an abomination. Kambe was happily singing Japanese fighting songs two hours after senselessly killing the cat and her kittens.

BY LATE SUMMER 1943 we were some seventy-five men fewer than before. After Chisuwa took over the camp, a group of Japanese doctors arrived and removed those prisoners who suffered most acutely from amoebic dysentery. They went to the hospital at Shinagawa Headquarters Camp and from there must have been relocated, because they did not return. Without them, and after our high death rate the winter before, about four hundred men called Yokohama Camp Number One home.

I was still being interrogated into July, if one could call it that—the "interrogations" had become a bureaucratic charade. The Imperial Staff officers and their smooth-running car and cookies were long gone. I was interrogated by various lower-ranking officers after my last session with the lieutenant colonel. By my last interview, my importance to the Japanese power structure was such that I was questioned by a second lieutenant of the interpreter corps who arrived in a coke-fed vehicle that he drove himself. Once that was over, I was simply a kitchen supervisor again.

The enlisted men's primary duty that summer was to repair damaged ships, both naval and commercial. The work bosses were Japanese civilians. They did not carry weapons. It was the camp guards assigned to the work details who were armed, and the work bosses turned to them if a problem arose. But there weren't many discipline problems at the shipyards—all of us POWs, whether at the shipyard or in camp, knew better than to cause trouble. Rebellion against authority requires energy and certain recognized rights, neither of which the enlisted men at the shipyards had. If a POW wanted to break some rules, he did so on the sly and took only private satisfaction in proving that the Japanese were neither omniscient nor omnipotent.

But the work bosses or camp personnel sometimes imagined a POW rebellion when there was none. A U.S. enlisted man named Harris was a scapegoat for the civilians because they were intimidated by his size—tall POWs like Harris were often picked on by Japanese personnel. One afternoon he was digging holes with a Japanese detail when a civilian worker took up his pick and smashed it across Harris's back, fortunately with the blade turned up. Harris was shaken, but not really hurt; he didn't think before wrenching the pick away from his attacker. This act of self-defense set the other civilians against him—they turned on him with fists and shovels and any other handy weapon. The guards rushed in once they saw the melee, but it took three of them and their guns to break up the mob. Harris later returned to camp to face a kangaroo court to which Colonel Lindesay, the POW-in-charge, was not invited. Harris was named as the perpetrator of the incident and ordered outside for punishment. Ikeda and Kambe both beat Harris while Chisuwa supervised—Chisuwa also beat Harris with the back of his sword. They then marched him to the guardhouse where he was given two buckets full of water to hold outstretched in front of him for two hours.

There were other shipyard incidents as summer moved into fall. All the workers at the docks were hungry all the time; understandably enough, the hunger made some men reckless. The men worked all day long by piers that were encrusted with barnacles. The barnacles were mildly poisonous and the men must have known that, but some obviously didn't care. POWs ate weeds, grasshoppers, worms, and dirt—some in the harsher camps in the south had even drunk their own urine. Barnacles could not be worse than all that, not to minds made irrational by hunger. Thus, some men broke off barnacles and stuffed them into their pockets to eat later. And barnacles were not the only things they attempted to eat. Any man who had access to the shipyard's garbage was liable to sift through it when unsupervised, looking for anything edible that might have been tossed away.

One of the guards discovered a group of three prisoners with some barnacles and garbage on them. On returning to camp, he informed Chisuwa of the incident and all of the enlisted men were lined up and searched. Those who had any garbage on them were taken aside and beaten on Chisuwa's orders. Daily inspections and punishments went on for the next few weeks. But crazed by hunger as some of them were, they continued to bring the garbage into camp and continued to receive beatings for it. Chisuwa never recognized the irony of his policy. POWs were beaten and sometimes badly hurt to prevent them from hurting themselves with inedible garbage. But we saw the irony. Chisuwa was no Nichizawa, but he was still dangerous.

Chisuwa was smarter than Nichizawa and far more observant. He quickly realized that Sherman was a crafty POW who learned much useful information about Japanese personnel as his orderly, so one of his first moves was to restrict Sherman's presence in his office. Chisuwa also began to watch Bracky carefully. For some reason, he particularly disliked him, and in September he discovered that Bracky was buying medicinal goods via the black market. He did not discover who Bracky's contact was; he only found bottles of vitamins and sulfa drugs among his things and immediately sent Bracky to the guardhouse after a brief interrogation and a beating.

Bracky spent ten days in solitary confinement on half-rations and with no blankets while Price attended to the ill POWs on his own; when Bracky emerged, he said that Chisuwa had personally beaten him during the interrogation. Chisuwa had demanded that he tell him who had sold him the goods, but Bracky refused. Bracky told Chisuwa that he had only bought black market items once, the time that Chisuwa caught him. This Chisuwa did not believe, and it was then that he had beaten Bracky. Throughout his confinement Bracky steadfastly refused to say a word about his dealings. He was eventually released because his services were too vital to leave him languishing in the guardhouse. But Chisuwa kept a close eye on him and obviously ordered his gunzokos to do the same, for he was watched constantly. It was two months before he could buy medicine for us again.

The most disturbing event of the fall arose partially because of Chisuwa's hatred of Bracky. Soon after Bracky's release, Chisuwa ignored Bracky's recommendation and ordered a young British enlisted man, J. J. Dressler, to work. Dressler was pale and unsteady on his feet; he was suffering from a malaria flare-up. Once at the shipyards, his work bosses assigned him to work atop a scaffold. After lunch, Dressler lost his balance and plummeted some thirty feet to the ground. He broke his leg in two places, which would not have been especially dangerous but for the snapped bone in his thigh. It was a compound fracture that had severed an artery. Price and Bracky agreed it would require immediate attention and care that they could not provide. Bracky asked Chisuwa to transfer Dressler to the Shinagawa hospital, but Chisuwa refused, saying that "a man does not die of a broken leg."

Bracky continued to try to persuade him that Dressler was in a dangerous condition, but Chisuwa wouldn't budge. He was in no mood to cooperate after Bracky's refusal to give him the name of his black market contact. He also ignored requests from Lindesay and Price. Thus Dressler remained in camp, growing weaker with each hour as he lost more blood, while Bracky and Price tried to comfort him.

Two days later, Dressler was unable to lift his head to eat. About that time, Chisuwa finally decided to get help for Dressler. But by then, Bracky and Price said Dressler was too weak to move—doctors with proper equipment would have to come to our camp. But Chisuwa wouldn't agree to this, and we had to load Dressler into the back of a truck.

Young Dressler, weakened by malaria and then suffering from a broken leg and a slashed artery left unattended, died soon after he arrived at Shinagawa Camp. Once he was dead, two guards loaded him back into another truck and brought him back to our camp.

It was a bleak experience, helping to remove Dressler's stiffening form from the truck. Later that same night, when the last roll call had been taken and the fogs had rolled in from the sea, I cried silent, useless tears and felt very alone. I could not, no matter how hard I tried, imagine a future in which I wasn't a powerless prisoner of war surrounded by emaciated men or, as on that day, helping to place them in wooden boxes.

DRESSLER'S DEATH HAD an unusual effect upon us. Many other POWs had died, several because of beatings inflicted by Japanese camp personnel, but when Dressler died because Chisuwa wanted to thwart Bracky, many of us rethought our actions toward one another. For most of that year, we POWs had not been particularly unified. But after Dressler's body went out with the burial detail, we drew together and cooperated more than ever before as a single mass of prisoners with one enemy. The Brits, Americans, Canadians, and Aussies quit hounding each other about which nation was more civilized. The Dutch mixed more easily with their English-speaking bunk mates. The enlisted men seemed friendlier toward the officers, and the officers curbed some of their patronizing behavior toward the enlisted men. We all had to come to terms with the thought of another winter together in a cold POW camp, and we had the sense to help each other through it.

The Japanese personnel had a bleak winter ahead also, but they had one way of keeping morale high. Once a month throughout 1943, the guards and gunzokos in our camp received an allotment of saki. We prisoners were envious of the Japanese "saki parties"; most of us had not had a drink for almost two years and could only listen wistfully as our captors noisily enjoyed themselves across the compound once a month. Any of us would have risked just about anything to drink a bit of the stuff.

Sherman, who of all the POWs was the most interested in acquiring some saki, went to some lengths to learn how it was distributed. He discovered that the usual procedure was for a detail from one of the camps to go to Shinagawa Headquarters Camp to get the saki. It was all quite official. They signed for it, made certain that both barrels were full, and witnessed the loading onto their truck. The soldiers then traveled back to their own camp and from there informed the other camps that they had their saki ration for the month; a detail from each camp soon arrived for their portion. The camps took turns sending a detail to pick up the saki from Shinagawa, and in early November, it was our camp's turn to get it.

The evening following the saki pickup, Sherman sent a cook to wake me from the nap I was taking before going on duty again. Sherman wanted to talk to me. As I drew near the workshop, I heard a conspiratorial whisper in the dark. "Captain, come into the workshop and close the door. Keep your voice down." It was Sherman. As I stepped in, he excitedly grabbed hold of my arm. This surprised me—Sherman always made a point of staying calm and impassive. His face, I noticed right away, was lit with a certain mischief, but this was not communicated in his tone. "Captain, sir," he said gravely. "The guards are to have their saki party tomorrow night. No one wanted to wait till tomorrow, but they have no choice."

I nodded, uninterested. Their frivolity did not affect me, although their hangovers the following day might.

Sherman paid no attention to my lack of enthusiasm. He continued in a quick whisper. "They're having it tomorrow night because they picked the saki up this afternoon, not this morning. They got the call to come to fetch it so late that they can't distribute it today. And they can't have their own party until it's been split. So it's tomorrow. One of the guards told me. He's upset about it, because he has late duty tomorrow night, and will miss it." He finished his speech with a somber nod of his head, as if his words were too astounding to be believed.

I was mildly alarmed for a moment, wondering if Yokohama Camp Number One was finally getting to this ingenious cobbler. Why was he so interested in all of this? "Sherman," I said gently, "who cares?"

His voice became tense. "They're storing it in the camp overnight, sir. They can't distribute it, so they're storing it in the camp." He gave another slow nod while staring at me, waiting for my reaction.

I only gazed back at him mutely, disturbed by his fixation on the petty affairs of the camp guards. He was becoming too close to them, perhaps, talking to them all the time, knowing their language so well.

Sherman must have sensed my concern, for all at once he made an impatient gesture and grabbed my arm again. "Don't you understand, Captain, sir? They don't trust each other! And there would be big trouble if those barrels were short tomorrow when the other camps' guards arrive. They've never had to leave the barrels overnight at a camp. All the gunzokos are upset about it!" As he said this, he dragged me over to his workbench and made me sit down. I was really concerned about Sherman by then.

Once I was seated, Sherman continued. "Think about it, Captain, sir. Where could they store it? They'd put it in the food storeroom, but you know they don't trust Arai—they think he's up to something. Too much food disappears. Kambe told me once that they all suspect Arai of taking extra food to sell or give to his family."

I smiled at this. Poor Arai. He swallowed our tale of mice and rats, but apparently his colleagues didn't.

"And they can't put it in Chisuwa's office," Sherman continued. "You know how fussy he is. He won't lower himself to drink with his men, so he wouldn't have their saki in his office. They don't dare even ask him. And they can't leave it in their own barracks either, or none of them would sleep for worrying about someone sneaking a drink of it. They need to put it in a place with a lock and key, someplace where no one will get to it." With this,

Sherman smiled triumphantly. "Sir, Ikeda and Shishido came to check out my storeroom here to see if there was any extra room. There is. Or rather, there was. Just now the storeroom is rather crowded."

I finally understood what Sherman was so excited about. There was a small closet in Sherman's workshop that stored the leather, nails, and other goods used in the shoe workshop. When Maddock or Sherman needed extra material, they were to ask the camp commander for more supplies, and he or a gunzoko would get them from the leather storeroom, for only the camp commander had a key to the room. Sherman had long before found this a tedious process. He reached into his pocket then and pulled out a makeshift wire key and dangled it before me. "You know, Captain, sir, about this?"

Sherman had fashioned the key some time ago with the help of the cook-thief who had made the key for the food storeroom. He had been discreetly filching extra leather and goods for months in order to repair the soldier-guards' shoes. The one place in camp that the gunzokos thought was safe was the storeroom that Sherman, that friendliest and most fluent prisoner, entered on a daily basis. A slow smile spread over my face. It was dangerous and foolish and unnecessary and certainly not a risk worth taking, and I didn't care—I would certainly be a party to it. I hadn't had a night on the town since before Pearl Harbor.

"Where's Maddock?" I asked. "Does he know about this?" For of course he would have to be included.

Sherman misunderstood my question, thinking I was hesitant. "Of course Maddock knows. Look, sir, we *have* to do it. They've put the proverbial lamb before the hungry wolves. When was the last time you had a drink? It's been even longer for me, and I've never tasted saki before. We've *got* to do it. It would be wrong not to."

I grinned at Sherman. "Of course we have to do it, Sherman. Count me in."

Sherman's face broke into a huge smile, and the two of us went to find Maddock and consult the kitchen crew on duty. We would need their help.

WE MET—Sherman, Maddock, the cooks, and I—late that same night, after the other prisoners were long asleep. We had chosen our accomplices carefully; only people who had a reason to be up so late could attend our saki party. Two of the cooks kept watch, one on each side of the workshop area. They were to strike up a loud conversation if a guard came near, while two other cooks continued cleaning in the kitchen as usual. Sherman stood at the entrance to the workshop, ready to delay any guard with chit-chat. I sat idly on the workbench, ready to pass on a whispered warning to Maddock and the other cook helping him should a guard walk by while they were in the closet.

The storeroom door opened easily with the makeshift key, and Maddock and his partner in crime crept in, each carrying an empty bucket. They pulled out the plug on the side of one of the large barrels and together tilted the heavy barrel over, spilling its precious contents into an empty bucket. They filled the two buckets with a couple of gallons of saki while I contemplated just what might happen if our watch system failed to stop an advancing guard. But no guard appeared, and with buckets in hand, the thieves emerged. Maddock grinned and gave a silent thumbs-up sign, then they slipped across to the kitchen. I followed, to keep watch should anyone come while they hid the saki.

In the kitchen, we had some forty buckets that we washed daily—at night we stacked them along the wall to dry. Some of the buckets at the back and bottom of the pile went unused and unnoticed, and it was there that we hid our saki. With a pile of empty buckets stacked on top, we didn't think anyone would notice that two of the buckets weren't empty.

Maddock and the cook then grabbed two buckets of water and returned to the storeroom. As they moved toward the door, a guard passed the galley. He only mumbled a few words to Sherman in his workshop and moved on, entirely unsuspicious. When the danger was past, the two thieves slipped into the workshop again, removed the peg from the barrel and poured in several gallons of water to replace the missing wine. The saki would be a tad weak, but the guards would blame that on a bad year or the bureaucrats in Tokyo; the saki had, after all, been stored in a safe place overnight.

We left our saki there in the kitchen, after each of us checked the hiding place to make sure it was secure. We then returned to our routines. The Japanese personnel would have to wait until the following night for their party, and so would we.

The next day went by without a hitch, but the cooks, cobblers, and I lingered in the kitchen area more than normal, a sight that anyone watching us closely might have thought suspicious. There was really no reason for me to be in the kitchen from dawn till dark, and Sherman and Maddock didn't need to pop into the kitchen two or three times an hour. That afternoon, we discreetly watched as gunzokos measured out their saki from the closet—if one of the guards had studied us closely then, he likely would have noticed that none of us were breathing correctly.

But in spite of our uncharacteristic behavior, the saki was distributed without anyone noticing anything awry. We had only to wait and keep our jubilation quiet until after all the others had gone to bed, which was not an easy task. Children waiting for Santa Claus to arrive could not have been more excited than we prisoner-thieves.

Night came and with it the fog and final roll call of the day. We in the kitchen area followed our usual routines, but we arranged to meet after midnight to begin our party. I felt somewhat guilty that our party was exclusive. I told only Bracky about it and waited until the last minute to do so. Had we told anyone else, we obviously would have been in a more dangerous position than we already were, for word might have gotten back to the Japanese personnel. Besides, we couldn't steal enough saki for four hundred POWs, and if we were the only ones who knew about it, perhaps only we would be punished if we got caught.

After midnight we moved to an unused corner of our barracks. With the removal of the seventy-five prisoners, that section was empty, frequented only by rats and spiders. We climbed atop the bed-shelf and adjourned to a dark nook. The shelf stood some ten feet off the floor, adding that much more safety to our chosen party area; a guard would not only have to search an unfrequented area but climb up a wobbly ladder to reach our makeshift speakeasy.

We didn't start drinking immediately, but instead sat in a semicircle in the dark, gazing at the black shape of the buckets that sat in the center while fingering our mess cups. We had to wait until the Japanese on the other side of the compound were going full swing before we could start—Sherman was to bring word when their party was roaring. He finally showed up about fifteen minutes later—the Japanese party was going strong, he said, and the guards were not likely to disturb us. There were only two soldiers on duty, and they reluctantly so; neither of the guards were very curious about the prisoners as they listened to their off-duty friends reveling on the other side of the camp. But in case a guard should wander by, Sherman sat next to the ladder, ready to intercept anyone who might be interested in us.

Our first toast of the night was I think to the key to the storeroom and its manufacturers, our second to the Japanese tradition of drinking saki. At least one of us stood and bowed ceremoniously toward the Japanese side of the compound, thanking them for generously supplying the honorable saki to their malingering prisoners. After awhile we didn't bother to raise our cups at all, only dipped them into the buckets, each refill becoming sloppier than the last. Bracky and Sherman drank very little—Bracky claimed that someone had to be sober to patch up our wounds after we were shot, and Sherman, whose determination to steal the saki had obviously been centered around fooling the Japanese and not getting hold of a drink, wanted a semiconscious head if he had to deal with a guard. So the other twelve of us drank the two gallons of saki, which was enough to leave us jolly. Our only complaint was that we couldn't laugh aloud, because it was the most screamingly hilarious event we experienced as POWs. We were reduced to short titters and muffled giggles—I'm certain we sounded like a group of teenagers at a slumber party.

But it was not an innocent slumber party, which suddenly became evident several hours after midnight. A guard opened the heavy door to the warehouse then, and stepped inside. When we saw him, we immediately froze. He carried a lantern, and swung its light over the sleeping POWs while studying them perplexedly. He had obviously heard something. He turned in our direction. Once a bit closer, he saw Sherman and one of the cooks where they sat motionlessly watching him, and he walked quickly toward us. The rest of us, immobilized with drink and fear, sat like cornered rabbits as his echoing footsteps drew closer. Sherman broke the paralysis of our group by shifting forward to the edge of the shelf while the rest of us encircled the two buckets, making them invisible from below.

"It's the guard I was talking to earlier," Sherman whispered, then tossed out a casual greeting to the guard in Japanese. He spoke in a low, friendly, and respectful voice, a voice that to me conveyed all the innocence of a thirteen-year-old girl talking to her awakened parents, but the guard was not impressed. He abruptly asked Sherman what was going on. Sherman shifted himself so his legs were dangling over the side of the ladder, making it all the more difficult for the guard below to climb up, and smiled down at him.

"Oh, not much," he said casually. "We're just talking."

The guard was bewildered by this amicable answer and pointed to his watch, saying that it was past lights out and that we should not be up there.

"But we couldn't sleep! It's so noisy!" Sherman protested. "It's just us, the cooks, and Maddock—you know Maddock, he works with me—well, we couldn't sleep. We couldn't sleep with all the noise your friends are making."

The festive guards and gunzokos *were* making a racket—we could hear shouts and bits of song from their well-lit barracks across the compound. Obviously, water does little to dull the effect of saki on off-duty soldiers.

"They sound like they're having a great time. Too bad you can't be with them," Sherman said sympathetically.

Sherman's ploy worked—he reminded the guard that he was angry about not being a part of the saki party, so he forgot his suspicions about us. The guard began to complain about having to watch sleeping men rather than drink saki with his friends. Sherman listened sympathetically; he was careful not to hurry the guard while he spouted off. After some minutes, the guard finally closed the conversation and turned away. Sherman remained at the top of the ladder until the guard was gone and the heavy door closed, then he hopped down from the bed-shelf. He went to the door and peeked out, making certain no one was around. He returned after standing there silently a few moments.

"If that guard had come up here," he said while sniffing the fetid air, "we would have been sunk. He wouldn't have had to find the saki—you can smell the stuff ten feet away."

We all sipped our drinks quietly for a moment, absorbing what Sherman had just said with various images of torture and execution in our heads. No one argued when Bracky spoke. "Let's drink up, chaps. I'm nervous about all this."

We finished our saki party with one final round of drinks and a silent toast to our escape from detection. We hurriedly discussed what to do with the damning buckets and their odoriferous scent, and decided to clean them right then rather than leave them hidden in the barracks where they might be found. We also got some towels to wipe up the floor.

With the mild suspense and the need for stealth while washing up, the effects of the saki were muted until we had finished at the sinks. But once the last bucket was clean, I fully realized that I had drunk some four cups of potent wine on a very empty stomach. It had been a long time since I'd had that much alcohol—my head began to reel as I headed toward my mat. I leaned on Bracky, who was sober, and stumbled forward after a subdued goodnight to my partners in crime; they too felt the saki and were moving slowly toward their own mats. I finally made it to my mat and with Bracky's help carefully lowered myself onto it. Then that straw tatami, which I had trusted to be a stable bastion against my dancing head, betrayed me. It seemed to take off as I stretched myself out upon it; I was suddenly on an airplane's wing that was bobbing and spinning through saki-soaked clouds in an attempt to throw me to the hard ground below. I tried to stifle a burp, failed, turned over on my side, and realized I was drunk.

I began to laugh quietly to myself while my head whirled. I made more noise than I should have, for a fellow officer next to me stirred in his sleep. Bracky admonished me to keep quiet, but I didn't care. The danger was past. Even if I laughed out loud, no one would discover what we had done. The noises from across the compound were muffled by then—the Japanese were also retiring to sleep off the effects of their watered-down party. It was this that made me chortle. They had sipped weakened saki, weakened by us, their prisoners, and they didn't suspect a thing. I giggled again helplessly. Chisuwa would likely have ordered us all shot if he had discovered we had stolen saki from the almighty emperor's army. They had certainly killed POWs for less, I thought, almost soberly, but still I grinned into the darkness. It was the most dangerous act I had taken part of as a POW, but I patted myself on the back for it. The Japanese, I now knew from firsthand experience, were not unbeatable.

With these final thoughts, I fell asleep. The next morning, a pounding in my head kept me close to my tatami all day. The night cooks and Maddock were also conspicuously lethargic, but no one remarked on our conditions. As we served up meals, we secretly smiled at one another, proud of our exploit. To this very day I am pleased to have been a part of that group of thieves, with only one or two shivers when I think of what would have happened had we been discovered. Only the desperate sterility and boredom of that camp could have induced my cronies and me to attempt such a foolhardy act.

IN ANOTHER MONTH, 1943 was over, my first full year as a POW. Chisuwa gave us our Red Cross packages so we had something to celebrate at Christmas, but that and the saki party of November were the only bright spots of 1943. As the year ended, my greatest task was to conquer a gloomy awareness that as the new year began, there was no sign of any sort that I wouldn't spend all of 1944 in a prisoner of war camp as well.

12. 1944: My Midway

JANUARY ARRIVED, and with it came a mass of arctic air that plunged temperatures. The sick rate soared. Chisuwa and the guards, who had been semidecent the month before, came down hard again. With the drop in the work force due to the cold, Chisuwa and the gunzokos became disgruntled with the "malingering" prisoners once more, and the sordid violence of camp resumed. The year did not feel like a new one.

January and February 1944 were my lowest months as a prisoner of war. The world became all black-and-white for me, with only shadings of melancholy gray skies for variety. It was as if all color, all brightness had been drained from existence. Many times I found myself searching for some relief from the dirty gray as I gazed out a frosted window, but I saw only slashes of black—the black fence, the pronged black wire atop parts of it, the black poles of the hooded floodlights. That January, for the first time, the fate of Christensen, Dressler, and countless other Allied POWs appealed to me.

I became an automaton. I worked through one day at a time, saying the correct things, moving in the expected manner, avoiding the guards and gunzokos with no thought, absolutely none, of the future. In previous months, I had fallen into thinking of my wife and our hopes for a home and family one day—those dreams I put aside that winter and would not allow them to return in conscious moments. The hopes only returned to me at night when I sometimes dreamed of happier days. I dreaded such dreams, because they became nightmarish in the morning when I awoke to a stark POW camp.

I could not be like Bracky. He allowed himself to care for prisoners around him—I don't know how he survived with that much empathy in him. I would not let myself think of those who had died or those who were dying. I did not allow myself to measure the small portions of food the men were receiving against what they should have been eating. I would not see the wasted bodies and diseased eyes that watched me tiredly as they moved through the mess line. I would not think about the fact that hundreds of men awoke every day before dawn to walk to their work—their slavery—at the Mitsubishi Shipyards with nothing warm in their bellies and only a thin, single layer of clothing on their backs. Most of all, I didn't allow my mind to dwell upon my own weary and aching body; I only noticed in passing that I had to cinch in my pants to the last hole of my frayed belt to keep them on. I tried not to think of the young carefree man I had been, because I wasn't that anymore and never would be again.

All of us were affected by the despair of another winter in a Japanese POW camp; two prisoners' methods of coping with it attracted much attention and proved a lesson in human nature that particular winter.

Homosexuality was somewhat prevalent, or at least feared to be so, in our early days as POWs, back when men had more strength and more marks of "civilization" still with them. But by 1944 the possibility of homosexual relationships had become irrelevant to most of us. Even if someone were interested in the idea, he didn't have the strength to perform. From what I witnessed, POWs under the Japanese simply did not have the energy for sex. We could talk and reminisce about sex, but even that required an interest and zest for living many of us did not possess.

At least, most prisoners did not possess such energy. There were several POWs who ate better than others and were healthier, stronger; one of the cooks was such a man, and he had a boyfriend. What was singular about this was not the couple themselves, but the reaction to them on the part of other prisoners. There were some who objected to the relationship, but most either ignored or accepted the couple. Today this would not be surprising, but fifty years ago, homosexuality was still firmly shut inside the closet. In fact, it was so taboo that several of us worried when the affair first became obvious that it would end in violence. But this did not happen. The cook himself was quite popular; he was recognized and liked by all, and few prisoners were concerned that he engaged in sex with a man. Where they actually engaged in their encounters, I do not know; I only know that their relationship became a camp conversation topic that winter. It was the source of many crude jokes, but even as we razzed them, the two of them became as popular as a couple as the cook had been on his own. I suppose their relationship added variety to sterile camp life. They represented feelings and affection in a world that seemed devoid of those essentials, thus most of us accepted them.

By 1944 we had been prisoners for almost two years—we had seen many immoral acts: executions, unprovoked beatings, diseases left untreated, epidemics allowed to run rampant, betrayal, intolerance, starvation, and more. We had learned what immorality really was, and most of us tacitly agreed that it had little to do with one's sexual habits.

Organized religion itself took a back seat in the camps I was in, which surprised me. There were some in the Yokohama camp who probably practiced some sort of worship or regular prayer, but this was not the norm. There were several Bibles in our library, and they were read, but not pored over. I myself read the New Testament as a POW, but not because of a deep faith in Christianity—I had always wanted to read it, and had time to do so while a POW. I suppose the Bible seemed rather inadequate to most of us. The problems it speaks of do not embrace gun batteries, torpedoes, and heavy bombers, and we didn't have a chaplain among us who could explain what seemed to be lacking in the book. We were entirely separate from the rest of the world and its religions, and while there may not be any atheists in foxholes, skeptical soldiers do emerge from such places. It seemed natural that we should be isolated from religion along with all other aspects of our former lives; it is an institution of civilized society, and not found in hell itself.

Since the war, I have had few fears of hell. I have already seen it, endured it. I simply cannot conceive of a more damned existence than that inside the fences of a Japanese POW camp.

DURING THOSE WINTER months, Okimoto and I often talked in the kitchen during free moments. We seldom spoke of the war. We talked instead of the States, of U.S. geography and character, and compared such matters to those of Japan. Okimoto loved the energy of New York City and several times inadvertently referred to it as home. As a result of his thirty-six years in the United States, Okimoto had lost some of his ability to read Japanese. He could understand the simple passages he was required to read and translate to the POWs, and he could write basic messages, but the English language, he confided to me once, was easier for him to decipher. As a result of this, Okimoto read the *Nippon Times,* because he could more quickly get through it.

The *Nippon Times* was an English-language newspaper published in Tokyo for those in their sphere of influence who did not speak Japanese—many people in the Pacific spoke English along with their native tongue, but not Japanese. In the *Nippon Times,* leaders and business people all over Southeast Asia could read how the Japanese were winning the war and converting the Pacific into a Japanese empire. The newspaper was obviously a medium for propaganda—it always referred to the Japanese and their emperor as a great people and condoned their efforts while the Allies and their Western culture were criticized and belittled. But in spite of its pro-Japanese slant, the paper was interesting for us to read, and Okimoto knew this. He thus often "forgot" it in the kitchen. He could not openly give it to us, but he would not be punished for accidentally leaving it behind if a guard were to find it.

We found a way to read beyond the propaganda in the *Nippon Times.* We discovered there was a pattern to the stories, a formulaic approach to reporting the glory of the Axis, and we realized that Japan and her allies were in trouble. Our first clue was found in the Japanese version of what happened in North Africa. In early 1943 the paper claimed the Germans had suffered a slight setback, but all was improving and the article suggested that it was only a matter of time before the Germans squashed the Allies there. This same story appeared in two later issues, but in the fall of 1943, all mention of North Africa ceased, as if the continent itself had disappeared, and boasts about the Axis powers' imminent victory in Italy took over the headlines. Those prisoners who knew their geography pointed out that though the Nazis and Italians were supposed to be winning, they were slowly giving

up ground, because they had obviously lost North Africa. The tiny published war maps were the final clue—the arrows showing Axis strength were
illogical and inconsistent if compared week by week. We could not be certain exactly what was happening, but it was clear that things were going
wrong for the Axis in Europe and North Africa.

These flaws in geographical logic made us wonder just what was going
on in the Pacific. On this subject, the paper never wavered in its reports: the
Japanese had the Allies on the run—the paper hinted that it was simply a
matter of time before the Australians would be speaking Japanese. We had
had our doubts about this before, of course. A few months after we Americans surrendered in April–May 1942, rumors had circulated back to us of
the events at Midway Island. There were said to have been great losses on
both sides, but the Americans had finally equaled the Japanese at Midway;
some informants even said we had beaten them. It was only old scuttlebutt
gleaned from the Filipino black market, but by 1944 many of us in our
Yokohama camp suspected that something had begun to go wrong for the
Japanese at Midway, for not since the summer of 1942, a year and a half
before, had we heard of any new Japanese victories.

We read a garbled report in an older issue, from spring of 1943, about a
place called Guadalcanal—the article attempted to justify heavy Japanese
losses there. Few of us even knew where Guadalcanal was (several Aussies
said it was off the coast of Australia), but we were certain that the Japanese
military machine had faltered there. Throughout 1943 and 1944 we read of
battles occurring at other unfamiliar islands: Bougainville, Tarawa, Eniwe-
tok. The only thing consistent in the reports about those places was their
illogical and vaguely inconclusive nature.

Quite simply, it was what *wasn't* in the *Nippon Times* that intrigued us:
the paper celebrated victories long finished instead of announcing new con-
quests. The fall of Indonesia, Malaysia, Bataan, and Corregidor along with
the ingenious attack on Pearl Harbor comprised the news we read, but those
stories were all at least eighteen months old. The saying "no news is good
news" took on a special meaning for us. We learned by omission just how
well the touted Japanese military was faring in their newly conquered empire, and it gave us great hope. There was at least a stalemate in the Pacific,
we suspected, and with the shortages of food and fuel in Japan, we thought
there might be a successful blockade somewhere as well. The *Nippon Times*

helped keep me going during those bleak winter months of early 1944; I didn't let myself dream of the future, but I let myself ponder whether the Allies were on the rebound. I wasn't the only one who was uplifted by the newspaper. Those of us who read the papers circulated the "news" about the struggling Japanese military through the camp, and such gossip had almost as positive an effect on morale as our Red Cross packages at Christmas had.

By early 1944 I had received an occasional blow from a guard and been shoved around many times, but I had never endured anything more humiliating or painful than that. Kambe changed that. Kambe and I had never been friendly with one another but he did know my name, as I headed the kitchen crew. Because I was considered one of the cooks, he tended to leave me alone. That was another benefit of being a cook. For some reason, the gunzokos were more lenient with the cooks, perhaps because we cooked for them as well. Thus, we often asked a favor of the gunzokos if the conditions seemed favorable: to skip morning roll call.

Roll call was a tedious procedure that took place twice a day. Every morning and night we lined up in small groups and counted off in Japanese. If the combined total number of men tallied up to the gunzoko's expectations, we were dismissed. If not, we repeated the process until the number matched or we discovered who was missing. The numbers were almost always off, so *tenko* (the Japanese word for roll call) was almost always an ordeal. Roll call was hardest on the cooks. A given shift worked until one or two in the morning; those same cooks had to get up to stand roll call at six. Although they gave up sleep willingly in return for the privileges of a kitchen job, the cooks hated having to wake up several hours after falling asleep. So I usually asked the gunzoko in charge if the shift that was going off duty at one could be excused from morning roll call after taking a night tally. I had to wake up to supervise the day cooks' count off whatever the gunzoko's answer, but I was usually willing to make the request for the night cooks.

One February day, Kambe was the temporary officer while Chisuwa was out of the camp. He was in a foul mood. He kept us at roll call for three hours that night and beat on whoever blinked in a way he didn't like. Because of the lengthy roll call, the cooks were still working after two. By then they were loudly complaining that they would have to wake up for morning roll call after less than four hours of sleep. They had noticed I hadn't asked Kambe to excuse us from tenko.

I ignored their complaints for as long as possible, but as I was leaving the kitchen, one of the cooks asked, "Hey, Captain, why didn't you ask Kambe to excuse us from roll call?" They all looked at me expectantly.

I was exasperated. "Are you guys out of your minds? Have you seen what's been going on out there the last three hours? I wouldn't go near Kambe and ask him to excuse you from roll call. He's out of his mind again."

The wily cooks were ready for this. "Oh, come on, Captain, he likes you. He's never bothered you. He'll do it for you. You're an officer." They also told me that Kambe had been quiet for a while, which was true.

Our debate went on for several minutes. When the cooks told me I was their representative, their only protection from unfair camp policies, I was done for. I was their officer-in-charge, I thought. If I didn't stick my neck out for them, who would? And how would I maintain their respect? I left the kitchen and found a guard to escort me across to the Japanese side of the compound to talk to Kambe.

I found the officer for the day in a small private room (a privilege of the day—the gunzokos normally bunked together). Kambe was not alone. Okimoto stood on one side of the room, looking pale and anxious next to a guard with a gun; two Dutch prisoners stood across from them. I recognized one as Lieutenant Boon. There was a third Dutchman in the room. I did not know his name, but I had talked with him several times. He was friendly and stood out in a crowd because he was quite tall, with very light blond hair. He had had a muscular frame once, but because of malnutrition he was now gaunt and ungainly. His awkward appearance made him the butt of many jokes in camp. The gunzokos especially picked on him; he intimidated them because of his height.

Just then, though, the good-natured Dutchman was miserable. As I entered the room with the guard, he was on his knees with his hands clasped behind him, his head lowered and thrust forward. His eyes were tightly closed. Just next to him stood Kambe in an executioner's pose—his sword was overhead, poised and ready to decapitate him. Kambe still wore his ribbon proclaiming him top dog of the day, an officer for twenty-four hours who had the right to abuse men in this manner. Boon and the other Dutchman were terrified—they obviously didn't want to see a murder enacted in front of them and feared for their own lives. This execution scene was likely one of Kambe's malicious games, but no one could be certain what he might do. We knew Kambe was equal to murder.

All in the room swung round to see who had come in as we opened the door. Kambe scowled at me. The Dutch prisoner opened his eyes and recognized me, then closed his eyes again, his face contorted with terror and shame. He was more than a foot taller than Kambe, and probably could have easily thrown him through the window, for his hands were only clenched together, not bound. But he had to kneel there, wondering if Kambe would actually carry out his execution fantasy. It is not pleasant to witness another's terrified humiliation—I wish I had not seen this young Dutchman's.

After glaring at me a moment, Kambe turned his back on the guard and me. He stepped away from the Dutchman with his sword still held high in the air, and then made slashing movements in the air with it, as if he were a warrior fighting off unseen foes. He stopped doing this after a few moments and spat out a few words to Okimoto.

Okimoto turned to me meekly. "He wants to know why you're here, Captain Grady."

The scene had shocked me so much that I was confused for a moment as to why I was there. But I long ago learned it wasn't a good idea to register alarm, outrage, or even surprise at an act performed by a guard or gunzoko, for those who did often were beaten for such reactions. I collected myself as best I could and bowed. "Good evening, honorable Kambe-san." I said in Japanese, while fervently wishing I had not allowed the cooks to talk me into this. But by then it was too late to leave and say nothing to Kambe.

Kambe ignored me and began to swing his sword back and forth again, but this time over the Dutchman's head, allowing his victim to see the flashing blade.

I lowered my voice and switched to English. "I came to talk to him about morning roll call," I said to Okimoto.

Okimoto translated this to Kambe. Kambe had the sword high over his head just then and was clutching it in both his hands with the sharp side down. He then swung it down with a fast thrust forward toward the Dutchman's neck. I winced, but Kambe stopped just before contacting the Dutchman's skin. He then took up the sword a few inches, deftly turned it in his hands, and smacked the prisoner across the head with the flat of it. It wasn't a life-threatening strike, but it was obviously painful—the young Dutchman flinched. Kambe struck him again with the flat of his sword, and then again. The heavy thuds of metal against skull bone hung in the air. They sounded incomplete somehow, for the Dutchman never cried out. He just knelt with his eyes still tightly shut.

Kambe repeated this mock execution before speaking again to Okimoto. "And what about roll call?" was the translated question.

I drew myself up. "The night cooks were wondering if perhaps they could skip roll call in the morning. The men have worked late—they're still working—they would have to get up in less than four hours for roll call. We were hoping that honorable Kambe in his fairness would see that the men need their sleep to cook for so many prisoners."

Okimoto's translation alarmed me. I partially understood what he had said and thought the request should have been more eloquently put than those brief words conveyed. After nearly forty years in the United States, Okimoto often neglected to use the ultrapolite Japanese form of speaking as an inferior to a superior; I was considered Kambe's inferior, so this should have been reflected in my translated request. But I didn't blame Okimoto for his terse translation. He was nervous. So was I.

Kambe turned to face me again, his face hateful and accusatory. He did not speak to Okimoto, but hissed several words directly to me that I did not understand.

"What did he say, Okimoto?" I whispered.

Okimoto shook his head miserably. "It wasn't good. He says you've insulted him," he said in a small voice while struggling to sound official.

My heart skipped. "Why should he be angry? He's let us skip roll call before." My voice was hoarse with fear.

Kambe then screamed something, demanding to know what I had said while not taking his eyes off me. Okimoto started at his shrill voice, but repeated my request. He then translated Kambe's next question. "Do the other gunzokos let you skip roll call?"

Kambe was not looking for a precedent, but prey. And he had me trapped. If I said yes, he would either inform Chisuwa, who would ensure that such leniency never occurred again and punish me, or he would call me a liar for insinuating that a gunzoko would ever have been so permissive, and he himself would beat me. If I said no, he would be insulted, for I would be asking him to be lax when no one else had been. I certainly did not want to insult

Kambe in his present mood. My predicament only took a second to register, but my answer took longer. Kambe impatiently shouted his question a second time.

"He wants an answer, Frank," Okimoto said quietly. Okimoto knew the answer—he had frequently translated this request to other gunzokos and Kambe himself.

The young Dutchman looked up at me from the floor, his head still thrust forward in that absurd position, ready to be cut off. His face was gray and tense and acted as a mirror for me; I am certain I was as frozen with terror as he was, and as humiliated.

I decided avoidance was the best strategy. "Honorable Kambe-san has been fair before. The cooks are tired and have to wake up early for roll call. We thought honorable Kambe might consider letting them sleep so they can work better and work more after their rest."

When Kambe heard my translated answer, he stepped across the room to stand right in front of me. He spoke again in a hissing voice.

"He said you didn't answer his question. He also called you a liar," Okimoto meekly reported from behind him.

I shrugged automatically, which was a mistake; Kambe took that as a sign of disrespect. His face became contorted again as he swung back and struck me hard across the face with his fist. I stumbled back, surprised by the blow, but quickly regained my balance and stood grimly in front of Kambe. I wasn't hurt badly, but for a minute I was furious. Though I was not as large as the young Dutchman, Kambe was still smaller than I; it would have been more of an effort, but I too could have thrown the despicable man through the window, or at least given him a hard shove toward it. But he carried a sword, and the guards held guns—those weapons promised the little despot respect and authority. I didn't move. Furious and afraid as I was, I had learned from the enlisted men. I had to stand firm if I wanted Kambe to leave me alone. I gazed straight ahead and said nothing.

At first my unwavering gaze irritated him, for he struck me with his fist again. Like the motionless Dutchman, I tried not to move a muscle or cry out, but I became angrier. I continued staring straight ahead and hated Kambe, and oddly, that hatred steadied me. It was easy to despise that vicious little man with the ridiculous ribbon tangled across his chest and his uniform all askew. He was a mad man caught in a daydream of power, and his current fury sprang from the fact that my intrusion had forced reality upon him. He was not a warrior, he was only a twisted man assigned to guard the ill and unarmed. The man wasn't even a soldier anymore. His own army had rejected him and his insanity.

These thoughts kept me from backing away from him. If I had relented then, let him see my fear, I think Kambe would have had me down on the floor next to the Dutchman as another actor in his sordid fantasy.

But Kambe backed down. After all, he already had a toy to play with. And I was an officer—it wasn't Lieutenant Boon that Kambe had on the floor but an enlisted man. My rank helped protect me. Kambe swung on Okimoto and yelled at him, swinging his sword high in the air. I didn't need Okimoto to translate that—Kambe had just refused my request and called me something very disrespectful. He made chopping movements with his sword next to the Dutchman's head again. After wildly slashing the air for a few moments, Kambe became oblivious to my presence, and I backed toward the door where the guard impassively stood. Okimoto nodded at him, and he opened the door. Kambe did not seem to notice as I slipped out behind the guard.

I nearly broke into a run across the compound—only the slow-moving guard kept me from doing so. He left me at the door to the kitchen and I burst in there. I was still furious. The cooks were finished cleaning by my return; they were only waiting for me to tell them they could sleep through morning roll call. One of them started to say something as I entered, then stopped after a glance at my face. He moved toward me. "Captain Grady!" he cried. "Are you all right?"

He was staring at my eye. I raised my hand and touched the tender temple and cheek where Kambe had twice hit me. It was swollen and sore—I could expect a nasty bruise by morning. I fingered it a moment, oddly losing much of my anger as I did so. It hurt, oh yes, it hurt physically, but the humiliation, the impotent sense of outrage combined with fear was far more intolerable than the actual pain. And others had seen my shame. Lieutenant Boon had seen it. The young Dutchman kneeling on the floor had seen it.

"Sir, you're bleeding," the cook said. The others had gathered around. "Kambe beat *you?*"

I tasted blood in my mouth and realized that I must have bitten my cheek when Kambe hit me. I hunched over the sink and spit, then wiped my face with my sleeve. This wasn't much, I told myself. Many men had been hurt far worse than I. "I'm all right," I murmured, more to myself than any of the cooks. I suddenly wanted to get away from them. This was all too humiliating, to be hit without cause or recourse. I moved toward the door and raised my voice. "You guys are standing roll call in the morning!" I swung out of the kitchen and headed toward our barracks.

I was too upset to sleep much that night. I found myself thinking of many things—of our collective humiliation, of our vulnerability, of our anger. I remember thinking many times that sleepless night of the fist fights I had seen in movies where a man gets up from a sharp blow without any apparent damage whatsoever. Never before had those scenes seemed more ridiculous. No one gets hit without feeling it—both physically and emotionally. I thought of this frequently as I walked around with a painful shiner for weeks afterward; I still carry the shame that Kambe's fists imprinted on me.

The next evening, Kambe was his friendly self again, the previous night's events forgotten. "Arigato, Grady," he said when I gave him the roll call figures. He smiled after thanking me, the same smile that beguiled so many men into trusting him. He did not seem to notice the deepening black blot around my eye.

Lieutenant Boon told me that Kambe had continued the mock execution scene for another hour but had not used the other POWs in the room as his props. The tall Dutchman, Kambe's victim, nodded at me as I spooned up his rice the next night, but said nothing; he was no longer pale, yet his face still had a slightly humiliated cast to it, along with several ugly bruises and slash marks. He only nodded again when I asked if he had seen Bracky about the cuts. He was obviously embarrassed and did not want to talk to me about what had happened. This made sense to me. I had seen his terror, and he mine; we had felt it together. Such knowledge, I discovered, tends to prevent friendship: intense humiliation and fear should not be shared between mere acquaintances. The Dutchman and I, acquaintances who had sometimes chatted before his mock execution, did not speak to each other again.

In late June 1944 we had more reason to hope that our days as POWs might be numbered: we heard rumors that U.S. bombers had hit southern Japan. We studied the *Nippon Times* more closely and noticed that the maps published of the world's battlefronts had shrunk to two-inch squares, which left absolutely no room for detail. This was a clever move on the part of the publishers, for one hundred miles became less than a millimeter difference on the tiny maps and thus losses of territory did not easily show up.

The *Nippon Times* itself had shrunk in length—it no longer presented page after page of glorious tales of the Japanese empire and the Axis. And in one of the tiny maps displaying Europe, we saw in late June that the Allies had landed on the coast of France. They were still in Italy, we knew, and now they had landed in France and had obviously not been thrown back into the sea, for the paper would have boasted of that. As to the rumors of bombings in southern Japan, the paper said only that a few planes had been sighted but were shot down or driven off by valiant Zeros.

But there must have been bombings occurring somewhere in Japan, because come summer 1944, the Japanese took the nightly blackouts more seriously. The four hooded lights around our camp were no longer lit at night, and the few lights that had faintly illuminated the quay immediately behind our camp were extinguished as well. At night, Tokyo and Yokohama became a hooded animal crouching silently, a conglomeration of millions of frightened people huddling in the shadows. There was an expectant silence over the city day and night, and I often found myself searching our tight horizon framed by the four high fences, looking for a change, for an end to this madness.

One August afternoon I was in the galley when I heard a chorus of shouts. I ran outside and looked up, and there, some distance to the south, was a high-flying squadron of airplanes. I do not know how they knew it, but several men yelled that they were American, and as I stood there, a high-pitched wailing ensued. It was the first time I had heard a Japanese air raid siren—I had only heard American and Filipino sirens before, and I had hated and feared the screeching sound. In Yokohama, though, I immediately loved the sirens, and I began to yell uncontrollably, tossing my head back and screaming vindictively into the air. The Allies had the Japanese running for cover, had them cowering in air raid shelters, just as the Japanese had done to us a few years before. There were not many POWs in camp just then as most of the men were at the shipyards, but those of us there all shouted and whistled, sending our support to the planes that flew overhead those many miles to the south. "Blow the shit out of 'em, guys!" "Blast 'em to smithereens!"

Just then, Chisuwa rushed from his office to order us into the barracks and away from the windows; anyone looking out at the planes would be punished. The order did not stifle us once we were inside, though—nothing could have. The Allies were striking back; our planes were in view; and we were jubilant. Some of my despair lifted from me like a damp and heavy blanket withdrawn, and I thought of the future for the first time in months: with planes within view, it could not be long before the bombers were hitting Tokyo.

The planes that day must have quickly disappeared, for soon the air raid sirens fell silent. Chisuwa visited the officers' area later and told us it was only a reconnaissance squadron and the planes hadn't dropped even one bomb before Japanese Zeros drove them off. It was nothing, he said angrily, nothing at all, only a lucky day for the Allies—the planes wouldn't be back.

Two days later, however, a work detail was assigned to begin digging slit trenches for the prisoners and Japanese personnel. Apparently Chisuwa's superiors were not so certain the planes would not return.

We heard more rumors of bombings as the summer ended, but it was difficult to tell which stories were true; from latrine gossip, one would have thought the entire Japanese nation was under air attack. As word of the Japanese bombings became more frequent, I found myself wishing that the pilots above could somehow know of the POW camp nestled in the warehouse district surrounding Mitsubishi Shipyards. Whenever I thought of our location, my feelings of jubilant vindication often turned to ones of frightened vulnerability. From the air, our unmarked camp looked like just another Yokohama warehouse in this industrial area. And any industrial area in Japan would be a potential target for U.S. planes.

Our guards and gunzokos turned to their scapegoats when they needed to vent frustration over the bombings of Japan. They came down hard upon any prisoner they could get their hands on that summer, and Chisuwa did nothing to discipline them. Men were beaten for smiling too often, for searching the sky in a guard's presence, for talking about the planes.

One night we were ordered not to look out the windows, not because planes were in the area, but because the gunzokos were pummeling a POW in the compound. Kambe slapped me several times that night because he saw me look out a kitchen window at the beating. The punishment didn't hurt much; it was only humiliating and added to my deep hatred of Kambe. I remember hoping there might be an Allied bomb somewhere that had

Kambe's name written on it. But I also pondered the significance of Kambe's attack. The Japanese personnel had never bothered to hide their abuse of prisoners before—why had they ordered POWs not to watch the beating of another POW? Why had Kambe been so intent on punishing a witness of the beating? The cooks and I all thought it important that for the first time the Japanese military appeared concerned that their abuse of POWs be hidden. Were they losing the war and afraid of our reports of Japanese abuse once we were released?

At about the same time we first saw the planes on the southern horizon, the prisoners working out at the shipyard were assigned a new project— they were to perform the final outfitting of a ship the Japanese had christened the *Horyoku Maru*. Apparently the supervisors at Mitsubishi had come to trust their slaves, for it was a first for the POWs—they had never done a final outfitting before. The ship was to sail the seas the coming fall, or such was the Japanese plan.

The ship was a large one, but not as big as an aircraft carrier. It would handle small planes when completed, but the planes would only take off from it, not land. The aircraft would be placed on the ship by huge cranes at dry dock and be prepared for takeoff once aboard. As the smaller ship was more maneuverable than the larger aircraft carriers, it was to sail in front as a sort of scout, and the planes that took off from its deck would land on the bigger craft that sailed behind it. Had all gone well, the ship would have been a valuable one for the Japanese. But some of the POWs working on it were inspired by the sight of U.S. planes and rumors of bombings to the south, and were weary of helping the Japanese war effort with their forced labor. That summer, a handful of POWs discovered firsthand the meaning of the word sabotage.

There were many different work details on the ship. A group of men might end up working on the bridge labeling gauges, switches, and buttons, or working in the engine room on the huge boilers. Others worked on the cooling and heating systems, or up on deck, or on the steering mechanism. Some POWs were left alone for as long as fifteen minutes without a work boss checking on them, and in those free moments it was possible to undo some Japanese technology, then conceal the alteration or damage.

The POWs who worked on the bridge probably had the most fun contributing to the ship's downfall. They were to label all instruments there with metal plates on which Japanese characters were written so that the ship's captain and pilots would know which switch, dial, or lever did what. The script meant nothing to the prisoners, but if they followed the diagrams, they could have finished the task easily enough. The bridge detail put most of the labels in their correct places, but they chose a few labels and affixed them wherever they wanted without a glance at the diagrams. Whoever eventually tried to navigate the ship would have to do so by trial and error.

The men working on the heating and cooling systems had access to large amounts of steel wool, a product they shared with their friends working on the steam and pipe lines. These prisoners wadded up large amounts of the thick insulator and stuffed them into any narrow tubing or duct they found. With the lines thus blocked, the steam needed to propel the vessel would not efficiently pass through, and the ship would likely be trailing the aircraft carriers it was supposed to lead.

Other groups made a point of not screwing down heavy plates wherever possible, only giving a bolt a few cosmetic twists to make it look secure, and on some important but unseen joints of the ship, they neglected to install a nut at all. Others left clamps loose, while the electronically daring redid the wiring in creative ways, guaranteeing that power on the boat would be capricious. By the time it was finished, the *Horyoku Maru* was a loosely bolted down craft that would only be able to move sluggishly through the seas. This was probably a good thing, for with the shape it was in, it would probably have rattled to pieces or exploded if it topped ten knots.

But the work bosses at Mitsubishi Shipyards knew nothing of this. They were pleased no end with their ship, for it looked just dandy. To the work bosses, it was a propitious event, the completion of the *Horyoku Maru,* one that portended a future in which the conquered worked happily for their superiors, the Japanese. The supervisors had likely noticed the unusual zest with which some of the prisoners approached their work each day, and this too probably pleased them. The work bosses were proud and patronizing toward the POWs, which made the saboteurs all the more gleeful as they worked.

In early September the *Horyoku Maru* stood in the harbor, allegedly complete, and ready for its first voyage. An assembly of local dignitaries, along with a few officers from the Japanese navy and senior officials from

Mitsubishi Shipyards, gathered to watch the ship's first trip out. The prisoners were also allowed to watch the events. So they too stood on the docks that day, I'm certain with faces of angels, watching their baby come to life.

The event, I heard later, took some time to get started, as the engines did not immediately fire up and were skipping. The work bosses frowned at this delay, but the ship finally freed itself from the pier. It slid out into the harbor, and the seniors of Mitsubishi smiled as they watched it move through the water. It was a majestic-looking ship, and they must have been proud those first few minutes of the voyage.

What I have always wondered is just how long it took the Japanese officials to realize that something was amiss with their pride and joy. At first they must have thought that its pace was kept leisurely to impress the viewers with the ship's size and potential. At some point, though, the audience must have divined that the pilots were not simply putting on a show with the slow pace, for the ship lumbered through the water with a conspicuous lack of prowess. They watched as the pilots rushed about on deck, trying to detect the trouble. But it was useless. The awkward ship continued to crawl pathetically through its maneuvers. After floundering about an hour on the water, the *Horyoku Maru* circled around to dock without showing any adeptness in the water.

The POWs, those three hundred vassals who had worked on the ship that summer, some of them more cheerfully than others, stood quietly, some showing genuine surprise, others only feigning that reaction. The Japanese officials cast a few suspicious glances in their direction, but only a few; nothing was clear that afternoon except that the ship hadn't performed well. The prisoners were ordered back to camp and left the docks with their guards. No wild rejoicing over the success of their sabotage could take place, of course. The guards were looking for jubilation over the ship's failure; they watched us suspiciously all night. So our celebration was muted, but it was certainly a celebration. The camp fairly rippled with hushed laughter that night, as the saboteurs passed word around of their success and patted themselves on the back for their ingenuity.

The Mitsubishi officials must have discovered what was wrong with the ship, but we never found out what their reaction was to the faulty workmanship. The POWs were not allowed near the *Horyoku Maru,* and they heard it would be completely overhauled. But no one was punished, for the

Japanese could not be certain what had happened. All they knew was that the ship was riddled with errors in labeling and construction, and though they obviously suspected the POWs, they could not pin the blame on any one group of prisoners. The work details had changed too often—the civilian bosses had not paid attention to who worked where and when. Besides, it would have been impossible to prove that all the snafus had been made on purpose. There was, after all, a difficult language barrier between supervisors and workers, and instructions could easily have been misunderstood.

The Mitsubishi work bosses were caught by the collusion of this mass of POWs and probably furious over it, but they could do nothing. That was the beauty of the sabotage: our captors were hoodwinked but no single prisoner caught the blame. Chisuwa could not cut our rations lower than they were and expect the men to continue working, nor could he increase the already heavy work load. There were several severe beatings after *Horyoku Maru*'s test run, but there was nothing unique about that; we were accustomed to such abuse. I am certain Chisuwa considered gunning down the whole lot to make certain he punished any wrongdoers, but this he couldn't do; his superiors obviously realized that win or lose the grisly war, civilized nations would not look kindly on the execution of three hundred men to guarantee punishment of several handfuls of possible mischief makers, and besides this, Mitsubishi needed the free labor the POWs provided. The saboteurs got away with tossing various wrenches into the engines of the *Horyoku Maru*.

13. Bombs over Tokyo

By September 1944 the rumors of U.S. bombers hitting Japan proved true—the air raid sirens went off often in Tokyo and Yokohama. Some parts of the city were being hit, but we never saw any bombs actually fall until early October.

The air raid sirens came on that day about noon. About an hour later, the sirens' sound changed, and we knew the planes were headed in our direction. On Chisuwa's orders, we grabbed our blankets and moved to our recently completed slit trench outside the camp. We had withdrawn to the trenches several times the week before, but it had been unnecessary; the planes had not come near our camp, though one squadron had hit the southern end of Yokohama. We were jovially unconcerned about the order to retire to the slit trenches that day, for it was just another sign that the Japanese were in trouble, and this we relished.

By order of Chisuwa, we were to hold blankets over our heads as extra protection while in the trenches. We were joking about how useless those blankets would prove in an actual bombing when we heard a loud rumbling sound. When we peeked upward between the folds of our blankets, we saw U.S. planes coming toward us. Soon they were directly above us. From that close range, I saw they were huge, the largest planes I had ever seen; I wondered how the heavy masses of metal had managed to get off the ground and move through the air. We learned later that the planes were B-29s, the new U.S. Superfortresses. But the crews flying the giant planes did not know who was beneath them, and we fearfully wondered the brief instant they were over us whether they would drop their bombs on our warehouse district. But the squadron passed over us.

We were just beginning to breathe sighs of relief when four of the planes separated from the squadron and came back in our direction. They had apparently seen something of interest, a target of opportunity. We saw that the planes were headed toward the docks where our camp's POWs worked.

The Japanese workers had continued working on the *Horyoku Maru* that fall but were not finished with it as October began. It still sat at Mitsubishi Shipyards. Though not seaworthy on the inside, it appeared to be so on the outside, and this must have attracted the four pilots' notice. The *Horyoku Maru*, an ill-fated ship if ever there was one, was their target of opportunity.

The planes banked just over the shipyards, still very high, as was their custom then. As they passed over the ship, two planes dropped their bombs. Huge cascades of water rose in the air as the explosives hit the water and docks, but they missed the ship. The two planes that had not discharged their bombs tried again from what appeared to be beyond reach of the ship, but the distance had skewed our perceptions. We heard at least two of those bombs hit their target as the ship exploded with a mighty blast that rushed to meet us across the short stretch of water. A muffled burst of triumph circulated under the blankets as we realized what had happened.

The prisoners who had been at the shipyards returned soon after that because of the bombing. They had been huddled in slit trenches close to the *Horyoku Maru*, but there had been no injuries other than cuts and bruises from flying debris. They were uncontainable that night, much to Chisuwa's chagrin and in spite of the guards' slaps, shoves, and oaths—they had actually watched the loathed ship blow up. The poor old *Horyoku Maru*, they said, listed, filled with water, rolled over, and sank. That ship would never lead any convoy to attack anyone. The men were beside themselves.

By November the wail of the air raid sirens was familiar to us. It was a sound that evoked an odd mixture of pride in our armed forces, awe at the huge planes and at the havoc the explosives wrought, and after the hit on the *Horyoku Maru*, fear for our very lives. The bombs were dropped from

high altitudes in fall 1944 and often missed their targets, but still they devastated parts of the city. We were always aware of how close we were to some
key targets: the shipyards and the industrial area that surrounded us. Irrational as it was, we were convinced that "our boys" would somehow know
where our POW camp was, and they would consider the area more sacred
than an ancient and irreplaceable cathedral. Such illogical beliefs in the
pilots' ability to know the unknowable—our camp was not marked—kept
most of us from panicking as the planes drew near.

The bombers had a pattern to their attacks that soon became familiar.
The planes came in from the southeast, then flew along the coast of Japan.
When they were sighted by coastal observers, the sirens were switched on.
The first sound emitted was a continuous wail that did not fluctuate in
tone. The planes meanwhile drew closer to the most populated area of central Japan. Once they were in sight of Mount Fuji, their initial point, they
turned either north or south. If they turned south, Nagoya was the target. If
they turned north, they were headed toward Tokyo and Yokohama, and the
air raid sirens' sound would shift to a fluctuating wail, which warned that
bombs might soon be falling.

The B-29s were vulnerable in the skies over Japan. They were spotted
long before reaching Tokyo, and the antiaircraft guns fired constantly at
them. Japanese Zeros were ready to meet them as well. Those smaller planes
were more maneuverable than the B-29s, and though not nearly as powerful, they could slip up behind one and put out an engine before the Superfortress could react. The plane could lumber away without one of its engines,
or perhaps two, but with three of the four out of commission, the plane was
doomed, and the crew was forced to jump. They then became some of the
most hated POWs in Japan, if they survived the parachute drop.

The planes were just as vulnerable during night raids. The B-29s could
successfully slip up to the coast under the cover of darkness, but once over
Japan, they had to find their way in inky skies over a blacked out country,
so they relied on the dim lights of the railway lines to plot their paths. The
Japanese accordingly had established searchlights all along the tracks that illuminated the planes for their Zeros and antiaircraft gunners. Along with
pinpointing B-29s, the bright glare blinded the gunners and pilots above,
and they could not tell whether they were over a target, let alone pick out
the darting Zeros among them.

As dusk fell one evening in November, the sirens broke into our dinner preparations. We made little comment as we filed outside with our blankets and took our places in the slit trenches. Air raids were common by then.

As usual, the planes flew in from the south, hugging the coast, but as they headed toward Tokyo, six planes separated themselves from the squadron and headed toward the heart of Yokohama and our camp. That night they looked more menacing than ever. They were giant birds of prey in the fading light, flying inexorably toward us. The Japanese people, we heard, were afraid of them, deathly afraid; they thought them swooping monsters of doom. I could understand their fear. By 1944 standards, they were huge and deadly.

But inexorable they were not, for out of that same dusky sky tumbled several Zeros, and the sky was in an instant full of them as they swarmed toward the six B-29s, looking for all the world like a cluster of mosquitoes attacking a flock of great birds. The Zeros proved their superior maneuverability. Two of the bigger planes were immediately hit. A moment later, we saw white splashes of parachutes against the dark sky—four, then five of them from one plane and five from the other. We heard the whistling of the abandoned planes as they rushed toward the ground and the ensuing thunder of their crash somewhere out of sight.

A third B-29 was almost directly over the camp. It was stumbling through the sky—an ominous trail of smoke foamed from behind one of its engines, and we could see amid the clouds of black that a Zero danced close on its tail, guns blazing. The pilot of the B-29 was trying to escape the Zero and get out to sea where he could perhaps ditch the plane and stand a chance of rescue, but the plane was a wounded giant, and the Zero a lithe young David; the Zero scored again with a hit to another engine. A great pall of smoke hid the plane from view, and then the B-29 appeared again just over Mitsubishi Shipyards at a much lower altitude. From where we were, we could hear its engines faltering. We watched as four white blobs emerged from the plane, which was odd. We had counted five from each of the other planes, and deduced that that was the normal size of a B-29 crew. We wondered where the fifth man was.

A few more moments passed and then we all realized who had not jumped from the plane, for the plane was not spiraling toward the earth but was still moving unevenly through the sky. The pilot was still aboard and had some control over the plane. We wondered what he could be thinking of, because he was guiding the plane toward downtown Yokohama—there was nowhere to attempt a safe landing in that direction. But he made a wide arching turn, dropped even lower in the sky, and suddenly he was headed toward us.

"What the hell is he doing, gonna dive bomb us?" someone yelled as the Superfortress rushed at our warehouse barracks. But after a few panicky moments, the plane changed its direction once more, and we knew it would miss us. The pilot moved that faltering plane purposefully, as if he had some inscrutable intention. As it lumbered past our camp, I fancied for a moment that I could see the grim face of the pilot, some young American thousands of miles from home, a man with a plan. But of course I couldn't see him, he was still far too high, and it had grown too dark. But the will of the man was almost tangible.

"What the hell is he trying to do?" a voice wanted to know. It took another few seconds of watching the plane before we understood what the pilot had in mind. On a bluff not far from our camp sat a huge power plant. From the air it must have stuck out as one of the more enticing targets in the area. The B-29 pilot had decided where he wanted his doomed plane to crash, and he was determined to ensure the burning hulk connected with the high voltage steel on the hillside above us. There was still no splash of white against the sky—the pilot obviously was going to stay with the plane to make certain he hit it. It was the first I had heard of an American kamikaze fighter.

Moments later the plane ducked out of sight behind a warehouse, the same warehouse that blocked our view of the lower part of the bluff and its power station. But a brief second later we knew the pilot had succeeded when a great explosion rocked the camp, deafening and violent—he must have hit the power station head on. A great plume of smoke rose over the bluff, engulfing it until it disappeared from sight. There was not one fire, but five, then six separate little spurts of flame. And then began a brilliant fireworks show, with accompanying blasts and bellows as thousands of megawatts of power exploded. The destructive show played on while we watched, guards and POWs alike completely awestruck. We POWs didn't yell in victory; it was too sudden, too loud, and too frightening.

The blasts and shooting rockets of fire went on for some fifteen minutes before the chaos of the exploding power plant settled into a steady burn. Then a strange solemnity crept over all of us, a relative quiet made up of the muted roar of the fire and the still-wailing sirens that warned of an imminent bombing. Loud noises these, but they were quiet compared to the explosions of the plant. A stillness seemed to pervade as we absorbed what had happened.

The burning power station was quite large—it had been responsible for much of the electricity in Yokohama. Its destruction would have little effect on us POWs, as we were not dependent on electricity for light or heat (we used candles, oil lanterns, and wood stoves in camp), but for the Japanese military, it was another defeat. Without power in much of Yokohama, one of Japan's great manufacturing centers would be handicapped. That one American kamikaze pilot had done more damage to the Japanese war effort than any single soldier could have inflicted in those days before the nuclear bomb. I still wonder if he realized the significance of his final act before he died.

ANOTHER JANUARY ARRIVED. We greeted the new year, 1945 and our third year of captivity, with the thought that it had to end soon.

We did not receive a Red Cross package that Christmas. From what we understood, even Chisuwa was not getting his hands on our goods from home. Japanese-held ports had been under an effective blockade for nearly a year by then, and the civilians had access to less food, so they were breaking into our Red Cross packages as they came in, which to me was more tolerable than the thought of the camp commanders doing so. The men who worked at the shipyards said the atmosphere at Mitsubishi was not good—for the first time since they had been working together, many of the civilian workers were openly contemptuous toward the guards in their uniforms. The military seemed to be losing its hold on the people.

And the military wasn't happy about this—our gunzokos certainly were not. As the bombings continued and the Japanese civilians became more rebellious, our gunzokos became all the more resentful toward us; January and February 1945 were the most violent months in camp. The beatings were no longer inflicted by only one or two gunzokos, but by four and five of them at a time.

At the shipyards one afternoon, U.S. Army Sgt. R. T. Sparks was working when his work boss, Oshee Shan, became furious with him for some unknown reason. Oshee Shan began beating on Sparks while screaming about sabotage. He accused Sparks of singlehandedly crippling the *Horyoku Maru*, and when Kambe, who was supervising at the shipyards that day, heard this, he began beating Sparks as well. This went on for several minutes before one of the Mitsubishi supervisors intervened and informed Kambe he would have to discuss this with Chisuwa at camp, for the punishment was interrupting the men's work. Kambe and Oshee Shan restrained themselves, and two hours later, the men marched home.

Predictably enough, Chisuwa decided that Sparks had caused the incident and was to be punished. Later that night, Kambe led Sparks to the guardhouse. While I worked in the kitchen after lights-out, I looked out the window once and saw Shishido headed toward the guardhouse; two other guards were just entering that little room. That made at least four men who were to take swings at Sparks. After I finished my work, I went to the hospital so I could help Bracky with Sparks once they were finished with him.

It was more than a half an hour later before we heard the guardhouse door open and heard a scuffling in the compound. Kambe and Shishido emerged, half-carrying Sparks as he stumbled toward the warehouse. The gunzokos dumped Sparks on the ground outside our barracks and then returned to the Japanese side of camp.

Sparks's buddies reached him before we did. They had been watching for him and violated the lights-out confinement to quarters to help their friend. They lifted him gently, carried him in, and placed him on a mat in the hospital. Sparks was sobbing loudly while feebly waving his arms to and fro, fending off imagined strikes. His face was almost unrecognizable from the blows he had taken; his mouth was swollen and bleeding. A trickle of blood oozed from one ear. Bracky asked him to open his eyes, but he did not comply. Bracky began to bathe his face. Sparks jerked at Bracky's touch, so another man and I held him still.

Sparks then began to yell weakly. "The sons of bitches, those fucking sons of bitches! I didn't stay down for them anyhow. I got back up. I got back up!" His voice trailed off and he began to weep again. Bracky asked someone else to attend to Sparks's face while he looked for broken bones.

Colonel Lindesay entered the room. He gazed down at Sparks silently for a moment before speaking. "Is he going to be all right, Bracky?"

Bracky didn't answer immediately, as he was still checking over Sparks's body for any bone breaks. A few minutes later he raised his head. "He'll live.

He'll be aching for awhile, but there are no broken bones. I'm worried about a concussion, though. He was beaten badly about the head."

"How many were there, Sparks?" Lindesay asked.

Sparks did not answer, and Lindesay repeated the question. Bracky looked alarmed when Sparks still did not answer. He went around to the other side of the mat and spoke loudly into Sparks's other ear, the one that hadn't been bleeding. "Sparks, can you hear me?"

"Barely," came the reply.

Bracky bit his lip. "Jesus God, what have they done?" He looked up at Lindesay. "His ear there was bleeding when they brought him back. He may not be able to hear."

By shouting questions into his better ear, we got the story. There were seven of them, seven guards and gunzokos beating on him. They beat him with sticks and also hit him with their fists. He kept getting back on his feet when they knocked him down, because they beat him more fiercely when he was on the ground.

Bracky and I stayed with Sparks much of the night, as did his buddies. None of us would have slept anyway after seeing what had been done to him.

The next morning, Sparks was forced from the hospital in spite of Bracky and Lindesay's protests and sent to work without breakfast. His hearing was not gone but was badly impaired. And there was nothing we could do. There was no one to turn to for help; it was just another barbaric beating. How much longer could such atrocities go on?

WE DIDN'T READ the *Nippon Times* that winter. Okimoto told me that he could not find any copies of the newspaper anywhere; he suspected it was no longer being published. I thought that likely. A periodical that was meant to glorify the Japanese empire would have been hard-pressed to keep its pages full at that point in their history. But I missed reading it, in spite of the propaganda, for it had been an important news source from the outside.

Okimoto said that even Japanese language newspapers were hard to come by—there were shortages of everything in Tokyo. He said the latest news was of a place called Iwo Jima, an island somewhere in the Pacific, less than a thousand miles from Tokyo. The fighting there was fierce, he said, and although the newspapers he could find claimed the Japanese were defeating the Allies there, Okimoto wasn't so certain they were. The battle had been raging for weeks by then—it was late February 1945.

And we all knew that the Japanese were struggling to hold the Philippines. In November we first heard of the return of Allied forces to Leyte Gulf. I wondered what had become of Joe, Pfaff, and James in Cabanatuan, of Virginia in Santo Tomas—how were U.S. POWs treated by the Japanese as they faced defeat and surrender?

As March began, it was clear that the Americans had adopted a new bombing tactic. Someone somewhere must have decided that high-altitude bombing raids were not doing the trick, for the B-29s swarmed in at a much lower altitude than before—perilously low.[1] Sometimes bombers came in as low as a few thousand feet from the earth to drop their bombs. And the bombs were not simply high explosives but incendiary bombs, burning drops of hell that transformed whatever target they hit into an inferno, be it a civilian's home, a factory, a school, or a hospital. The B-29 pilots took great risks in flying so low, for they were more liable to crash at that altitude; the Japanese antiaircraft gunners could also more easily hit them. But there was no ignoring the fact that the strategy worked. It wreaked havoc with the Japanese industrial might while sapping the civilians' support of the war as they watched entire neighborhoods go up in flames.

On 9 March 1945, about midnight, a huge squadron of the Superfortresses flew over our camp—hundreds of them. The planes were headed toward Tokyo's *shitamachi* (downtown) in the southern part of the city, a densely populated and vital center of Japan's industrial complex. At that time, the shitamachi district was made up of wooden buildings and homes and thus was especially vulnerable to an incendiary bombing. The planes made many passes over the area, and it went up like a pile of kindling. The raid proved to be the most damaging strike against Tokyo and the most devastating bombing in world history up until that time. We POWs were in the slit trenches as the bombing took place and unable to see much, but it wasn't long before we smelled smoke and saw a bright glow in the sky—it seemed that all of Tokyo was on fire.

That night the B-29s' incendiary bombs wiped out much of Tokyo's industrial capacity, for many people in the shitamachi district had set up minifactories in their homes. But that U.S. victory had come at great cost to Japanese civilians. Thousands died in their burning homes, trapped by the flames that quickly engulfed the houses as the bombs hit. And the slit trenches were no refuge because of flame's great thirst for oxygen. In places, the inferno was so intense it sucked up all available air, leaving hundreds suffocated in the narrow pits. Burning to death or ghastly suffocation—both fates were ugly, and women, children, and the elderly died that way along with laborers and soldiers.

There was less resistance from antiaircraft fire and aircraft that night, but the B-29 pilots struggled to keep their planes aloft because of the hot, turbulent air masses created by the heat beneath them. Several planes crashed into the burning pit they had created.[2] The night was a holocaust, utterly unimaginable in its destruction and indescribable in its horror.

But that night we knew nothing of the destructive bombing raid aside from the fact that it lit up the heavens for hours. We watched the glowing sky from our slit trenches for some time and then were ordered inside. The next day progressed like any other, but many of the guards were away from camp—we learned later that they helped dig for survivors and bodies in the ashes of southern Tokyo. When they returned, they spoke of massive destruction—the whole of the shitamachi had apparently been leveled. Such decimation had been wrought in the Philippines and other parts of the Pacific by the Japanese, but they had required months of incessant bombing to destroy places like Corregidor Island, while the new U.S. war machine had obliterated the downtown area overnight. It was utterly incomprehensible.

As it happened, I was one of the few POWs who saw the immediate aftermath of the shitamachi bombing. A few days after the attack, our grain supplies were low. But most of the gunzokos and guards were still helping with rescue and clean-up efforts in Tokyo, so there was no one to get more staples for us. Because of this, Chisuwa sent me and another cook with a guard to collect the grain. Our trip by truck would take us through the shitamachi district of Tokyo.

There were hundreds of people on the streets of Yokohama and Kawasaki as our truck trundled from camp—more than I had ever seen on those ever-crowded avenues. Many carried large packs on their backs—it was a few minutes before I realized that these people were the survivors of the bombing raid; they were crowding into the still-habitable sections of Yokohama and Tokyo. I wondered where they would go, where they *could* go, for Yokohama and Tokyo were already crowded cities. I saw their faces as we went by but, as usual, not their eyes; the refugees walked with their heads customarily averted, with who knows what thoughts of the Japanese army truck as we slowly passed.

The crowds of homeless survivors grew thicker as we drove along the outskirts of southern Tokyo. I had never seen that part of the city, and on that March day I could not develop even an idea of what it had looked like. There was so little left there; I could not imagine that a teeming city had existed there two days before. It was a vast, blackened plain, still smoldering, with only a few spectral structures standing among the devastation. A smoky stench hung heavily in the air that I identified with defeat, death itself even. And no wind would lift that smell from Japan soon, I thought; these people would ache from the wounds of 9 March for years to come. For it was obvious to me as I viewed the shitamachi that Japan had lost the war. The event that I had long hoped for had come to pass. The killing would continue, of course, and the bombings, but the war was over for the Japanese after that raid. Not even a miraculous kamikaze wind would help defeat the foreign devils. That magical wind that had saved the Japanese in the past had only aided the Americans during the bombing raids, helping to spread the fires and fan the flames higher.

There were people everywhere among the blackened rubble, digging through the ashes with shovels and picks, searching for bodies and salvageable materials. Soldiers traipsed out of the wreckage with stretchers in between them; the stretchers held unmoving and uncovered clumps of what had been human beings—sometimes there were two of the charred hunks on the narrow stretchers. I suppose they had removed the wounded by then and were only collecting their dead for identification, if possible, and final cremation.

I felt a great remorse mingled with a gnawing uneasiness that day as I gazed at the city that was no more. The feeling returns to me, but there is no proper label for it. I believe it is related to anguish, the anguish of the human race as a whole as it realizes its failures, its demons. As I watched the attempts of the Japanese to find life in the ruins that day, I too failed with them to find it. I too was defeated by our human ugliness. For a few moments I ceased to be an angry POW held by the Japanese. No one wins these things, I thought; no one ever wins. We all lose something together in any war.

I learned later that a hundred thousand people had died in the shitamachi district of Tokyo during the 9 March bombing raid.[3]

THE PERIOD AFTER the shitamachi bombing was anticlimactic as yet another spring arrived. We expected the war to come quickly to an end after the devastation in Tokyo, but it dragged on. The incendiary bombing raids continued; each week news trickled into camp about another one. We heard rumors of much death and destruction all over the country, starvation, and shortages of everything. But the Japanese military refused to surrender.

Several facts we were finally certain of, for Okimoto confirmed the rumors. The Japanese had lost the Philippines and with it much of their naval power. MacArthur had made good on his promise to return to the Philippine Islands, or rather, thousands of enlisted men had made good on his promise to return, and Manila was once again in American hands.

We heard other rumors about the Philippines that spring, but the news didn't leave us hopeful. Several unmarked Japanese ships that were transporting POWs north to Japan had been attacked by U.S. planes. Hundreds of weary and sick POWs who had managed to survive the Bataan Death March and Cabanatuan had drowned. Many POWs who survived the sinking were shot in the water by Japanese guards in lifeboats who claimed the POWs were attempting to escape.[4] The reports made me shudder—in spite of their proximity to the tropics, the waters north of the Philippines would be a cold and desperate place to die. I thought for the thousandth time of Joe Iacobucci, of James and Pfaff, of my wife.

In early April our schizophrenic gunzoko, Kambe, was transferred out of the camp. He went to a camp in Tokyo, one of the detention areas set up exclusively for the B-29 crews who had crashed in Japan. There were rumors circulating that B-29 crew member POWs were regularly being tortured in special camps set aside for them. And now Kambe was a guard among those Superfortress crews. I shuddered. I envisioned them, those unwary pilots and navigators, warming up to friendly Kambe, surprised to find among their torturers such a nice guard who offered them cigarettes while passing on camp gossip. They would trust him until acute pain took over his personality, and then he would share his agony with them. Nevertheless, we were relieved once Kambe was gone.

Meanwhile, in Yokohama the civilians were becoming even more openly rebellious, but with a new twist: they were often openly hostile toward the enemy in their midst. An oppressed and starving people, they were losing all patience with the war effort as they lost families and friends in the incessant bombings, bombings made possible by our brothers and sisters across the seas. The men said that labor on the ships did not flow along as it had before. The work bosses were testy, the civilian laborers resentful. Beatings of

POWs took place more frequently at the shipyards, but the gunzokos weren't doing it, the civilians were. This left us aware of just how isolated we POWs were—four hundred Dutch, British, Australian, and U.S. POWs would have nowhere to run among millions of Japanese should angry civilians become a vengeful mob.

But finally, when it was obvious that they were going to lose the war, the Japanese military paid attention to their POWs. They gave us more vegetables that spring, which helped make up for the fact that by then we were receiving smaller allotments of grain. In mid-April they even allowed about fifty officers to send radio messages home. And most importantly, they decided to break up some of the POW camps in the Tokyo area; the POWs would be removed to supposedly safer places in Japan. They claimed they were afraid that one of the camps might become an accidental target of an Allied bombing squadron. We saw through that. If they had genuinely been worried about our safety, they would have painted a huge sign designating our warehouses as a POW camp or they would have moved us long ago, when the bombings first began. We knew the real reason they were finally moving us: we POWs were a possible catalyst for rioting. If civilians became so full of hate that they attacked a POW camp, the fury unleashed could prove contagious and unstoppable. They hated us, but they also hated their military. If they were to rebel en masse, it might not be just the Allied prisoners who suffered.

As our camp was disbanded, we were generally segregated by nationality. The Dutch prisoners went off in one direction, to camps in the north of Japan. Because there were so many of them, the British were divided into two groups—most of the officers and half the enlisted men made up one group. They would end up in a camp called Hanawa, or that at least was Sherman's last news before our move. The remaining British enlisted men formed another group, and they, with some Aussies and New Zealanders, joined our American group. Bracky was with us—he was assigned to us because the other British group had Dr. Price, and as the camp we were going to might not have any medical personnel, we might need Bracky's services. There were about a hundred of us.

Our departure from camp was a brief procedure, for we had practically nothing to pack. Buddies who were going in separate directions wept and hugged each other, with many promises to meet in one country or another after the war was over. I was filled with a sense of widening distances that evening as the first British group marched out of camp; I sensed that many of our goodbyes were final. Sherman and most of the cooks were in the first group to exit the camp. I have neither seen nor heard from any of them since.

I also said goodbye to Okimoto, that kind man who had tried to make our captivity more bearable. We promised to meet again, but not in Japan, in Brooklyn; he would show me around. I only hoped that he and his family would survive whatever Japan had yet to face before the war's end.

Our group's move took place later that night by train; we rode in cars with the shades down. We were not allowed to look out. We headed north along the coast. The train was crowded, but not unbearably so; the ride was luxurious compared to others I had taken as a POW. Sometime during the night we stopped at a darkened station where another group of POWs boarded the train. We learned the next morning that there were a hundred of them, Americans and British, and they too had been at a camp in Yokohama. We were two hundred strong now.

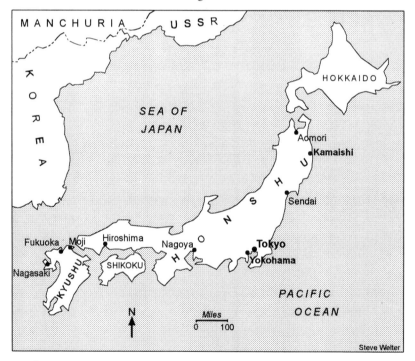

Japan, 1941

About an hour after daybreak, we pulled into a small town that sat between lush hillsides next to the sea. We saw a huge factory a short distance up the valley and the air smelt of some sort of manufacturing. We could see coal mines up the valley as well. A guard told Maddock that the town was called Kamaishi, and that we were about 250 miles north of Tokyo.

As we marched along, I wondered what day it was. I asked Bracky if he knew—it was the fourteenth of April 1945, he thought. Unbeknownst to us, Germany was on the brink of surrender, and the Italians were by then long out of the picture. Japan was fighting the Allies alone. And I was walking toward my fourth camp as a prisoner of war.

14. Kamaishi: Spring 1945

WE ARRIVED AT A small, fenced-in camp just outside the town of Kamaishi, down on the harbor. There were two long rows of barracks, one of them unoccupied, which was to be our home. A fence ran down the center of the compound, separating the POWs from the Japanese personnel. We marched in and assembled on the prisoner side while the camp commander, an interpreter, and a gunzoko walked toward us.

Our new commander stood in front of us with his hand on his sword. He introduced himself as Lieutenant Inaki and told us we were now at Sendai POW Camp Number Five, Kamaishi. Inaki spoke English fairly well—much better than Chisuwa or Nichizawa had. He gestured toward the men next to him and introduced them. The gunzoko was Matsuura, and the interpreter was Fukumura. After the introductions, Inaki studied us silently, his eyes flickering across our various uniforms. He fixed his eyes on me momentarily, then focused on Bracky and several other officers in our group. "I will talk to all officers alone when I finish the rules," he said.

Inaki then told us the camp procedures. He told us several times that he ran an honest camp and we would receive "honest management" but that he would punish any "incidents." He went on to inform us that the enlisted men would work in several places: the steel mill, the sawmill, the harbor, the cement mill, coal mines, or on locomotives. They were to work every day, with a rest day every two weeks, as in the Yokohama camp. He pointed out the guardhouse, the latrines, bathhouse, and our barracks. He told us that the other prisoners in the camp were Dutch.

After he finished talking, the enlisted men moved toward the barracks while we officers stayed where we were, per Inaki's orders. He still stood with his hand on his sword as he spoke to us. "There are 183 Dutch in camp," he said. "The highest rank is first lieutenant. Who is highest rank here?" Capt. Eric Marsden, who was from England, and I identified ourselves. Inaki continued. "Marsden, you are prisoner-in-charge of the British prisoners, and Grady you are prisoner-in-charge of American. You Grady are fire chief of camp. You Marsden are assistant fire chief. You both must prevent fires. This is your responsibility."

Marsden and I glanced at each other briefly, both a bit amused. Never had I thought that my commission would bring me such a noteworthy responsibility—Marsden and I were now two upstanding firefighters in a POW camp.

Inaki went on a while longer, giving us orders and describing the work details of the enlisted men. He informed us that officers were to work as well. There was a garden for the prisoners, and we were to tend it, along with searching in the fields for edibles to supplement our diet—again we would consume "weeds you can eat." We were also to search the seashore for edible seaweed. And officers were responsible for cleaning and maintaining the camp.

Bracky asked about the hospital—where was it and was there a doctor in camp? Inaki stared at Bracky somewhat angrily when he spoke up—he didn't seem to like answering questions. But he answered. "The hospital is there," Inaki pointed to one of the barracks. "There is a Dutch doctor."

Bracky identified himself, said he had some medical experience, and he had been acting as a medical officer at Yokohama. As the doctor, Dr. Pijma, now had two hundred additional prisoners to attend to, Bracky volunteered to help in the hospital. Inaki said nothing to this but still seemed angry. I added that Lieutenant Brackstone had been indispensable at Yokohama. With this, Inaki nodded curtly toward Bracky and accepted his services.

Inaki had finished with his orientation, so with hand on sword he marched back to the Japanese side of the camp.

Bracky slapped me on the back when Inaki was out of sight. "Well, Frank, this move hasn't been bad for you! From head cook to senior American POW officer! And fire chief! Congratulations!"

I laughed with Bracky, but I was concerned. "Why do they need a fire brigade here? No other camp commander has been that concerned about fire, not in any camp that I've been in." We debated this point and other matters for a few moments. When we began discussing our new camp commander, Bracky announced, "I don't like this Inaki fellow." This surprised me, as had the angry looks Inaki had cast in Bracky's direction. The two seemed to have taken an immediate and distinct dislike to one another. Bracky went on. "He seems awfully proper and strong on rules. What does his 'honest camp' and 'honest management' mean? I don't trust him. He might be better than the Yokohama Japs, but still I don't trust him. Honest camp indeed. No POW camp is honest."

IT BECAME CLEAR that the Japanese military had issued a handbook on how to run a POW camp, because procedures and conditions were very similar at Kamaishi camp and the Yokohama camp. Our barracks were simple, again made up of a huge warehouse with wide shelves as beds. The officers slept on one side of the building, the enlisted men on the other. The latrines were filthy, the bathhouse grimy, and the mess room basically a barn. With the dirt and scanty provisions, nothing was different—our new camp quickly became familiar.

The cooks in the camp were Dutch. They did not enjoy as many benefits as the Yokohama camp cooks had because they were closely supervised by Matsuura. Matsuura was wildly protective of his food stores—he checked them several times a day. There was no unauthorized key to the food storeroom at the Kamaishi camp, and our cook-thief wasn't there to make one— he had marched off with Sherman and the rest of the Brits to another camp. POWs still vied to be cooks, though, for one could always manage to gobble up an extra bite of food behind Matsuura's back, and it was easier to cook than to work in the factories and coal mines. The Dutch cooks were firmly established in their positions; no Brits or Americans became cooks at Kamaishi.

I was soon convinced that we were in a more vulnerable position at Kamaishi than we had been in Yokohama. There was an antiaircraft gun battery across a narrow dirt road just outside camp, and with the area's factories and coal mines, U.S. bombers were sure to find Kamaishi inviting. And as in Yokohama, our camp was unmarked. Any plane above would assume that our POW camp was simply a warehouse sitting next to a prime target, an antiaircraft gun near the town's docks. Several of us officers went to Inaki three days after our arrival and requested that he move the camp to a safer area. He refused. We then asked that he at least mark the buildings as a POW camp, but Inaki would not entertain this idea, either. He said that marking a POW camp was unprecedented and therefore impossible. We did not give up trying to get the buildings labeled, but our requests were all denied.

I was not enthusiastic about my title as a POW officer-in-charge. After watching Lindesay struggle with Nichizawa and Chisuwa in our last camp, I thought POW officer-in-charge a useless title. It wasn't as if I could change anything. I could not improve the conditions we all endured, and the position did not bring with it any perquisites such as extra food or clothing—in fact, in Kamaishi, my rations were smaller than they had been at Yokohama, for I was no longer in the kitchen. All my title affected was my ability to sleep those first nights, for I felt burdened with my responsibility. Any suffering the men endured was reported to me or to Marsden with hopes that we could somehow better the situation.

Thus began our daily visits to Inaki, whom I came to despise for the same reasons Bracky did. He functioned well as long as no one rocked his little world, but when anything was amiss, he grew as sullen and unresponsive as a spoiled child. He was obsessively miserly—he was ever convinced that a bit more could be squeezed out of an empty barrel. I never enjoyed my sessions with Inaki because they always ended in arguments that I could not win. But I soon realized that the 382 men whom I represented were quite able to take care of themselves; after surviving three years in such conditions, they had to be. And the other officers, most notably Marsden, Bracky, and Lt. Francis Van Buskirk, an American, helped me argue with Inaki. I was not alone against him—none of us felt alone against the Japanese by then. We had been through too much together to imagine ourselves alone anymore. We could see no God, and images of peacetime and our homes seemed mere fantasies, but while immersed in that hell, we found strength where strength really is and always has been: in one another.

Beatings were not as frequent at Kamaishi as they had been at Yokohama. Inaki did want free hard labor from his POWs, but he was not particularly vicious in his attempts to get it. When he beat POWs, he did not do it with the premeditated malice and obvious enjoyment that I had seen in the gunzokos and camp commanders at Yokohama. It is little to say of anyone, but for us it was a break. Inaki enjoyed the beatings less than our other camp commanders, and he didn't encourage his gunzokos and soldiers to abuse us. And most thankfully, we had no schizophrenic Kambe at our new camp.

When we first arrived, we ate a bit better at Kamaishi than we had at Yokohama. We got about 650 grams of rice or millet a day, which was slightly less grain than we had received at our last camp, but in addition to it we were given vegetables more often. Several times a week there was also fish to eat, though only a few bites of it per prisoner. On our biweekly rest days, we were given some flour, and the cooks were allowed to make an unleavened bread for us—it wasn't very tasty, as they had no butter or milk to add to it, but it was a change and added extra calories to our diet.

Inaki was decent in one other way: just after our arrival, he gave us five days off from work. He did this because unlike Chisuwa and Nichizawa, he recognized that sick men cannot work well. So he granted us a rest period, during which the Dutch doctor, Lieutenant Pijma, examined all of us. Predictably enough, he declared that we were all walking skeletons who were vulnerable to any virus or injury. His assessment changed nothing—we were still expected to work after our five-day break, but the diagnosis gave us a grim satisfaction: death should have claimed us, but had failed.

Pijma was able to help a few of our group, however. Some of the men who were dangerously emaciated were given a protein milk made of crushed soy beans and water to help them regain some of their strength, which they did. But once the men who received it were better, Inaki withdrew it.

Dr. Pijma was an interesting man. Like Price at Yokohama, he was older, but he was not fearful of the Japanese camp personnel as Price had been; on the contrary, he voiced his opposition to the maltreatment of POWs whenever he could. By the time we met him, Pijma was very tired of being a POW. He was impatient with the Japanese commander and guards, pushy with them even—his age and position as the only doctor gave him a sense of authority that even Inaki respected. His uncompromising devotion to the health of the prisoners and impressive sense of dignity could sometimes sway Inaki when nothing else could. Pijma and Bracky got along well together and made as fine a medical team as we could have hoped for.

The Dutch POWs at that time went to several job sites. They did locomotive and car repair, loaded gravel cars, and worked at the cement mill and iron smelter in town. The Americans and Brits were assigned to various locales. Some worked at the sawmill and iron smelter; some worked with the Dutch, stevedoring and fixing automobiles; some were assigned to dig a tunnel that was to connect the steel mill to the port; and some worked in the coal mines. About twenty enlisted men remained in camp each day and acted as medical orderlies under Pijma and Bracky or worked around camp.

Maddock managed to do fairly well in Kamaishi. When Bracky and I vouched for his shoe-making ability, Inaki assigned him a large closet in our barracks as a workshop, for the Dutch POWs at Kamaishi needed shoes— Pijma had in fact requested several times before we arrived that Inaki provide shoes for them. Maddock received a small supply of leather and tools, and he was in business. He made the same simple sandal-type shoes he had made at Yokohama, and he produced them by the dozen. He also tried to work the guards as Sherman had in the Yokohama camp. He didn't enjoy the trust of the guards that Sherman had, for his Japanese was not so flowing and full of charm as his mentor's, but he did manage to acquire some money or food from the soldiers at times.

As one of the senior officers, I heard the enlisted men's reports about their working conditions. Most often they complained to me of hard work at the factories. The foremen were irritable and abusive, they said—much more so than the civilian work bosses had been in Yokohama. Most of the maltreatment only left bruises, but once there was a more serious incident: a foreman grabbed up a shovel and hit a Canadian, Earl Jacobson, across the head with it. The prisoners were at the time loading ore into the furnaces, a heavy task for their weak bodies, which was exacerbated by the heat and noxious sulfur fumes of the ovens. When Jacobson stepped back for a breath of fresher air, a foreman grabbed a shovel and struck him. Jacobson required stitches when he returned to the camp later that day. Inaki's ruling was that Jacobson had somehow provoked the foreman. He ordered him to spend fourteen days in the tiny guardhouse, where he would receive half-rations and sleep without a mat. And he would get no vacation from work—every morning he was sent back to the steel mill where he faced the same angry foreman.

Jacobson was not the only one to spend nights alone in the guardhouse without bedding and on half-rations. In May and June several prisoners were sentenced to that bleak shack, all on weak pretenses. One supposedly insulted a guard, another did not work hard enough, two were lazy, and so on. Inaki did not encourage wanton beatings of the men, but the guardhouse was a busy place under his command. And the hearings that Inaki staged were for appearances only—he had no intention of ever questioning the actions of his fellow Japanese, no matter what the circumstances.

During Jacobson's "hearing," I noted the resigned dejection on his face, and it worried me. I tried to reason with Inaki, not because I thought it would help, but because I thought it important that Jacobson see someone was concerned about him. I told Inaki that he was being unfair and that he was ignoring the laws of the Geneva Convention. Of course, this was futile. And though he thanked me for my efforts, Jacobson's face remained dismally fixed as he was marched to the guardhouse.

Resigned, despairing faces were common by then. There was a lifelessness encroaching on the camp, an apathy that was taking over us all. We had endured three years of physical deprivation, abuse, and hard labor, but I feared that some of us might not survive this loss of interest in living.

Soon after Jacobson's sentence, I went before Inaki with two prisoners who had been reported by their civilian foreman for not working hard enough. The foreman had beaten both of them severely at work that day. Once we were in front of Inaki, the POWs on trial tried to talk but were silenced immediately with the clipped reminder that enlisted men were not to speak to the camp commander. Inaki asked me for my account of the men's behavior.

Because my usual defense of the prisoners never worked, I tried a new tactic. "Lieutenant Inaki-san," I began, "whether these men have been working well or not is not important here. They say they have worked hard and I believe them, but this is not the point. Honorable sir, the foremen at the sawmill are beating the prisoners constantly. It isn't right that civilians are striking prisoners of war, Lieutenant Inaki-san." I paused, letting him absorb my words, then continued. "Civilians cannot strike prisoners. It is against the Geneva Convention. That is the rule at other POW camps, should it not be the rule here as well, honorable Lieutenant Inaki-san?"

As I finished, Inaki began to twitch angrily in his chair, and I knew my strategy had not worked. He jumped up and swung around his desk, his fists flailing the air. "If civilians cannot strike, then I will strike these men!" He attacked each of them as they stood there, pounded them on the shoulders and face as they flinched under the blows. The beating went on for a few minutes while I watched, shocked. It was the first time we had seen Inaki react violently. I worried again about the victims' lack of emotion or resistance to this outrageous beating. They should have put up an arm in defense, drawn back, or at least cried out as they were struck. But such beatings had become so predictable that the two men were not moved out of their resigned despair.

When Inaki finished venting his fury, he stepped back and screamed our dismissal from his office. The episode ended with no real injuries—one prisoner had a cut lip which he dabbed with a filthy handkerchief, and there would be bruises, but fortunately there was no other physical damage done.

I apologized to the two men as we walked across the compound. My ploy had not worked, and I was ashamed that they had had to suffer another beating because of my bad judgment. The man with the cut lip only shrugged; his companion mumbled something about it being a better defense than none. I felt as if I had beaten the men myself, and I vaguely wished that Inaki would have slapped me once or twice as well. With my own physical pain to bear, it would somehow have been easier to handle the unfairness of it all.

THERE WERE NOT many POW officers in the camp, but those there were worked every day. We sometimes roamed the fields and beaches looking for edibles, but usually we tended to the camp garden, a sorry affair about a mile from our barracks. There were few vegetables ever harvested from the garden, partially because of the events of the summer 1945, but also because of theft—hungry Japanese civilians raided our unfenced garden by night and dug up the fruits of our labor.

The garden work was not objectionable but for the fertilizing detail. The fertilizer was compost à la Japanese—human waste, the dung dug out from the POWs' latrine. The fact that it was our own waste made the detail abhorrent, for many of us still suffered from dysentery and other digestive disorders that resulted in a repulsive muck. We first shoveled it out of the latrines and into buckets, then hung the buckets between two poles, and two of us carried it to the garden. The mile walk with that pail of night soil was an odious experience—the smell hung on my nostrils and with each step the slimy excrement was liable to splash from the bucket onto my worn trousers and shoes. I told myself when it was my turn to help carry the vile bucket that it could be worse; I could be shoveling iron ore into hot furnaces and inhaling noxious fumes all day. Sometimes such thoughts made the work less repugnant, usually they didn't.

About a month after we arrived, we saw the depth of the personality clash between Bracky and Inaki. Bracky and I went to see Inaki to protest when he sent two men to the sawmill after Pijma had declared them too ill to work. As usual, Inaki sat in his chair, staring impassively at us as we presented our case, and then he dismissed us without even a word, only a flick of his wrist.

Bracky, though furious, had allowed me to do the talking. After Inaki's dismissal, however, he leaped forward and pounded his fist on Inaki's desk.

"Lieutenant Inaki, are you listening at all?" he shouted. "Have you listened to a word we've said? You must listen—these are men's lives here!"

Inaki looked up, for a moment frightened—Bracky was at least six inches taller than he and loomed over his desk—but he regained his composure after placing a hand on the sword at his waist. Once his fingers were in contact with the metal, his eyes became calmly dismissive again.

Bracky continued yelling. "Have you listened to a word we've said? These men are sick. At home they'd be in a hospital! They cannot work! They could faint and fall, hurt themselves on the equipment! It's murderous to send them to the mills!"

Inaki gazed at Bracky blandly, but there was a touch of malice in his eyes. I stepped toward Bracky and grabbed his arm, trying to lead him away.

He shook me off. "We've got to do something, Frank; this is murder. We can't just sit back and take it anymore."

Inaki finally spoke. "You object, Brackstone?" he asked in a cold tone.

"Yes! I object! Captain Grady objects! Captain Marsden objects! Any human being would object! You're killing them!"

Inaki stood and came around the desk. "You are no doctor, Brackstone," he said quietly.

"But I've eyes in my head! You don't need to be a doctor to see those two men are not well!"

Inaki ignored him and continued. "You are no doctor, and you act as one no more. No more. You will do no more work in hospital. No more."

Bracky didn't hesitate a moment. "Pijma is overworked. He needs my help. You can't order me not to help him."

Inaki puckered his lips, allowed a long minute to pass while he stared at Bracky. He seemed to consider this fact, but his voice was unrelenting when he spoke again. "Dr. Pijma will work without you. He work before with no other one."

"Pijma has two hundred more prisoners now!" Bracky yelled. "One doctor to see to nearly four hundred men! As sick as they are? You can't order me not to help him!"

Inaki calmly folded his arms across his chest. "You will not enter the hospital again."

Bracky stared at him with an intense malevolence that made me step close to his side for fear he would lunge at Inaki. Such a move would be suicide, and the prisoners needed Bracky. I needed Bracky. Inaki again placed his hand on his sword hilt, and I thought I saw a hopeful gleam in his eye. An attack from a POW, even if an officer, would justify the sword's use. With that thought, I grabbed Bracky's arm and began to drag him toward the door.

As we left, Inaki confined Bracky to the officers' area for a week and reduced him to half-rations. Bracky was fuming. I made sure he stepped out of the room in front of me. I didn't think Inaki would stab me in the back with his sword, but I wasn't certain what he might do to Bracky.

Once outside, Bracky took a deep breath of air. "How I hate that man." He uttered a string of curse words as we headed for our side of camp and muttered over and over that Inaki couldn't do this. "He can't; he just can't. They've lost the war. It's over. He just can't do this."

We reached our barracks and stood outside the door. After a long silence, Bracky raised a hand to his forehead and rubbed it, and in that gesture I saw the same hopelessness I had seen in the enlisted men of late, but there was a difference. He might have felt hopeless, but Bracky still cared. After three years of this, he still cared. Deeply. Too much. It was dangerous to care that much. But Bracky, the most compassionate man I have ever known, kept on caring.

Bracky spoke in a small voice while a tear rolled down his face. "Yes, he can. He can do this. He's going to do this." He caught himself before breaking into sobs, and asked the question I was already asking, "Shit, what will Pijma do?"

A RESTIVE BRACKY spent the week inside our crowded barracks; he was only allowed outside three times a day to use the latrine, which was a punishment in itself—Bracky had a mild case of dysentery along with the rest of us and needed to use the toilet more often than that. He ate his half-meals in the barracks as well, and the guards would not allow any of the other prisoners to eat with him or visit with him. Meanwhile, Pijma worked many more hours a day taking care of all the ailing POWs in camp by himself.

Inaki had chosen the perfect punishment for Bracky. He saw that Bracky liked nothing better than to be a vital part of the camp, to be aiding other prisoners. Along with meeting his sense of social responsibility, helping his fellow POWs was Bracky's way of passing the time. I think Inaki so hated Bracky that he was trying to cut his lifeline, and had Bracky been confined to quarters for much longer, Inaki might have succeeded. Bracky was in silent despair that week. Once he was allowed to move about more freely, he did so, but the guards had orders to prevent him from entering the hospital area and to tell Inaki if he tried. So Bracky wandered about uselessly for another week, for he was not allowed to join any other work detail, either. Inaki correctly guessed that Bracky would be happier doing any work, even the night soil detail, so he was ordered to remain idle. Bracky was miserable.

After two weeks, Pijma, who had gone to see Inaki every day to complain about the loss of his right-hand man, finally convinced Inaki that he simply could not keep up with his patients without some help, and Bracky was restored to duty. The hatred between Bracky and Inaki did not dissipate, however. On Bracky's part, it became more subdued, but I suspect more intense; Inaki meanwhile lost no opportunity to humiliate him in front of the prisoners. This rendered Inaki even less popular with the POWs, for Bracky was as beloved by the prisoners at Kamaishi as he had been at Yokohama.

One of the new aspects of life in Kamaishi was the quiet. No air raid sirens went off, and we didn't see any U.S. planes. I had not realized while in Yokohama how the appearance of Allied bombers lifted our spirits; we sorely missed seeing them, as the bombers' strikes suggested that we wouldn't be captive forever. But as June began it was as if the Allies did not exist. Again we felt alone in Japan.

Some POWs at Kamaishi were so depressed that their priorities became scrambled. Cigarettes had always been a valuable commodity for POWs, but at Kamaishi they took on new importance because the supply had tightened. Kamaishi was in a remote area where fewer civilians smoked, and fewer guards had access to cigarettes. This shortage demonstrated itself almost immediately after our arrival—the price of a single cigarette skyrocketed. They had always been expensive, but now they were positively priceless. Men clandestinely sifted through trash bins while at work, searching for cigarette butts to smoke or sell. And though each of us were only fed several handfuls of grain with a few vegetables every day, some prisoners were actually trading their small meals for cigarettes. When Bracky and Pijma told me that a man had become ill because he habitually traded his food for cigarettes, we set out to put a stop to it.

We first declared it illegal to trade food for cigarettes. This did no good whatsoever; we could not watch each and every prisoner who smoked, and besides, we could levy no punishment if the rule was broken. So several of us nonsmokers began supervising meals, making certain each man ate his meal then and there. We threatened to take the food back if someone didn't eat his food. Bracky was the most determined mess supervisor. He stood over the prisoners, a gaunt mother hen; if a POW tried to trade his food for a cigarette, Bracky usually was the one who caught him. Those who were caught cursed Bracky and claimed they should be able to do what they wanted with their food, but Bracky was adamant. He made them eat while they called him all sorts of foul names.

In retrospect, I see that even those curses were proof of Bracky's camaraderie with the enlisted men—they would never have cursed me or any of the other officers in camp. Bracky was a magic and cohesive factor in the midst of a camp ringing with dissonance and frustration. He, not the food rations or allotments of cigarettes, was the most valuable asset at Kamaishi.

15. Under Allied Fire

FINALLY, IN MID-JUNE there was a sign that we weren't abandoned in Japan: the air raid sirens sounded. We first heard the alarm one afternoon when most of the enlisted men were at work. Those of us in camp let out wild yells at the sound. But we did not see any B-29s that day, and Inaki would tell us nothing about the air raid. Two days later, however, the sirens went off again and we did see planes. They cut across the harbor, flying high, and passed on to the south.

The alarms became more frequent as June progressed—by the end of the month, the first-stage warning blast of the siren announced planes in the area six to eight times a day. But the planes didn't seem interested in our corner of Japan. A couple of squadrons flew directly overhead, but most were headed toward Sendai and the southern population centers.

Inaki lectured us early one morning about how we were to behave during air raids. We had heard it before in Yokohama. We were not to cheer when we saw the planes, nor were we to try to signal them, and we weren't to look at them. "And you must know," Inaki finished, "you are losing the war. Allies are losing. Japan is winning again. Soon war over, and we win. You are not good fighters, all losers."

An enlisted man in formation perked up. "Oh yeah? So then where are all the Zeros, Inaki-san?" he cried. It was a good question. We no longer saw Zeros tagging the B-29s. The Superfortresses seemed to be attacking the beleaguered Japanese with practically no opposition. The only Japanese response to the planes came from their antiaircraft guns. And these, like the land-bound antiaircraft guns on Corregidor so long ago, were woefully inadequate.

Inaki, of course, became furious over the question. "Who said that? Who said that? You tell me who said that!" He pounded a foot on the ground and grabbed for his sword. The guards sprang to life and slapped a few men, demanding they tell who had spoken, but we remained silent. In actuality, few of us knew who had said it, but we were all glad he had. It was delicious to see a prisoner retaliate for once.

After swearing at us for awhile, Inaki called the guards off and dismissed us. They hadn't found the impertinent POW.

Later, after the enlisted men marched off to work, we officers discussed the situation. For the first time in three years as POWs, a prisoner had openly harangued a camp commander. Spirits were certainly picking up, we decided. We also talked about our apathetic guards, for they were inattentive and very nervous. And Inaki had not punished us all for the POW's insubordination—this was a surprise. All this made us wonder what was really going on in the world outside the small town of Kamaishi.

WHEN WE FIRST arrived at Kamaishi, there was only one slit trench for the prisoners, which was adequate for the Dutch POWs, but not for two hundred more bodies. We had pointed this out to Inaki on our arrival, and after several weeks passed, he decided to allow us to dig a new one. It was to be a hundred feet long by twelve feet wide, and it was to run along the American-British barracks. At first, the enlisted men worked on it only on rest days, for Inaki did not deem it important enough to assign a regular work detail. After a couple of air raid warnings, though, Marsden, Bracky, Van Buskirk, and I along with some other officers began to work on it every day after we finished our other work.

Sergeant Mikawa, a blustering Japanese guard whom we all despised, took an interest in the trench. Mikawa had just arrived in camp and was out to gain points with Inaki. With this as his goal, he decided that the bomb shelter needed a cover on it, and told Inaki of his plan to stretch a roof over the trench. We all agreed a cover was a good idea, but not one that stretched clear across as one single roof, as Mikawa wanted to do. Bracky, though a fine medic, was an engineer first, and he pointed out that if that single stretch of roof collapsed or exploded during a bombing, it would prove a death trap for anyone under it. He proposed constructing many small roof-covers, each one independent of the others, so if one was hit, other prisoners would not be trapped inside. Mikawa refused the plan, so Bracky and I took it to Inaki. Mikawa was there when we discussed our proposal, standing sullenly next to Inaki's desk as Bracky spoke.

Once Bracky finished detailing his ideas for a safer bomb shelter, Inaki leaned back in his chair and frowned. "Brackstone, you must tell me, are you a doctor or engineer?"

Bracky had beforehand sworn to me that he was not going to lose his composure, no matter how Inaki goaded him. He remained silent.

I tried some diplomacy. "Honorable commander, Lieutenant Brackstone studied both medicine and engineering while at university. He chose engineering, but still knows much about both. We think his plan for the bomb shelter is best. We're concerned about the safety of the prisoners."

Inaki rose and came around his desk to stand in front of Bracky. "So Brackstone knows about everything?"

Bracky and I remained silent. Both of us stared straight ahead. There was something ugly creeping into the room. Sergeant Mikawa whispered something to Inaki, who nodded.

Bracky spoke up then but still stared straight ahead. "That one cover will prove a death trap for anyone left alive under it if it's hit. Please consider this, Lieutenant Inaki, sir. Many prisoners could be killed because of it."

"Brackstone, if some prisoners are killed, that will leave us fewer to feed, won't it? We'd save food, give it to Japanese people."

Bracky shifted his gaze to stare at Inaki incredulously for a moment, then looked away. "Jesus Christ," he mumbled.

"What was that, Brackstone?" Inaki asked imperiously.

Bracky stared straight ahead. "Nothing, Lieutenant Inaki, sir."

Inaki shrugged and went around to the front of his desk. He told us we would use Sergeant Mikawa's plan. He then walked to the door and stood there behind us, but didn't dismiss us.

Mikawa moved to stand in front of Bracky, staring at him with baleful eyes. Mikawa was one of the guards at Kamaishi who loved a good beating, but before that day he had been too intimidated by the POW officers to hit them. Mikawa glanced toward Inaki, then asked a question of Bracky that he could not answer—neither of us spoke Japanese well enough to comprehend his quickly spoken question. He then said something vicious, a word we both recognized, and I took Bracky by the arm. "Let's try to leave," I whispered.

But as we started to bow and request dismissal, Mikawa grabbed hold of Bracky's shirt, reached up with a doubled fist and struck him hard across the temple. I froze. Bracky did too; he tried hard not to cry out or pull back, for we had seen Mikawa on the rampage before. Mikawa struck Bracky again in the face with his fist, a blow that caught him in the lip. Blood appeared seconds later. The sight seemed to delight Mikawa, for he struck Bracky again, and then proceeded to beat on him for a full three minutes.

I stood there, my head averted to hide my shame and rage, and witnessed my friend's beating. Officer-in-charge of prisoners? I could not stop Mikawa, could do nothing for Bracky, nothing for any of the prisoners whom I had seen Mikawa strike. A sense of great humiliation and hatred engulfed me as I stood there, trying not to hear the thuds and slaps connect with Bracky's face and body. I turned at a sound behind me—Inaki had just slipped out the door. Apparently he had witnessed enough of the beating.

Bracky took a step back from the sergeant when Inaki left, and put up a hand to block a blow. I grabbed Bracky then and the two of us backed toward the door. Mikawa slapped me across the shoulders, but didn't go for his sword. The beating was over. Without Inaki in the room to condone his actions, Mikawa once again was intimidated by our rank and dropped his fists. He glared at us, spat out some obscenities in Japanese, then ordered us to leave.

I helped Bracky back to the hospital while trying to mop up some of the blood on his face with the back of my hand and sleeve. The few POWs around fell silent as we came in the door but moved quickly to help. Bracky sat down and gingerly touched his swollen face as Pijma arrived to attend to him.

Inaki's sanction of Bracky's beating turned out to be a mistake. The prisoners gathered sympathetically around their beloved Bracky that night, then the next day they began to retaliate. At work, they became openly rebellious toward the guards and civilian bosses and committed as many anonymous acts as possible to demean the Japanese. They were surly when ordered to do something and muttered insults while in crowds of prisoners that the Japanese could hear. Surprisingly, no one retaliated, and few of these incidents were reported to Inaki. With this as encouragement, the men became all the more irrepressible. When the air raid alarms went off in camp one evening, they openly cheered, and the bored guards only struck two or three of them. And we officers began to demand more of Inaki. He did not grant many of our requests, but the fact that he even listened to us was significant. Something had changed. The Japanese were adopting our apathy and we their aggression.

In spite of all this, Bracky did not go across to the Japanese side of the compound again for weeks. And for some reason, Inaki finally left him alone.

THE ALERTS BECAME more frequent as July began, and the planes were showing more interest in our little valley with its smoke stacks and antiaircraft guns. By that time, the whole camp was buzzing with news. Another camp five miles up the valley, Ohasi Prison Camp, sent POWs out to join our prisoners on work details; the Ohasi POWs had access to more outside information than we did because they had managed to find a radio. On a clear night, they could actually hear broadcasts from Honolulu. The war was coming to an end, the radio reports declared, and the Allies were the victors. Germany had surrendered and the Allies were in full control of Europe. And Hitler was dead.

In the midst of this good news from the outer world, we POWs had to cope with worsening conditions: there was less food for us. Because of the pressures on Japanese food supplies, by late June food was becoming scarcer in Japan. Our POW garden added little to our diet—Japanese citizens ate much of the produce, and the garden was never productive anyway. For a good portion of that summer, my dependable buddy Maddock came through for me. He shared the extra food he got in return for fixing the soldiers' shoes with me fifty-fifty.

On the tenth of July, I asked Inaki once again to move the camp up the valley because of the Allied planes in the area, but he still refused. That same day, Bracky and Marsden came to me and said something was up—the

Japanese were grouped around a radio on their side of the camp. Later that afternoon, two guards crossed to our side of camp and climbed atop the hospital barrack to get an unobstructed view of the harbor. One guard eventually climbed down, but the other stayed up there until he was relieved by another soldier. From that day on, there were guards manning the makeshift observation tower all day. They only came down at dusk, when their naked eyes could no longer warn of an impending attack. But they had the radio on twenty-four hours a day. We heard the staccato reports drifting across the camp on the night air, all of it unintelligible because of the distance and the rapid Japanese. But the message behind the incomprehensible words carried to us. The Japanese were scared, and if they were frightened, we had reason to be jubilant.

The next morning, Lieutenant Blystra, a Dutchman, asked me whether I would like to fill water tubs with him. The task did not thrill me, but I went with him, for I knew the real reason we were going to fetch water. The well was on the Japanese side of the camp, and from there Blystra could listen to the radio reports unhindered by the distance between the buildings. Blystra understood Japanese almost as well as Sherman of Yokohama camp had; I was curious to hear his translation of the broadcast.

We grabbed up several tubs and went across to the Japanese side of camp. We could hear the radio clearly there as we slowly filled the tubs. We were there some ten minutes—we "accidentally" knocked over two of them and had to refill them. As we lugged our heavy buckets toward our side of the camp, Blystra turned to me, his eyes fairly dancing.

"They've reason to be upset. The news is from Sendai and it's saying, 'Enemy warships in the area.' They're all over the place—the Hokkaido area, I mean, and they're close to Aomori. They're only a few miles from us, Captain! Enemy warships! They're American!"

We left the buckets in the kitchen area, then grabbed a couple more to fill. We returned to the well several times that day, and each time Blystra came away excited. He said the Japanese were being told to prepare for any eventuality. It was finally happening—American ships sailed nearby. The island of Hokkaido and the city of Aomori were north of us—that meant the Allies had control of the sea to the north. Before we left Yokohama we knew the Allies controlled the area south of Japan. The country was surrounded.

On the thirteenth of July, the prisoners came back from work early with no reason given as to why they returned with so much daylight left. Inaki called us all together for an early roll call and a speech. His talk was about proper behavior during an air raid, a lecture we had heard before, but it had a new twist.

"You will listen to guards' orders and obey. Guards carry guns, and we will shoot you if you not obey every word we say." Inaki had never threatened to shoot us before. "Do not look out the windows, or we will shoot you. There will be no crazy in this camp. No incident. No dishonor. You remember this, or we will shoot you." When several officers approached Inaki for more information after the speech, he angrily waved us away. We retreated to the barracks with the enlisted men.

Although he prohibited us from looking out windows, Inaki did not mention anything about peepholes, and our rickety barracks were full of them. The back of our barracks looked out directly on the harbor, and through cracks in the wood, we could see what was going on there. Bracky watched the events going on outside long after the lights were out and most of us had fallen asleep. Several hours later, he shook me awake.

"Keep quiet," he whispered. "Something's up. Jap troops are right outside. They've manned the ack-ack batteries."

I followed him over to his peephole. From there I saw soldiers on the docks to the east of us, moving quietly in the dark. We could hear their muffled conversation and the clank of their guns and equipment.

I stayed there for an hour more, watching the shadowy figures move along the dock, then returned to my mat. Bracky, who appeared not to require sleep, would awaken me if something momentous occurred, but I didn't think that would happen. The Japanese soldiers were preparing for something, but I doubted it was an invasion. Many more men would have been there had that been the case.

The next morning, 14 July, a first alert acted as our alarm clock instead of the 6:00 reveille. After that, the roll call that was usually held outside took place inside. The men normally went to work at 6:45, but they weren't ordered to fall out after breakfast. I went to speak to Inaki as he stood with two of the mill foremen.

I waited until he finished with them and turned toward me. "What is happening, sir?" I asked. "Why are the men not at work? We have the right to know what is happening, sir."

Inaki glared at me, then turned away without answering.

The men were lined up in front of the barracks when I returned. A few minutes later, the guards led them off to work. A while later, the second alarm went off, meaning that enemy planes were headed directly into our area. There were only forty-five men in the camp that morning—fifteen were sick in the barracks, ten were in the hospital, and the rest were officers or camp personnel—orderlies, cooks, and Maddock the cobbler. Inaki ordered us into the slit trenches, which still had no overhead cover, so we each grabbed up blankets and jumped into the unfinished bomb shelter.

We remained there for several hours, with the sirens wailing incessantly. We were beginning to think the alarm a mistake when two formations of U.S. planes appeared from the east. Once over land, the two groups separated and went in opposite directions. Just then a tremendous volley of explosions made us all duck our heads under our blankets, but no bombs fell; it was the Japanese antiaircraft batteries next to camp shooting at the planes, which escaped unscathed. We noticed that one plane separated from its formation, though, and took a long pass over the town, as if it had forgotten something, then flew out to the open sea.

When the planes disappeared, we expected to hear the all clear bell from the observation tower, but it didn't ring, and we stayed in the trench. About half an hour later, we heard the bell announcing an imminent attack, but we only saw a single shipboard fighter approach. It passed over us, flying low— it swept over the camp, then up the valley toward the coal mines. I didn't immediately comprehend the clue, for although the plane was obviously a shipboard plane, I didn't recognize the markings or design. We only knew that it was American. The U.S. obviously had many new war toys since we had become incommunicado.

Just then a great explosion sounded immediately outside camp, but not from the antiaircraft batteries. The ground shook beneath us as a huge geyser of water and debris shot into the air. The bridge outside the fence had been blown to pieces and was crashing to the earth around us. I looked out from beneath the blanket after the strike to find the plane, but it was long up the valley by then—it couldn't have dropped the bomb, and there were no other planes in sight. We all began to wonder what the hell was going on when we heard a sharp whistling sound, and I dove under my blanket again. All at once I knew the source of that mysterious bomb that had destroyed the bridge: the sea. And it wasn't a bomb; it was a shell. There was a ship somewhere out there, beyond our line of vision, and it was shelling the industrial town of Kamaishi with its steel mill, coal mines, antiaircraft guns, and unmarked POW camp. We were under attack.

We saw the guards run toward their side of camp, abandoning us in our unfinished pits. I jumped from the trench. Three years before I had learned that one could count on delays of at least thirty seconds between salvos during a shelling, so I tried to find Bracky and Marsden—we had to make certain that all the prisoners were accounted for and in the shelter. Bracky was in the narrower trench (it was actually a drainage ditch) close to the American-British barracks. He was just climbing out as I arrived.

"Are all the hospital guys there?" I cried.

"Yes, all there," Bracky yelled. "I'm going to get some tatamis! They'll stretch across the ditch and give us a bit of cover." He was running by then, but called a question over his shoulder. "Where's Marsden?"

I thought this a good question—I was also wondering where Maddock was. But I couldn't ponder these mysteries long because a screaming whistle rushed through the air again. I jumped into the trench. The shell hit a shack across the road; it caught fire and would burn to the ground during the shelling. Just after that shell hit, I renewed a habit over three years old: I looked at my watch. I used to do this on Corregidor to ascertain just how much time I had between explosions to recover my wits before the next shell. I noted my second hand's position at the time of impact, then climbed out and began searching for Marsden and Maddock. I ran back to the main shelter, but did not see them, so I ran toward the drainage ditch again.

Before I reached it, another shell flew over and hit somewhere in town. I looked at my watch again as I threw myself down on the ground—fifty-five seconds between that one and the previous shell. I jumped up and dove into the drainage ditch. Before the next one arrived fifty-five seconds later, Bracky and friends returned, each carrying an armload of tatamis. We stretched them over the top of the trench. The thin mats certainly wouldn't save anyone from a direct hit or flying shrapnel, but they would cushion the blow of stones and keep some of the debris from landing on us. In between shells, we ran across to the main trench and gave them some mats, but it was too wide for the mats to reach across, so the men there simply put them over their heads as we did our blankets—they were shawls against the shells.

While we were passing them out, Marsden and a few other POWs scrambled into the trench. I started to ask him where he had been, but then I saw Maddock, who was with him. He cradled his left arm with his right hand; it hung at an awkward angle, and he was covered with dirt.

"What in the world happened to you, Maddock?" I asked.

"I think my arm's busted, Captain," he said with a ridiculous grin. "It's OK. I'm almost glad. It'll keep me from working. I'm kinda tired of fixing everybody's shoes."

Marsden explained that Matsuura, who was ever obsessive about his food stores, went berserk when the shelling started. He came to the trench and ordered Marsden and a detail to help move the food from the storerooms into the trenches. As they were climbing out, a salvo landed nearby and scattered debris everywhere. A large rock hit Maddock in the arm and broke it. But Matsuura still made Maddock help with his good arm.

I shook my head affectionately at Maddock, who just stood in the trench grinning. I was so happy to see him alive that I wanted to hug him and cry, but there was no time. "Go find Pijma or Bracky when the shelling's over, Maddock," I said.

He gave a sloppy mock-salute and hunkered down in the trench, still grinning the inimitable Maddock grin.

Shortly after this, someone reminded me that a Dutch POW was still in the guardhouse; he of course couldn't get out and was in grave danger there. Marsden jumped from the trench to go get him—it was some fifteen minutes before they returned. The Dutch prisoner had been terrified in there, listening to the shells explode all around him.

The salvos continued to thunder into the valley at a rate of one every fifty-five seconds. We could hear them hitting along the walls of the ravine and in the town; the echoes of each strike resounded against the hillsides and found their way back to us. It was an eerie sound, a terrifying one. The next echo might emanate from the crater blasted by the shell that had killed one of us.

Just before each fifty-five-second interval, I held my breath, hoping to hear the screeching whistle of a shell passing over as a voice came back to me: "It's the one you can't hear that will kill you, sir." I had first learned that on Bataan just before my army surrendered. Chaos—I had found chaos again, but this time there were no stone barriers to protect me from it as there had been at Corregidor, only a flimsy blanket and some light straw mats. And this time, the shells were not Japanese, but American.

Fortunately, that morning only a few shells did not announce themselves first with a loud whistle. Several of these hit a few feet short of the fence surrounding our barracks, and another exploded in the harbor just east of us, sending a great cascade of water into the air. Another actually hit the camp, smashing into the south end of the American-British barracks with a cacophonous blast. Debris flew everywhere with this strike, shattered bits of wood and metal and glass.

After an hour of the fifty-five-second lulls between shells, the intervals stretched to seventy-five seconds of quiet before explosions. This went on for about another hour. Then early in the afternoon, the shelling stopped. We waited in tense silence for another shell after the initial seventy-five seconds had passed, but none came, and the quiet lengthened. After about ten minutes, we cautiously emerged from the trenches, without any orders from the Japanese—there was not a guard to be seen.

We crept carefully around the camp, picking through the debris—we found several fragments from exploded shells and saw that some of them had been 16-inchers. Marsden and I turned toward the trenches and began checking for casualties. There were some scrapes and bruises, but nothing more serious than Maddock's arm.

About an hour later, six prisoners were brought into camp by a couple of guards—three of them were on stretchers. They had been at the steel mill, which was apparently the prime target for the shelling, and had taken shelter in one of the tunnels in the adjacent hillside. The tunnel had been hit and had collapsed, burying several POWs and many Japanese civilians. The other work details straggled into camp after that in small groups. Many of those who were able volunteered to help rescue those trapped in the tunnel. A detail left the camp shortly afterward with two guards.

The men told of hundreds of Japanese leaving the city as they went to work that morning. One of the men said the civilians paid no attention to the Japanese soldiers. "They had their little bundles with them and just walked away. The road was full of them—the guards shouted at them to move so we could pass but they ignored the guards. They ignored them! There weren't many civilians at work, either."

It appeared that everyone in the area had been aware of an impending attack except us POWs, we who sat in the midst of so many enticing targets.

That evening, the tunnel rescue detail returned to camp with six surviving POWs who had been in the tunnel when it collapsed. They brought with them a young Dutchman, dead. Two other Dutchmen and an American were still buried in the tunnel. The American was Sgt. R. T. Sparks, the man who had been beaten so severely at Yokohama camp that he lost most of his hearing.

Pijma and Bracky treated as many wounded as they could. Some twenty prisoners needed attention, and several were seriously injured. I stayed in the hospital long after midnight, holding a candle for Pijma as he operated, extracting shrapnel from wounds and bandaging cuts. We had no electricity in the camp and no water—the well was covered with debris. We asked Inaki for a small fire to sterilize the instruments, which he grudgingly allowed us —it was against regulations for POWs to have a fire in camp.

Late that night Inaki was still in camp, which was unusual; he usually left after sunset. He came to check over the wounded prisoners and let us use a flashlight. He gazed at one of the injured for some time. The man had been retrieved from the tunnel area and was in critical condition. His foot had been crushed by a huge rock and was almost cut off by it. What remained of the leg had been broken in two places, one of them a compound fracture. It was Pijma's unenviable task to remove the rest of the leg.

"This man is very bad, Lieutenant Inaki," Pijma said in his formal and forceful English. "He needs proper medicines and a quiet place to rest. It is not safe for him here. We could be bombed again, and he cannot be moved into the slit trench."

"Shelled," Inaki corrected him. "We were shelled, not bombed. Shelled by American ship outside the harbor." Inaki glanced at me accusingly, the only whole-bodied American present in that ill-lighted facsimile of a hospital.

He turned away after saying nothing about moving the prisoner. I handed my candle to another prisoner and followed him out the door to his office.

"Dr. Pijma is going to need help," I said when he was seated behind his desk. "He needs another doctor—two would be better. There is a POW doctor at Ohasi Camp up the valley, and perhaps some Red Cross supplies. Will you send for them?"

Inaki studied me silently for several moments before speaking. "My house was destroyed today. I will be in the camp all the time now." He glared at me.

I wasn't sure what to say about the loss of his house. Did he expect me to apologize for the U.S. ship's attack? I remained silent.

Inaki continued, repeating himself. "So I will be here all the time, every night. I will sleep here." He then addressed my question. "And no, I cannot request a doctor from Ohasi. Enough has happened. I will request nothing."

"Sir," I said in a tight voice. "Some men are badly wounded. Several might die if not treated correctly and immediately. We must at least have medical supplies!"

Inaki rubbed a hand through his short dark hair. "Grady, today many Japanese have died." He scowled at me again. "Many Japanese have died; many have lost their homes." That sentence, he obviously assumed, was enough to explain any neglect of the POWs that night.

"Lieutenant Inaki," I said, leaning forward onto his desk, "prisoners have been dying for years, and many more could die if you do not do something. We've already lost four today." I felt a furious wave boil up inside me. I slammed a fist down on the table. "Do something! Vacate this camp! If another shelling occurs, we will be in great danger because we have wounded to move now." My words were bold—the Allied shelling had given me new courage.

But Inaki was adamant. "We cannot move; we will not move. It is prisoners' duty to save food and protect the buildings from fire. This is the only place, Grady. We will not move. Sendai tells me what I do, not you."

I left Inaki's office before I got myself thrown in the guardhouse. I was at my wit's end. There were four fewer POWs that night than there had been at dawn, and our damaged camp was still a sitting duck, waiting for the next shelling or a bombing to blast us into oblivion. And Inaki didn't care. I wondered why he had brought us the flashlight—it was an act of decency, and yet he ignored our requests for medicines and a move to a safer area.

I walked back into the hospital. Pijma had amputated the mangled man's leg, and now stood gazing down at him. He looked at me tiredly when I came in. "I believe that this man," he said with a gesture toward the still body, "also has a skull fracture. And unless he gets to a hospital soon—by tomorrow—he will die. I can do nothing more for him."

Pijma and I remained silent for several moments. After that I gestured him away from the dying man and told him about my conversation with Inaki. "They won't give us any medicine," I whispered. "I doubt if they'd even consider moving him to a hospital."

Pijma nodded. He said nothing. He turned back to work. "Dr. Pijma," I said, "if you don't get some sleep soon, you won't be able to help anybody."

Pijma nodded again, but did not leave the hospital. He moved to another patient, and I grabbed a candle to help him.

A few hours later, Pijma left the hospital to sleep. I put the candle down and nodded to Bracky as he worked, then crossed the room to where Maddock was slumped against the wall, his arm held in a sling. He was sound asleep. It had taken the doctors some time to get to him, as his injury was less serious than many others, and afterward Maddock had sat down there. He always wanted to be in the middle of things, and that night the hospital was where the activity was.

I helped Maddock stand up, and we slipped outside into the warm night. Another July night in Japan. As I inhaled the fresh air, I wanted time to analyze the situation, time to appreciate the fact that a U.S. warship was in the harbor, its presence a guarantee that this would be our last summer in a POW camp. But I could not consider what the shelling meant, not yet. In my mind just then, it was simply one more indecent hardship for us to endure.

After helping Maddock to a tatami, I found my own, and a few seconds was all it took before I was deep in a dreamless sleep, the shelling and nearby U.S. ship all forgotten.

16 · Rising from Ashes: August 1945

Most of the prisoners stayed in camp the next day—the only work detail was one we POW officers arranged. A hundred volunteers went to the collapsed tunnel to find the POWs buried there. Those of us in camp kept busy cleaning up and repairing the buildings. We filled in the shell holes as best we could and mended the well on the Japanese side of camp so we had water again. And we finally received permission from Inaki for a permanent full-time work detail to work on our bomb shelter. That day, nearly 150 men worked furiously at it—we wanted a completed trench should our allies come back.

That afternoon the air raid sirens went off again, and we climbed into our unfinished trenches as another squadron of shipboard fighters flew toward Kamaishi. They skipped us that day and bombed the mills and factories in town instead. The men who had been on the tunnel recovery detail later reported that the roads were still full of Japanese civilians, all headed for the hills.

That evening our tunnel detail returned with the other three bodies; with them, all POWs were accounted for. When I saw Bracky at dinner, he was tired and dejected. Pijma sat silently next to him. They said that another prisoner had died, the one whose leg had been crushed and skull fractured.

That brought our total dead to five, all of them because the tunnel they took refuge in had collapsed.

Bracky had been with him when he died, risking his own safety to do so. He and an orderly stayed with the unmovable wounded in the hospital when the rest of us took to what little cover the unfinished trenches offered.

"His body's still in the hospital, Frank," Bracky said.

I nodded and scraped up the last rice grains from my kit, then left the room. We had built a huge bonfire for the dead in a corner of the camp— we had to feed it one more body.

THAT NIGHT INAKI summoned Marsden and me to his office. When we arrived, he asked us about our preparations for fire. Were we ready for any eventuality? Did we need any more drills? His questions were ridiculous. Inaki himself had drilled us many times and knew that we were as ready as we would ever be. Our fire brigade's equipment consisted of buckets of water placed in strategic locations all around the camp—we were to put out any flames by dipping mops in the water and blotting out the fire. We had been practicing the procedure several times a week ever since our arrival, but the drills were always absurd. The idea of extinguishing a major fire with a mop had become such a farce that the prisoners openly howled with laughter during the drills. I could not blame them, for it was indeed a joke. A mop and a pail of water might put out a small campfire, but they would be useless against the inferno that Inaki seemed to expect.

Inaki had instructed us that during an attack, all POWs were to search the buildings on both sides of camp for signs of fire. (How we were to do this when we were forbidden to remove the blankets from our heads during an air raid was a perpetual puzzle to us.) If anyone saw one of the wooden structures catch fire, they were to alert me, the fire chief, or Marsden, the assistant fire chief, and we would then order the firefighters to man the mops and rush to the rescue. Inaki was convinced that his plan was foolproof; thus the strategically placed water buckets were always to be full to the brim (half-rations for all responsible if they weren't).

We performed a drill the next morning to satisfy Inaki. It was even more of a charade than before, for during the shelling everyone had seen just how quickly the wooden shacks would go up if hit. And it was raining and had been for two days, so fire seemed unlikely. That drill in the rain was a piece of exaggerated theater. Every part of the drill, whether it was the melodramatic discovery of fire or the victory dance on a rooftop after drowning an imaginary ember, brought guffaws of laughter from the drenched POWs.

After the drill, Inaki was angry over the show but he restrained himself. "Do we need more drills, Grady? Are you ready for fires? Maybe we should practice every day?"

It would certainly keep spirits high if we could put on a show like this every day. But we were getting out of hand—somebody could get hurt prancing around on a wet rooftop. "Lieutenant Inaki, sir, I think we prisoners are ready for anything."

Marsden also agreed that we were ready.

Inaki wasn't satisfied. "You are certain, Assistant Fire Chief? And you, Grady? You are certain? It is your duty as prisoner to save the camp and food stored here. Bombs can come again any time, Fire Chief Grady."

This annoyed Marsden. He too had been emboldened by the Allied ship in the vicinity. "Yes, we could be bombed again at any time. You know this. You also know that four hundred men here are in grave danger if a bombing occurs. You knew it before the shelling. And you've still got ack-ack batteries on either side of us!" He leaned forward to meet Inaki's eyes. "Why do you not evacuate this camp, Lieutenant Inaki?"

Inaki said nothing. He turned his back on us and walked away.

The next day, the prisoners returned to work in the heavy rain that continued to fall. A detail was assigned to clean up the tunnel that had caved in, and others were put to work inside the steel mill—their job was to make the plant functional again, as it had only been partially destroyed in the shelling. Those prisoners in camp continued to work on the bomb shelter, in spite of the pouring rain, and we officers had our garden work again.

That afternoon, I was on the night soil detail. While helping to carry the reeking bucket, I surveyed the town. All was quiet, with only an occasional figure on the streets. The many bicyclists were gone, as were the children and the mothers bent over by babies on their backs as they shopped or worked the fields. Though many structures still stood, it was the blackened sentinels that caught my attention that day. Several scorched buildings had collapsed into heaps of rubble, and debris still littered the sidewalks and streets. Kamaishi, a small city that had once housed thousands of people, had become a ghost town overnight. I wondered where all the inhabitants had gone, what sanctuary they had found.

That night when the enlisted men returned, I asked some of them if they had seen where the civilians had gone. Up the valley and into the hills, all reported, to camp out until the threat was over. There had only been a handful of Japanese civilians at work that day. Some of the foremen seemed afraid also—some of them were missing from work as well; they were presumably up the valley too. The work bosses complained to Inaki, but the soldiers could not force the people back to work. They couldn't even find them.

As July ended, more Japanese troops moved into the area. They brought portable batteries with them—five 5-inch dual-purpose guns were set up on the south side of the harbor, about two hundred yards from our camp. The antiaircraft battery just across the road from us was removed—it was placed in the hills to the north, giving the Japanese firing power from both sides of town. In place of the battery, they left two wooden facsimiles of guns, dummies that to a U.S. observation plane would appear to be the real thing. With the new guns in the area, along with the dummy guns, we POWs in our unmarked camp were more vulnerable than ever. I protested along with the other officers about the false guns, but they stayed where they were.

In the last days of July several high-flying U.S. planes buzzed the area without dropping any bombs. They were obviously reconnaissance planes, American Photo Joes, and we knew they would soon discover that the steel mill was only partially destroyed. We rushed to finish our bomb shelter, but Inaki had by that time become anxious as well and had assigned twelve POWs to dig another slit trench for Japanese personnel. We officers continued to work on the shelter, hammering planks together to give us a partial roof and digging, forever digging. But in spite of our labor, our bomb shelter was only two-thirds completed as August began.

In early August Inaki was his most decent with us POWs. He rewarded good workers with Red Cross supplies and even tried to be pleasant with the officers several times. And for the first time in our three months at Kamaishi, he listened intently to what we had to say. He didn't concede anything, but he was amicable in his refusals. The guardhouse was empty, and no beatings took place.

In those first days of August, we were attacked again by smaller carrier-borne planes that machine-gunned the town. We were constantly moving in and out of the slit trenches. Meanwhile, the Japanese personnel became as skittish as they had been before the shelling. We noticed that they were again listening to their radio late at night. Bracky and Pijma heard the reports as they worked late in the hospital.

"They're scared again, Frank," Bracky told me one morning. "My Japanese isn't very good, but last night I caught a couple of words: 'American navy' and 'American ships.' Another ship is out there somewhere. And all this," Bracky gestured toward the demolished half of our barracks, "could happen again."

An American sergeant standing nearby grinned at Bracky's grim prediction. "Yeah, it could, Bracky. And I wanna see it! Hit us! Blow this smelly camp to hell!" The young man swung at the air with a clenched fist, his face jubilant.

Bracky gazed at him quietly. "The hospital too, sergeant? Who's going to help those men escape in a shelling? How will they get out if a ship blows this camp to hell?"

"Oh, they'll be OK, Bracky! You worry too much! We'll get them out!" With that, the conversation ended because Bracky shrugged and walked away. In spite of what had happened to the camp, many of us still believed that U.S. shells and bombs would sense POWs and miraculously avoid them.

That same afternoon, Inaki himself climbed atop the makeshift lookout tower to scan the ocean and sky. The sky was clear—the rains had finally stopped—and not a ship or plane was in sight. It was the fifth of August.

The next day, 6 August 1945, a day that forever changed human existence, passed without special incident in our camp. We heard nothing, saw nothing, felt nothing. Our work details went out to work and later returned to camp; we stood roll call; we ate; we slept. Nothing of any import occurred in our little corner of Japan when Hiroshima was bombed.

On 9 August, however, the planes returned. A first alert sounded at 6:45 as the men stood in line for their march to work. Inaki rushed out of his office and ran across the compound. He pulled aside several of the gunzokos and talked to them in low but agitated tones—his arms were wild with gestures. After a five-minute conference, Inaki rushed over to where we stood in formation and dismissed us.

"You return barracks! Get ready for air raid!" he cried.

We set off toward our barracks to get our blankets.

We were still in the barracks when the second-stage alarm went off a little after seven. We hurried out to the trench with our blankets. From there we saw several high-flying formations of planes pass overhead, and we heard the gun batteries open up on them from the hillside north of us. They caused no damage. The fighters didn't drop any bombs; they were headed south again, toward Sendai. But we stayed in the trenches because the all clear bell never rang.

Just a bit before nine o'clock, the camp interpreter Fukumura found me and said that the work parties should prepare to go to the factory. No one wanted to be caught between camp and the factory in an attack, so they quickly climbed from the shelter and hustled off with their guards in the lead.

When the first alarm had sounded, we had placed the wounded in the completed portion of the bomb shelter. Though it was uncomfortable for them, we left them there all morning, for the all clear bell still had not sounded. We then tended to our usual work around camp. Our only reminders of the early alarms were several high-flying planes on the horizon.

Just before noon, a huge explosion occurred just outside the fence, a few feet from the dummy guns. Air raid sirens screamed out seconds later. We all scrambled toward the slit trenches, blankets in hand, and jumped in while scanning the sky for planes. There were none. We were being shelled from the sea again.

The shells were coming in at a faster clip this time—and they seemed better aimed. They were only barely missing the dummy guns, and the factory area was again taking a beating. We huddled in the trench and hoped our unfinished bomb shelter would stand up to the attack. About an hour passed like this before several men yelled out simultaneously, "Fire!" Flames danced on the roofs of the bathhouse and barracks—they had been caused by hot embers from the former site of the antiaircraft battery; a shell had ignited the abandoned ammunition there, making for a loud fireworks display and many small flames. Those of us in the fire brigade jumped from the slit trench at the alarm and ran to our strategically placed pails of water. We quickly found it was easier to put out the small fires by stamping on them or smothering the flames with our blankets, and did so. Marsden was up on the roof of the hospital investigating some smoke rising there when he began to yell at the top of his lungs.

"I can see them! I can see them! It's a bloody huge battleship, and it's only just outside the harbor! An *American* ship, just outside the harbor! I can see their guns flashing!" Marsden began doing a little jig there on the roof, whooping and hollering all the while. Moments later he climbed down. "It's over; it's got to be over. That ship's firing away and there's no one to stop it! Their ack-ack guns can't hit it. It's over!" Marsden hugged a prisoner next to him, and started to describe the ship again in his excitement.

As we stood there, we saw smoke rising from the bathhouse, and ran to take care of it. Once that fire was out, we returned to the trenches, but we weren't there long. The shells still whistled by, and another fire had broken out. I looked at my watch—it was three minutes after two. I jumped from the trench with my blanket, thinking that this was another small fire that I could smother, but found that it would be useless to try. A building on the Japanese side of the compound had taken a direct hit and was burning furiously. A light wind from the sea gently fanned the inferno and helped spread the fire. As I ran toward it, I saw another shack burst into flame in front of me. I grabbed a bucket and threw some water on it, but it was futile; the fire was raging too high by then, although it had only taken me a few moments to reach it.

I turned just then to the sound of screaming behind me—it was Inaki. He ran toward me with his sword held high while howling like a madman. I didn't know why he was in such a fury, and couldn't get him to explain himself in English.

"Inaki," I yelled. "The fire's out of control! We tried to put it out but it's out of control! We have to get out of here!"

Inaki didn't understand my English just then any better than I did his Japanese, so I left him there waving his sword and screaming. The fire was growing rapidly, and it might at any moment spread to the prisoners' side of the camp. That was where my responsibility lay. Once back on our side, I saw prisoners climbing from our slit trench and fleeing the camp. No guards attempted to stop them. Flames were engulfing every building, and all was chaos. Some of the healthy POWs were helping the wounded out of the bomb shelter and leading them out of the camp. Two other whole-bodied prisoners had knocked a hole in the fence—they saw the spreading flames and wanted an escape route. I noted the hole's location, and ran to make sure there were no trapped POWs anywhere.

I ran between the hospital and the shoe-repair shack and glanced at my watch again—it was six minutes after two. I rounded the building and was suddenly caught in a thick cloud of smoke. I stopped, caught in a panic. The entire compound area was enveloped in smoke and flame, for the on-shore wind was still spreading the fire. Suddenly Matsuura, the gunzoko in charge of the kitchen, rushed at me with rifle in hand. "Rice, rice!" he shouted, waving me toward the food stores with his gun. I stared at him, ut-terly bewildered, then realized he was demanding I help him move the food stores to safety. Matsuura was capable of shooting me in order to protect his rice, so I complied and ran with him to the grain storeroom. I found a British seaman named Willison there; apparently Matsuura had roped him in too. Willison and I hurried into the smoke-filled room; we found the rice and pulled at it. The bag weighed some fifty kilos and was too heavy a load for our emaciated bodies. It was a ridiculous sight I'm sure. First Willison grabbed hold of one end and started to lift the bag, then dropped it as I took hold of the other side. I promptly dropped my end in a coughing fit. Just as Willison was bending down for a second go, the entire room seemed to implode upon us as it burst into flame.

"Bloody hell!" Willison yelled as he straightened up. "Matey, I'm getting out of here!"

We grabbed each other to make certain we both made it out and rushed out of the burning building. Matsuura and his gun had disappeared. From some twenty feet away, we both turned. The barracks were a sheet of flame that was fast closing upon us. Willison took off running toward the hole in the fence, but I wasn't certain that was still an open escape route. I ran be-hind the storehouse, heading toward the camp's front gate. I found one of our fire-fighting buckets of water sitting there, quickly soaked my blanket in it, and threw it around me. I looked up toward the gates and saw Inaki again. He had sheathed his sword and was waving his arms wildly, trying to draw us in his direction. POWs and Japanese soldiers were streaming out the camp's gate and across the road. I ran across to the gate and slipped out, one of the last to escape, for the wall of fire behind me became impenetra-ble a few moments later.

As I ran across the road, a loud explosion some fifty feet distant reminded me that our burning camp was not the only threat: we were still being shelled. The burning buildings were probably visible from the ship, but my countrymen didn't know that POWs lived in them, and they were determined to knock out the steel mill once and for all. The dummy guns still stood as well, as did the all-purpose guns that were blasting away just down the road from us. The U.S. Navy still had plenty of targets in Kamaishi.

All of this, of course, took only a fraction of a second to register in my mind—I was very vulnerable out there. I ran to a pile of railroad ties, thinking they would afford at least some sort of shelter if I could lie between them. Somebody else had thought the same thing—the first gap I found was occupied, so I stumbled on two or three steps and found another two POWs between two other ties. They stared up at me, mutely apologetic, and didn't budge. I ran on to the next ties and found two prisoners there, their heads hidden beneath a scorched bit of blanket.

"Hell," I mumbled and ran on. There were obviously no vacancies among the railroad ties. I hurried to a turnout area for trucks with a cement floor that was just opposite our barracks, or rather, opposite where they used to be; I squashed myself against the revetment on the oil-smudged concrete and covered myself with my blanket. It wasn't as safe as the railroad ties would have been, but it was better than nothing. I took a quick assessment of myself. Was I hurt? On fire anywhere? After a brief investigation, I knew I was all right but for a few bruises and scrapes. Once I calmed down, curiosity got the best of me, and I tugged the blanket from my head.

From where I was I had an unobstructed view of our camp. The buildings on the POW side were all burning—only a few blackened structures stood, their walls still crackling and snapping with fire. Another shell whistled overhead, which was a sound I was glad to hear. I glanced at my watch to time the next one—it was thirteen minutes past two. Although the chaos of the camp's destruction seemed interminably long, only ten minutes had passed since it had began.

Shells continued to fly, and heavy rocks and debris flew through the air—this went on for another hour. Throughout all of it I felt so alone. The isolation of that shelling still haunts me. I felt as though I were the only person left alive in the world, in the midst of mass destruction, while I listened to whistling shells pass overhead or nearby explosions. In retrospect it seems odd, but I felt lonely more than fearful during that attack, though I was afraid, very afraid. I must have been dazed by my loneliness and fear, because when a piece of shrapnel hit nearby, I unthinkingly reached out and touched it, and burned myself.

Some three hours after it began, the shelling stopped. Ten minutes after the last shell flew over, I cautiously crawled from the revetment and examined the area. Small fires burned nearby, and piles of shattered wood and stone were everywhere. I walked stiffly toward the railroad pilings, calling out as I did so. Those POWs without disabling injuries slowly emerged from their makeshift shelters. A long, sustained blast of the sirens startled me, but it was reassuring when I recognized the sound. It meant the attack was over.

None of us able-bodied prisoners spoke as we searched the vicinity. I saw the first mangled body huddled next to a cement block; it was soon obvious that many men could not leave their shelters for their wounds. Some were burned, others torn by shrapnel, all were calling out for help. Those of us who could pulled men free from the wreckage and placed them on their blankets on the road.

One of the wounded men was Maddock. He looked up at me dazedly as another officer and I pulled him from between the ties he had sought shelter in. I wasn't sure whether he had been hit while there or in the burning camp, and he couldn't tell me, for he could not speak. I thought in despair that Maddock would probably not live. His head and face were badly burned —the tops of his ears were missing and all his hair was gone. He had burns all over his torso, and his broken arm hung limply by his side, the sling gone. One of his legs was badly torn up by shrapnel. I wished he were unconscious, for he was obviously in great pain, but he was aware of us as we tried to help him. He kept glancing down at his mangled and burned body incredulously, as if he would perhaps be magically intact the next time he looked. We placed him in the road on a blanket.

Someone next to me was helping a burn victim get comfortable on his blanket. "Don't worry, I'll get Pijma and he'll take care of you." I suddenly wondered where Pijma was. As efficient as he was, I expected to see him there helping.

"Where's Pijma?" I called out to no one in particular. No one had an answer. And Bracky—where was Bracky? I began to run from shell hole to railroad tie, looking for the two of them. Down the road I found Bracky helping a man up and nearly hugged him in relief. He was whole; he said he only had a few scratches.

"Where's Pijma?" I asked.

Bracky hadn't seen Pijma. We immediately began to search for him. After some time, we found a moving body in a shallow hole. It was Pijma; he couldn't stand up because he had been badly burned. We helped him onto the road where he lay staring up at the sky. The entire upper part of his body was burned—much of his hair was singed off. He gazed at me stolidly as I squatted down next to him in the road. I tried to utter some consoling words to him. Though later we learned he could speak, he remained grimly silent.

A nightmarish haze cloaks the rest of that day's events and discoveries. After collecting the wounded onto the road, we organized ourselves for emergency medical care under Bracky's supervision. We were on our own as we did this—Inaki was busy with his own crisis and paid no attention to us. Several hours later we reentered the camp, once all the fires were out and the scorched buildings had cooled. We searched the buildings, calling out among the blackened foundations, but no answers came. There were no survivors there. We found Cpl. Earl H. Gaskin, an American, in the uncompleted part of the bomb shelter. With distended eyes he stared at the sky, dead. It looked as though he had fallen while trying to climb from the trench and the smoke had overwhelmed him, for there were no severe burns on him. We found another body in the compound area that was burned so badly we could not identify him—we determined who he was by a process of elimination after roll call: J. F. Gaspers, a Dutch prisoner who had survived the first raid but had suffered second-degree burns. Gaspers would have been unable to move as quickly as the rest of us as we evacuated camp, so he could not escape, and in the chaos no one could help him. Bracky openly cried over the unrecognizable form. Gaspers, he said, had been healing; Gaspers would have made it home.

After looking a bit longer, we gave up our search. If a POW was still in the camp, he would not need immediate attention. Anyone who had not escaped during the shelling was now a corpse.

BEFORE THE LIGHT faded that night, we moved the wounded into the camp compound and placed them in the slit trenches. Bracky attended them all, some thirty wounded men. He had practically nothing to work with, only a few basic first aid kits—there were no drugs, no disinfectants, and only a little morphine to ease pain. After dusk fell, Inaki ordered Bracky to go with him to the steel mill. There were casualties there, Inaki said, and they needed a doctor. None of us mentioned this irony, the fact that Inaki finally recognized Bracky's medical skills.

Once Bracky was gone, all those who could took over his duties. We boiled water over a small flame and by candlelight did what we could to disinfect the burns. On Pijma's orders, we picked away dead skin, leaving the burns open to the night air so that they might begin healing. With many of the men, even this primitive treatment wasn't possible. Their burns were too deep to do anything to comfort them. The wounded men whimpered softly all night, some breaking out into screams of agony from time to time, and we, the relatively healthy prisoners lying on the ground above them, could do nothing to help. They were cold, but we had no blankets to offer them. They were uncomfortable in the hard trenches, tortured by their burns, and we had no morphine left to administer to them. And we all were hungrier than usual—we had gone without lunch and dinner.

The next morning, some of the POWs who had been working at the steel mill returned. They reported that another tunnel had collapsed on workers who had withdrawn there during the shelling—many prisoners were trapped inside. We sent volunteers to help them dig out, and the results were predictable: seventeen had died, all Dutch. We brought the bodies back to camp for cremation, along with thirty-two men who were badly injured in the mill itself; we put the survivors into our new hospital in the slit trenches.

The U.S. ship had succeeded. The steel mill was completely destroyed.

All of our food had been burned during the shelling. We salvaged what we could from the vacant Japanese side of the compound, which hadn't been burned as badly. There we found three pigs that the Japanese guards had been tending for future meals. One was ready for eating, as it had been roasted alive by the fire—we only had to carve it up and pass it around. Another pig had been utterly destroyed by the fire and was only barely recognizable. The last pig was alive, remarkably enough—we saved it for a future dinner.

Inaki was staying in a house nearby. He called the POW officers together to meet with him that morning, the tenth of August. He said he was searching for a building for us. Marsden and I demanded that he send medicines and doctors from the Ohasi POW Camp, but Inaki said he couldn't promise anything. He would have to get permission from Sendai before asking for a doctor, but he said he would try to get us some medicines. At that, Marsden and I yelled that conditions were far more serious than Inaki realized; other officers joined in. We didn't bother to be polite anymore, and Inaki did not reprimand us for our open rebellion. He stood silently while we shouted at him. He only reacted when someone asked for a Japanese doctor.

Inaki stared at the man, shocked. "Our doctors are busy, very busy. They have no time come here. And you cannot go them. You must stay here until we can move you."

"But you can't just forget about us here!" the man yelled. "We need medicine and doctors! We haven't any food or shelter or clean water!"

Inaki backed away as the man spoke, leaving us to shout after him.

A short while after our encounter with Inaki, the sirens went on again and a formation of planes reappeared. We took to the trenches again, crowding in next to the wounded stretched out there, and watched as the planes bombed the factory area of Kamaishi again. But they did not drop any bombs near us, nor did we take any more shells, for obvious reasons. The Photo Joes saw that there was no reason to attack the blackened area along the docks. The antiaircraft guns were silent, the dummy guns blown to pieces.

That day, all jubilation over the unanswered air and sea attacks was gone. We simply groveled in the crowded pits, tense and very afraid that the planes might take an interest in our area. There were several hundred filthy and closely packed bodies in the shelter, and with the uncremated corpses lying in a pile near us, the stench was overwhelming.

Later we collected another pile of wood and combustibles and doused it with kerosene. We then placed our dead atop the heap, and set it ablaze. We watched in silence as they burned, their last remains transformed into a dark smoke that slipped away into the atmosphere. We offered no eulogies. No words could convey our despair over the fact that so many POWs had died in the midst of an Allied victory. None of us wanted to think much of it, let alone speak of or cry because of it. We had never seriously considered that our comrades from the skies and sea might bring this much death with the promise of liberty. And each of us left alive knew we had survived our nineteen dead companions purely by chance.

That afternoon, Inaki told us to place the wounded on improvised stretchers—we were moving. An hour later we headed for the devastated ghost town of Kamaishi. We marched around shell holes and collapsed buildings, and all the while I did not see one Japanese person who was not in uniform. There were more Allied soldiers—albeit captive ones—that day in Kamaishi than there were Japanese civilians.

We soon reached a small schoolhouse, which was to be our temporary home, and there met four POWs who had been working up in Kamaishi during the attack the day before. They carried the body of an American who had been killed. They placed him outside the schoolhouse. He was number twenty.

The school consisted of two buildings; uninjured prisoners were assigned to the gymnasium, and the wounded were placed in a smaller building adjacent to the gymnasium.

That night, Bracky returned with more wounded, ready to drop from exhaustion and despair. He said they had spent the night in a field with no medical care or supplies but what he could provide—few of them had slept; he certainly hadn't, and he had a full night's work ahead of him in our camp.

Bracky went right to work. On Pijma's orders, he smeared a small amount of antibiotic ointment, a contribution received from Inaki that afternoon, on the burn victims. I was with Bracky when he moved a severely burned man next to Pijma for special advice. The wounded man was still; what parts of his face that weren't burned were a chalky gray.

Pijma studied the man a moment, then spoke as Bracky began to scrape out some of the precious ointment to apply to the man's face. "Do not waste your time, Lieutenant Brackstone," he said in an even voice. "And do not waste the ointment."

Bracky stared at Pijma, surprised, but Pijma turned his attention to me. "This man's name is Downs. He is British. You are keeping a list, Captain Grady?"

I nodded. The list I had of deaths and casualties was growing long.

"Downs. And you should know, somebody should know, that this man is a hero. I saw him. He was an orderly, always helping me, very helpful. He helped you, Lieutenant Brackstone?"

Bracky peered at the prisoner's face. Downs had worked by Bracky's side for many weeks, yet Bracky had not recognized his burned face. It was

Downs who had stayed with Bracky in the hospital to tend to those who couldn't be moved during the air raid after the first shelling. Downs's dedication to the wounded was matched only by Bracky's.

"Yes," Bracky murmured after studying the man a moment. "My God. It is Downs."

Pijma nodded his head jerkily, wincing. "Yes. I saw him. He could have escaped. Everybody else was running, but he didn't. He stayed after I left—I saw him behind me—he was helping evacuate the wounded from the trenches. He got out finally, but he had helped too many. He was badly burned. He was hit by shrapnel also, as you see, along his leg." Pijma paused momentarily. "Look at him, Lieutenant Brackstone. You know enough of medicine. You know. Do not waste the ointment." Pijma dropped his voice and turned away from Downs's burnt form. "I am very sorry for him. He was a good man, a hero. But I am pragmatic. He will not live. Move on to someone you can help. He would have wanted you to," he finished tonelessly.[1]

Bracky started to say something to Pijma—he looked mildly angry. But he caught himself and studied Downs's face again, then felt for his pulse. Though Downs's heart was still beating, Bracky later told me, it was erratic. There was practically no breath under his nostrils. Bracky removed the identity tags that hung around Downs's neck and rubbed them between his fingers while studying them.

"His first name was James," Bracky said quietly. "James W. Downs, Frank. For your list." After a long silence, Bracky handed me the tags and moved to another burn victim.

James W. Downs, a hero who would not leave his wounded companions behind, died that night, 10 August 1945.

TWO DAYS LATER, on 12 August, a Japanese doctor arrived at the schoolhouse with three nurses. They dressed the burn cases and put on an oil-based sulpha compound. They returned the following day to open and drain the prisoners' blisters—literally quarts of pus and liquid were drained from the wounds. Another POW, a Dutchman, died that same afternoon. Our death count from the second shelling was up to twenty-two.

Despite my initial fears, Maddock was still alive, but he was in constant pain. He suffered second- and third-degree burns over half his body. He had also been hit by flying debris during his escape and had many lacerations. His handsome young face was swollen and pale—much of the skin was gone from his forehead and around his eyes. His wounds appeared to be improving slightly, but he talked to no one, not even to me. He only stared at the ceiling all day long; I wondered if he even recognized us. This burned man was not the Maddock I had watched heal himself at Bilibid, for he seemed to be giving up. And he wasn't the only one.

In the five days since the shelling, our world had fallen strangely quiet. The Japanese guards were negligent in their jobs—most of them were gone. Inaki avoided us and only spoke to us when he had to. The skies were clear and the valley completely free from the wail of sirens for the first time in months. The men no longer went out on work details, and there was no talk of assigning new labor to them. The factories and the coal mines appeared vacant; the steel mill was destroyed; and the antiaircraft batteries were abandoned. The Japanese troops that had been quartered along the harbor were no longer there, and the civilians still had not returned from the hills. It appeared that we were the only inhabitants of Kamaishi—and we were completely isolated, wondering what had happened outside our private little hell to cause this great silence, this great solemnity. The birds chirped; the sun shone upon green hillsides; but the somber atmosphere belied the pleasant weather—something was different, and we wondered what it all meant.

On 15 August, Captain Tucker, an American doctor from Ohasi POW Camp, arrived at the schoolhouse. When we heard he was coming, we were hopeful that he might bring medicines and a few medics with him. But Tucker came alone and empty-handed. We officers introduced ourselves as he began his rounds among the wounded in our small hospital area.

"My God, they look horrible! Don't you have any medicine at all?" he asked.

We had none, a few of us said in unison.

"They should have told me!" Tucker threw his hands up in disgust. "They didn't tell me anything! I asked if I should bring extra personnel and medicine, but they said no. We have plenty of supplies at Ohasi. We were never hit—none of our medical supplies have been used."

Tucker helped Bracky on his rounds that afternoon, cursing the Japanese military all the while. "Well," he finally said. "It won't be long now. They read the Imperial Rescript in camp today."

Several of us asked, again in unison, what the Imperial Rescript was.

"Some document the Jap officers read to their men. They didn't read it to us—we don't know what it means exactly. But it's over we think. The Japs came away pale after hearing it. That night a bunch of them disappeared. We don't know if they went AWOL or were discharged or what. But on our radio we've heard reports from Honolulu, something about a big bomb. Sounds like there were some huge bombing raids somewhere, bigger than anything we've ever seen up here."

I had watched formations of hundreds of planes fly over Yokohama and had seen the remains of southern Tokyo—I couldn't imagine any bigger bombing raid than that. Captain Tucker, I thought, had never seen such things while in rural Ohasi, distant from any real targets. I was certain there could be no greater destruction than that of the shitamachi district of Tokyo. We isolated POWs with our pre-1945 minds no longer fully understood warfare; much had changed since we had left the world behind three and a half years earlier.

That night, Inaki read the Imperial Rescript to the few soldiers left in our camp. We saw them dispiritedly walk away; the next morning most of them had disappeared. But we knew nothing, and Inaki offered no information. He only said something about how incredible it was that the Japanese emperor appeared to be so like other human beings.

The world was shifting somewhere; we sensed it, but we were still separate from it, still prisoners of our situation. We had nowhere to go, and feared for our lives if a mob of angry Japanese civilians should catch any one of us. And with the death and deprivation still around us, our war continued —we could not relish these most promising signs of our eventual liberation. While America celebrated Japan's surrender, we still did not know that the Imperial Rescript was an order from the emperor to Japanese soldiers to lay down their guns.

17. Freedom

On the day after we heard of the Imperial Rescript, Inaki told us that we would move to Ohasi, the POW camp five miles up the valley from Kamaishi. We marched away from the schoolhouse the next day without fanfare, leaving behind another hell-home. We walked to the railway station, where we learned that healthy POWs would go by train and the wounded would go by truck with the doctors and myself. Captain Tucker and I climbed into a truck with Maddock and a few other POWs.

We soon discovered that transporting the wounded by truck was a mistake, for the ride was bumpy. The road, unpaved and neglected for several years while Japanese resources were diverted to fight the war, was now badly damaged by the shells and bombs that had fallen for the last few weeks. We bounced all over that truck, wounded and healthy alike.

Maddock looked pale and grim. He stared at the top of the truck, still silent. I sat between him and Wilkin, a man who had also been burned, though not as severely as Maddock. Wilkin began to hallucinate when the truck started off. He babbled incoherently, his eyes glazed and unfocused. This went on for some twenty minutes before he fell silent and, like Maddock, stared at the top of the truck. The silence was better, and with it sanity returned to Wilkin's eyes—he even looked thoughtful. Ten minutes passed quietly, then Wilkin spoke again.

"How ya doing, Maddock? You all right?" he asked.

Maddock grunted.

Wilkin continued. "I'm not doing so good. I just ain't doing so good." He paused as I sat up, concerned.

"What are you talking about, Wilkin?" I demanded. "You're getting better."

"No, I'm not, Captain. I'm not. I can feel it. I'm all burned up." His voice shook as he spoke. "They've burned me up." Tears welled up in Wilkin's eyes.

"Wilkin, you're OK. Listen to me, you're going to be fine, the war's over, it's just a matter of time—"

"I don't care," he interrupted. "It's too late. I want to die. Look at me. Skinny, a skeleton, and burned to the bone. I'm gonna die. They've got me." He turned away.

I spoke firmly to Wilkin as Maddock stirred next to me. "Don't talk that way, Wilkin. You're going to be fine. We all are. The war's over."

Wilkin turned back to face us. "They didn't give us any medicine, Captain. Or any doctors. They just left us, those damned Japs just left us. . . ." Wilkin's eyes were lucid, but full of hatred, which wasn't good; hatred saps energy that should be used for healing.

Maddock spoke up then. It was the first time he had said more than a few words since the shelling. "Wilkin, you can't talk that way," he said, weakly but clearly. "That's what'll get you. Don't talk that way. I'm worse than you, and I'm getting better, so you'll get better, too."

Wilkin didn't want to listen—he continued to say he was all burned up and doomed.

Maddock interrupted him. "Be quiet, Wilkin," he said tiredly. "Don't talk that way. None of us want to hear it. I don't want to hear it. Just shut up." Maddock pulled the blanket up close around his singed ears and closed his eyes.

Wilkin shut up. Five minutes passed in a silence broken only by the noise of the bouncing truck and men moaning softly. I watched Maddock with some satisfaction. Wilkin's attitude was dangerous, but I was glad he had voiced his fears because it had brought Maddock around a bit. He sounded more like his old self when he told Wilkin to shut up.

As I thought this, Wilkin shifted again to speak to me.

"It's true, Captain," he whispered. "I'm gonna die." Wilkin stifled a sob. "And you know what gets me? I never even was in the army. I was a civilian. And now I'm gonna die cuz I was a POW."

Tucker moved over next to us, just in time to hear Wilkin's prophecy—he began to argue with Wilkin as Maddock and I had done, but Wilkin turned away. He listened to no one while feeding angry and frightening visions of his own death.

WHEN WE FINALLY arrived at Ohasi, the wounded were placed in the camp hospital and were treated by Bracky, Tucker, and Lieutenant Epley, another doctor. The hospital there amazed me—it was efficiently run and had ample medicines. There was even blood plasma for the worst burn cases. The Japanese commander at Ohasi camp was a decent soul—the storerooms were full of Red Cross medical supplies, and these were actually given to the prisoners, as were their food packages. As a result, the POWs at Ohasi were in better shape than we were.

The healthy prisoners among us were housed in an abandoned theater across the street from Ohasi camp. It was very crowded, but we assumed we wouldn't be there long. Inaki, Mikawa, and the few remaining camp guards took up residence in a building next door, but they paid little attention to us. They still carried guns and made menacing sounds from time to time, but it was out of habit mainly; they knew it was over. In fact, several of the guards had become somewhat servile in manner, smiling and sharing food with the prisoners. But Inaki still carried his sword.

Two days later, this all changed. On 17 August 1945, 1,199 days after Gen. Jonathan Wainwright's surrender of the U.S. forces in the Philippines and 8 days after the shelling that had destroyed our camp in Kamaishi, we heard via the radio that the war was over. The report was in English; it came from Tokyo; and it was Gen. Douglas MacArthur who spoke: the Allies had defeated the Japanese.

We were prisoners of war no longer.

We went wild. We tossed any object not nailed down into the air and sent up a volley of deafening shouts that lasted an hour, hugging one another, laughing, swearing, screaming at the news. It was over. Our brothers and sisters across the seas had won the war. We were free. We ran outside and danced in the streets, shouted our victory at any Japanese face we saw, and howled all the more at their sudden fear of us. Someone turned up the radio broadcast full blast when MacArthur's message was repeated, and we stomped our feet in time to his rhythmic recorded speech.

Some time later, I went across to celebrate with Bracky and Maddock, my friends for so long. But I found Maddock asleep and Bracky across the room from him, sitting on an empty cot. Bracky was pensive, even melancholy—he couldn't have heard MacArthur's announcement.

"Hey, Bracky," I exclaimed, rushing toward him. "Did you hear? It's official! It's really over! MacArthur's on the radio in Tokyo! It's over! We've won! We're free!"

Bracky nodded without smiling. "I heard. I saw all of you in the street."

I stopped dead in my tracks. "What's wrong?"

Bracky stood slowly. He walked over to Wilkin's mat and stared down at him. "Wilkin has been bad the past few days. Hallucinating, crying in his sleep." He gestured around the room. "Most of the rest of these men will live, with the care they'll get now. But still I can't celebrate." Bracky then told me of something he had been concerned about for several months. "Think about it, Frank," he said. "What will all these men do now? What happens when they haven't a common enemy to hate and give them reason to live? Many of these men are young; they were young when they became prisoners. Will they know how to cope in a world without a Jap guard in it?"

I had never even considered this.

"I'm not sure the war is over for us. Now we've got to learn how to live in a normal world. And I'm not sure that will be as easy as we all thought it would be. You should see how all of you look out there dancing in the street, so young, so unconcerned. I worry for us."

I didn't know what to say, but I didn't want to see Bracky glum. I tried to be cheerful. "Come on, Bracky. We'll be all right. You're just upset because you won't be around to take care of us anymore." I clapped him on the back. "The war's over, Bracky! We're not POWs anymore!"

Bracky sighed and smiled finally. "Oh, I'm glad it's over. I'm glad we're free. I just wonder what will happen to us now, after the celebrating is over."

I lapsed into silence then with Bracky. The men in the street were still hooting and hollering—I could hear their singing and laughter. After Bracky resumed his work, I walked over to where Maddock lay and stood watching him. I suddenly understood what Bracky was saying. Maddock was doing better now; ever since his rebuttal to Wilkin's hopeless words in the truck he had been improving. But after being a POW for so long, would he adapt to a complicated world that would put so many different demands on him? He only wanted to ride his motorcycle and find some women after liberation—he had said this for years. What would happen when that ride was over, when his new battle began, that of finding a place in a civilized world outside the fences?

The former POWs dancing in the street were tough; they were adaptive; they were smart, survivors all; but life back home, more subtle and just as competitive, might be overwhelming. In a way, they were all as helpless as sleeping Maddock, and I too was afraid for them.

The shouts of joy wafted into the stillness of the hospital. I walked toward the door. While we were in Ohasi, I would have to help take care of these noisy men, these former POWs. The war had been over for days; now that I knew it, my responsibilities returned. I was no longer a powerless POW officer-in-charge. With a sigh and a glance back at Maddock, I left the room.

I FOUND MARSDEN, discussed a few things with him, and then the two of us went together to see Inaki in the tiny office he had organized. Sergeant Mikawa was with him. The two didn't seem to be doing anything when we entered the room.

"Lieutenant Inaki," I began, "the war has been over for several days. The Allies have won the war. You knew this. You did not tell us, just as you did not tell us of our danger at Kamaishi. Because of you, many POWs died. You have treated us unjustly and inhumanely our entire time at Kamaishi." My words were so calmly spoken, so different from what I had fancied I would do once the Allies had achieved victory. Unlike my fantasies of the last few months, I did not grab Inaki or Mikawa and beat them; I did not threaten or yell.

"Many of the men are angry and will want revenge. We will appoint MPs to control them, but you have treated us abominably, and they may get out of hand." Inaki may not have understood everything I was saying, but I didn't care. "Your guards will turn over their guns to the MPs we appoint. Any guard or soldier who beat the prisoners unnecessarily in these past months," I allowed myself a hateful glance at Mikawa, "should be held by you for punishment and their own protection. There are many ex-prisoners here, and it will not be easy to control them."

By then Inaki was staring at me apprehensively. He asked me in a timid voice if I would like to sit down. I refused. But I tried to remember then that they weren't all bad, that most Japanese citizens were good people. We had been victims of a rigid military regime, not of the Japanese people. I would have to remember this in the coming weeks, and I would have to frequently remind the former POWs of the same.

When I spoke again after thinking this, my voice was surprisingly soft, almost a whisper. I said what I had wanted to say to him for a very long time, but, again, I didn't say it as I had imagined I would. "Lieutenant Inaki," I said softly, "I'll have your sword."

His eyes widened in anger at my mildly stated request. He started to argue with me, but then he recovered himself. He stood slowly, stared at Marsden and me a long moment, then lifted the sword from his belt and handed it across to me.

I nodded, and with another ugly glance at Mikawa, I turned away. I left out much of my long-planned speech. I did not tell Inaki that I would report his crimes against us or gloat about the fact that the founders of the Greater East Asia Co-Prosperity Sphere would pay for not adhering to the guidelines of the Geneva Convention that all civilized nations recognized. The vindictive spirit had deserted me while talking to Bracky in the hospital and after gazing at Maddock's sleeping and wounded form. It would come back, but that afternoon I realized that too many people had died because of seething emotions and unbridled hate. Too many of the Allies, too many Japanese, too many POWs, too many people. And nothing would bring them back. I do not know how Marsden felt just then, but he too refrained from giving a long speech about the injustice of our captors. Instead, we left Inaki's office together with Inaki's sword between us.

Several ex-POWs died after we learned the war was over. Robert Wilkin, a civilian captured and put into a POW camp because of his nationality, the same man who had predicted his own demise on the way to Ohasi camp, died on 24 August. Wilkin was able to prophesy his own death because he gave up. I had seen it happen before, the power of the mind to resist or invite death, but never so clearly as with Wilkin. Two Dutch prisoners died

25 August as a result of wounds sustained during the shelling: Teunis Ruiter and Ch. Vermeulen.[1] The deaths hung over us as we celebrated, a grim irony while we toasted the victorious Allies. They had won the war and liberated us, but at great cost to Kamaishi's POWs: twenty-nine men died.

MY FIRST ACT of command after we took control of the camp wasn't popular. As I had told Inaki, Marsden and I rounded up several men whom we knew were trustworthy and appointed them MPs. We continued to take roll each day, and every man was to be accounted for at night to keep anyone from wreaking havoc. This was an easier task than I had thought it would be, for the camp personnel who had abused us—Mikawa, Matsuura, and a few soldiers—had disappeared, which left any vindictive former POWs with no one to vent their anger on. Some minor incidents did occur, for there was much intensity of feeling in the camp, but the MPs managed to keep order among 350 men.

We labeled our camp as a POW camp, then confiscated several radios from Inaki to enlighten ourselves further as to what was going on in the world. On just about every major station, we heard messages to ex-POWs from MacArthur. "Stay where you are!" his authoritarian voice bellowed. "Do not leave your camps! We know where you are, and we will rescue you as soon as possible. Do not come to Tokyo! I repeat, do not come to Tokyo! We will come to you."

Apparently Tokyo was inundated with former POWs seeking food, entertainment, and revenge, and all was chaos, which left Marsden and me yet more determined that none of our guys would join them. If they didn't get hurt, they could get tossed into a makeshift brig. Waking up in another prison, one established by the Allies, was no way to greet freedom.

We listened to other reports on the radio and slowly pieced together just what had happened over the last four years. We heard of abominations committed in Europe, millions of Jews killed by the Nazis—the stories were ugly, unbelievable. They sickened me. It was worse than our own ordeal. For the first time we heard of gas chambers, mass executions, and incessant torture. What was most unbelievable was the fact that people had managed to survive that hell at all, for apparently there were walking skeletons who stumbled out of the concentration camps in Europe. My respect for the tenacity of human beings grew all the more.

And the mysterious bomb that Tucker had spoken of, it became a capitalized word, the Bomb. It was a different weapon from any used before, and two were dropped several hundred miles south of us. The Bomb had rendered devastation in Hiroshima and Nagasaki that matched the work of hundreds of fire bombs in the shitamachi district of Tokyo.[2] Again, I was incredulous. The world was demanding great adjustments from my sense of reality.

Though all our news came via the radio, we had company in our remote corner of Japan—U.S. reconnaissance planes flew overhead repeatedly. They waggled their wings at us in friendly hellos, signaling they knew we were there. They dropped heavy boxes of goods to us by parachute—in them we found food, comic books, cigarettes, chewing gum, magazines, medical supplies, and other items.

The crates were huge and the parachutes that lowered them to the earth capricious; more than once a crate fell to the hard ground freely, exploding upon impact and flinging wooden shards and food supplies everywhere. On one occasion, we were all in the streets of Ohasi, waving at the pilots above when they dropped supplies to us. After a few seconds, those of us on the ground realized the parachute had failed to open, making the crate a wooden bomb hurtling toward us. We scrambled to get out of its path, and watched it explode upon impact. Some kind soul had packed various canned goods in that container—beans, sauces, preserved meats, vegetables. I most especially remember the canned peaches, for a large can of it smashed open near me, and I was covered with the stuff. I arose from the ground with peach dripping from my nose and forehead. I wondered as I scraped the sticky fruit from my face just how ridiculous life would get before we got out of Japan. Everyone who had been happily waving just a minute before was now oozing various mixtures of food from head to foot while cursing the pilots whom they had moments before praised. And the goods they dropped to us were destroyed. Some of the men licked the food off their clothes, but most of it was unsalvageable.

A Japanese civilian was killed during a food drop—a gallon can of some foodstuff slipped from a crate and struck him in the head. I added yet another rule to the growing list of regulations for ex-POWs: they were to stay indoors during food drops. And I recommended to Inaki that he advise Japanese civilians do the same.

WE WERE ALL impatient with our situation—none of us wanted to just sit tight until our allies found us. Many men were ready to simply start walking toward the coast or Tokyo. Anything, they claimed, was better than dull Ohasi, which was even more rural than Kamaishi. One afternoon a young American corporal named Crandall accosted me, a man whose cheerful disposition I had grown to like in our years at Yokohama and Kamaishi. He was a clever fellow, a man full of ideas.

"Have you heard what's going on in Tokyo, Captain?" he exclaimed. "It's a great time there! Everybody's talking about it. Food, dancing, music, women, everything."

I eyed him warily. I knew the resourceful young man well enough to be immediately suspicious of his intentions. "How do you know that? No one's been to Tokyo. The last time I was there, it was a bombed-out city full of Japs who hated Americans. Doesn't sound too good to me."

"But our guys are there now, Captain! And it's a great time! You arrive, they put you up in good hotels, feed you, find you a bathhouse and a woman, give you medals even! Wouldn't you like a massage and a warm steam room? And a hot dinner? Why are we staying here?"

"Obeying orders. You heard MacArthur's message. If we all went to Tokyo, the city would become a giant madhouse. It probably already is."

"Yeah, but Captain, *some* of us can go." With this comment, the man's eyes became devious. "*We* can go, Captain," he said, lowering his voice to a conspiratorial whisper. "You and me and some buddies of mine. It's simple. I have a plan. All we have to do is go over that hill," he pointed toward a small rise just behind the camp. "Five miles away we'll find a train to Tokyo. We'll board the train, take it over, and go to Tokyo. We'll be heroes! It'll be grand!" Crandall was grinning triumphantly, his eyes dancing.

I was exasperated. "Are you crazy? Take over a Japanese train? Do you think the Japs are happy about losing the war? A few unarmed ex-POWs board a train and they're gonna turn it over to you? And how do you know there's a set of tracks over there?" I tapped the man on the head with my forefinger. "You've been a POW too long, Corporal. It's gotten to you."

"No, Captain, it's true! I'll prove it. Let's go tonight. All we have to do is go over that hill." Again he gestured toward the rise and repeated his story. I listened to him once more, and again told him he was crazy, but he wouldn't let up. "Captain, listen, all we have to do is go over that hill. . . ."

"Don't tell me that again!" I believe he would have talked about going over that hill ad infinitum if I had given him the chance. I took a firm tone. "Look, if you leave tonight, if you *ever* leave before our transport arrives, I'll prefer charges against you, and then testify at your court-martial. I mean it."

"A court-martial!" the corporal said, incredulously. "For what?"

"For disobeying a direct order. I order you to stay put. I order you not to go near that damned hill. Don't even look at it. Forget about Tokyo. We're all going to stay here until they come get us. We can't all go to Tokyo, so none of us will. You leave camp, and I'll report you."

The man became his most beguiling self. "Ah, Captain, you wouldn't do that. We've been friends. . . ."

"I would. This is a direct order. I order you to stay put."

The twinkle in his eyes did not fade, didn't even falter a moment. "You're missing a great time, Captain," he said.

I ordered him to remain in the camp again while he politely listened, then he saluted and walked away while gazing up at his beloved hill.

Perhaps my disciplinarian's voice had wavered after three and a half years, or perhaps we had simply been POWs too long. The next day, Crandall and three of his buddies were gone. I worried about them a little, but I remember being more envious than concerned. At least they were doing something.

On 8 September we moved from the Ohasi camp back down to Kamaishi, where we took over the seacoast battery barracks. Our former camp sat as we had left it, a charred and leveled testimony to the U.S. Navy's shelling abilities. I walked among the blackened heaps one day, expecting the camp to bear a few ghosts or memories of the men who had worked and died there, but there was nothing. It was a silent, empty ruin without whispers of the abuse and deaths that had occurred there so recently—time does heal, and quickly. Or perhaps I was simply numb still and could not feel the pain that lingered there.

We were rescued from Kamaishi a week later, on 15 September. All of us boarded hospital ships where we would be examined and cared for while we sailed. We Americans headed back to the Philippines; from there we would be sent home from the replacement depots in Manila.

Bracky and I parted on the docks before boarding the ships. I was awed by the huge ships in the harbor and jubilant that we would soon be on one. When I saw the American flag flying from one of them, I wept and laughed at the same time. But Bracky was quiet. He watched the proceedings with a curious look on his face—a look that I remembered later. I passed over his expression at the time.

Our parting was brief, unmemorable; it is our friendship that I have saved. We promised to keep in touch, to get together in Britain or the States before too long. I remember a few superfluous words: "It's been a privilege to know you" and "You were a great help, couldn't have done it without you." With that, I stepped toward my ship. I only glanced back once and only for a second, for I was excitedly talking with someone next to me, but I know Bracky watched me board, all the while with that curious expression. And I am certain that when Bracky finally stepped on his own ship's gangplank, he did look back, long and hard, and probably more than once. Bracky knew long before I did that we former POWs could not easily walk away from Japan.

MADDOCK WAS ON the same ship with me, but he had a permanent bunk in the sick bay. Most of his burns were healing, and his arm was bound up properly at last, but he would present many scars to the world once he was able to walk again. Along with his wounds, he was seasick, which was odd for Maddock; he hadn't been seasick once on our way to Japan. I dropped by to see him often, but he still wasn't inclined to chat much.

There were about seven hundred former POWs on board. Each man had all the food he wanted; they gave us cigarettes and candy and medical care and, most importantly, time to rest. A naval vessel is not usually considered comfortable, but for us it was paradise with its clean linen and cushioned bunks. We gained weight with each passing day, and laughed and talked and played cards. Great healing took place on that ship.

We arrived in Manila several weeks later.

It seemed as though the entire city had turned out to greet us, though we could not have been the only shipload of POWs who arrived. We were treated as heroes. The Filipinos waved joyfully as the ship came to dock, while U.S. personnel, regardless of rank, saluted each and every ex-POW as he stepped ashore. The replacement depot was aswarm with nurses and volunteers serving cakes and beverages to us—a band played and laughter filled the air. When the band stopped, a radio blared forth the latest hits from Stateside. Young women in pretty dresses flitted among us, and U.S. soldiers in pressed uniforms and polished shoes helped us with our gear. Many celebrations were planned, and we drank all the wine and beer we wanted. My group of ex-POWs were processed through the 49th Replacement Depot.

We passed Corregidor on the way into Manila Bay. Corregidor had seen more battles as the Americans took back the Pacific, as had Manila, and both places showed it. Although light vegetation already covered Corregidor and Manila was being rebuilt, the scars of war were still clearly visible. Indeed, parts of Manila looked as leveled as the shitamachi of Tokyo.

We learned that all former POWs were to receive back pay for their time in the camps, part of which was given to us in Manila. We also all received promotions—I was suddenly a major. It was the first promotion since I had earned my commission that I felt I actually deserved.

I remembered my last promotion with Joe Iacobucci and again wondered where he was, where Pfaff and James were. I asked many questions, but my initial investigations in Manila turned up nothing. There was no news of them anywhere. I knew that my wife, Virginia, was already back in the States; she had been sent home soon after MacArthur's forces had retaken Manila, but there was no sign of my friends.

I did find another missing face, however, or rather, he found me.

"Captain Grady," a man called from behind me one afternoon during a social event for former POWs. It was Crandall, the corporal who had disobeyed my orders and left Ohasi. He was dressed in a sergeant's uniform and was grinning from ear to ear. "How are you, Captain? Oh, excuse me. *Major.*"

I grabbed toward his hand to shake it, but he threw his arms around me in a bear hug. Both of us began to talk and laugh and cry at the same time. "I should have reported you," I said when we released each other and wiped away our tears. "You disobeyed a direct order! I told you not to go to Tokyo and you left a few hours later. You might have been hurt!"

"But I was fine! It was great! It happened just like I told you it would. We went over that hill and there was a set of tracks. We jumped a train and were gonna take it over, but it was going to Tokyo anyway, so we just went along. The Japs gave us food and smiled and bowed. And Tokyo! Captain, you shoulda come! It was the best! They treated us like heroes! They pinned medals on us and gave us food and drinks! It was great!" He launched into a lengthy description of his days in Tokyo that pretty much matched what he had predicted when he tried to persuade me to leave Ohasi. I wondered about scuttlebutt—sometimes it was right on the mark.

On parting, I tried to be gruff. "Don't you go ignoring any more direct orders, Sergeant. And keep in mind I may report you yet."

Crandall ignored my gruff voice and just smiled. "No you won't, Captain. You wouldn't. You couldn't." He paused, and his voice became almost reflective. "You never would have reported me. We went through too much together up there." He waved northward, in the direction of Japan. After that he said a hasty goodbye and was off to enjoy himself in Manila.

FOR ABOUT A WEEK after my return to the Philippines, I walked around in a fog; I had a difficult time absorbing my liberty and my status as a respected officer. I had gone up to Manila from the replacement depot to give an affidavit as to what had happened to my cryptographic machines before our surrender. I was billeted in a hotel that had once offered luxurious rooms, but now it could only provide a roof and a clean bed. I awoke there one morning to somebody's radio—through my open window I heard a new song from the States, "Sentimental Journey." I was still drowsy with sleep, and for several frightening moments thought that maybe the light notes wafting in were only part of a dream and I would awaken as a POW again with no promise of a good breakfast. But as the light melody continued, and no guard intruded, I knew my freedom was real.

I stood slowly and peered out the window as the song promised to renew old memories. The lyrics weren't written with a former POW in mind, of course, but they seemed to me appropriate to the moment. I was going to take a journey, which could only be sentimental, for I was going home soon, a place I had many times given up all hope of ever seeing again. I felt tears well up and did not fight them. I let my tears fall and savored reality as a U.S. citizen and not as a prisoner of war. It was a reality that for the first time in almost four years did not gouge or cut. I leaned my elbows on the window sill, and gazed at an American flag fluttering in the breeze, and cried like a small child.

Several times I tried to find Maddock in Manila, but failed. In the excitement of our arrival in the Philippines, I had lost touch with him, the man who had helped me through those long years as a POW. I have not yet forgiven myself for not locating him in Manila, for I lost track of him after that. I only know that he emerged from the hospital several weeks after I left the Philippines and was shipped back to the States, to California, and presumably, his motorcycle. I had told him many times in camp after our victory that it was up to him to keep in touch with me, as he had no fixed address. He promised to do so, but he didn't.

A few weeks later, after filling out countless reports and affidavits, I climbed onto a huge plane, something related to the B-29s I had watched fly over Tokyo and Kamaishi. That plane was bigger than any plane I had ever been on before, and it was bound for Honolulu and San Francisco. It was early October 1945.

AFTER A SEVENTY-TWO-HOUR trip with several stops, the plane landed on 12 October outside San Francisco, a city I had never visited. But I felt as though I knew it from all the stories I had heard from Christensen. I didn't want to think of those stories anymore. Whenever I thought of Christensen, I thought of Joe, and then I wanted to weep. He had said he'd find me and he hadn't. And I couldn't find news of him anywhere. I had to suspect the worst.

I was mulling over these somber thoughts when I heard my name mentioned by two army medics who were standing next to the entry gate. They were looking, one said in a low voice to the flight crew of my plane, for a Major Grady, an ex-POW who was very bad off and had to be taken immediately to the hospital. The crew members stood, scratching their heads as I walked up—no, there had been no stretcher-cases on the plane, but they'd check their records for Major Grady.

"I'm Major Grady," I said, pulling myself to my full height to help establish my healthy state. "Can I help you?"

One of the medics turned to stare at me, surprised. "You, sir? We were told you were very sick and had to be rushed to the hospital. We have an ambulance waiting."

"Someone made a mistake," I said. "I'm skinny, and I understand I'll have to take some tests, but I'm healthy enough."

"Right, sir. Well, I guess we don't have to rush anymore. I'm to give you a message. Your wife received your letter. She's waiting for you at the hospital. I'll take you there now, sir, if you like."

He turned and led the way to an ambulance parked just outside the terminal. His companion stayed behind, as his services weren't needed for the ailing Major Grady.

"This is awfully embarrassing, sir," said the orderly as we climbed into the ambulance. "They said you were awfully sick. I don't know what the mix-up was. You'll just take a few tests at the hospital and then you'll be released."

He started up the ambulance and swung it out into traffic. There were cars everywhere that I didn't recognize, bigger and sleeker cars. American traffic lights stopped us, then bade us to proceed. Americans walked by on the sidewalks under signs written in familiar script advertising American products. It was a typical day in the States, commonplace and untroubled by war. I had dreamed of this homecoming for years. For too long, perhaps —my arrival home after ten years in the Philippines and Japan was shrouded in a melancholy dreamlike haze, and still is.

"Have you been to San Francisco before, sir?" the young attendant asked companionably as he drove.

"No. Are we near downtown?"

"Oh, no, we're north of the city yet. We'll have to go over the bridge before we're downtown."

"Is that the Golden Gate Bridge?"

"Yes, sir. Golden Gate. The bridge is beautiful, especially at night. You'll have to come back after dark and look at it. San Francisco is a great place. It has some good night places, good dancing, wonderful food."

"I've heard that." I was quiet a moment, listening to a man now dead talk of the food to be had along Fisherman's Wharf. Christensen. Joe. Pfaff and James. Bracky, Maddock, and Sherman. I couldn't stop thinking of them. And I couldn't stop wishing that Christensen were my guide in San Francisco and not buried in a shallow mass grave outside a vacated POW camp near the Philippine town of Cabanatuan.

"Tell me, Sergeant," I said after a long silence, one I'm sure the sergeant didn't understand, "what has been happening in the States for the last ten years?"

The sergeant, a young and agreeable man, turned his untroubled face toward me. He was happy to hear me talk again. It was obvious he had never been hungry. He had never had cholera or dysentery or beriberi or malaria. He had never heard an enemy shell explode nearby, never been bullied by an enemy soldier, never watched a friend die. And because of that, I loved him. I loved him and his potential because of what he had not seen. May he and his generation never suffer such things, I thought to myself, for one does not really recover from such events. Not completely.

"Ten years, sir?" the young attendant asked. "Is that how long you've been away?"

"I was a POW for three and a half years, and in the Philippines for six years before that. I'm not sure I'm even American anymore, or married, for that matter. I haven't seen my wife since the spring of forty-two. And it wasn't a happy spring." As I finished speaking, we came over a rise and I saw a new world before me. San Francisco and the bay loomed up from behind the Golden Gate Bridge. I had never been to California, and I was surprised by the beauty of the place—it all lay ahead of us on that clear day, serene and unmutilated by bombs, the most beautiful city I had ever seen. Christensen had barely mentioned the loveliness of the area; he concentrated almost exclusively on the food.

The sergeant wasn't looking at the view—he had obviously seen it many times before. He was more interested in our conversation. "Geez, not seen your wife in all that time? This *is* an emergency." With that, the sergeant leaned forward and switched on his red flashing lights and siren. "I'll get you to the hospital in record time, sir—your wife's waiting for you!" He stomped down on the accelerator and the ambulance lurched down the hill toward the bridge.

I started to say that the siren and speeding weren't necessary, that after more than three years I could wait a few more minutes, but I checked myself. I enjoyed the young sergeant's energy and his interest in my life. I was fairly certain that on that day he was more excited about my life than I was.

And thus I first crossed the Golden Gate Bridge, with sirens blaring in a speeding ambulance. Cars pulled obligingly aside for us while the innocent sergeant told me as best he could what had changed in the United States since 1936. I only half listened to him as my thoughts meandered elsewhere. Nineteen forty-five was coming to a close, and I was speeding toward a new life. Even as I sat there in that melancholy mood, I felt a few wounds heal. After ten years, it wasn't exactly home, these United States of America, and it would never again be the America I had known, but America has always had its potential. With some time—and I was ever so patient now, equal to any wait—I would find a home again.

Epilogue

MAY 1985—In a hot hotel room we gathered, the former Signal Corps personnel who had worked on Bataan and Corregidor before the fall of the Philippines. The surviving American Defenders of Bataan and Corregidor were having a reunion in Albuquerque, and our group met for drinks and conversation in this crowded bedroom. The 228th Signal Operations Company was an older group, all heavier, all healthier. While age had brought ailments, they were relatively minor compared to what we had known as prisoners of war.

Many faces were not there. I knew they would not be—I had learned their fates long ago. Some fifty-seven of every hundred men taken prisoner on Bataan or Corregidor did not survive their years as POWs, and the numbers held true among our group: twelve out of twenty of us who had become POWs on Corregidor died while imprisoned.

I told the group that I had returned to the Philippines in 1982. I looked up certain names while there, for there is a memorial in Cabanatuan to the Filipino and American POWs of World War II; the memorial bears all the known names of those who died while imprisoned in the Philippines. The first two names I found easily enough: Lt. Andy M. James and Lt. Robert W. Pfaff. They died while en route to Japan. In the last days of 1944 the

Japanese tried to remove their POWs to Japan in crowded and unmarked transports. James and Pfaff had been on one of those ships, but theirs did not get far from the Philippines before being attacked by U.S. planes. They were either killed in the attack, shot in the water by Japanese guards, or drowned.

I found other familiar names on the memorial. There was Christensen, who had promised over innumerable bridge hands to show us San Francisco once the war was over. And there was Major Hart. His attempt to save himself by betraying us hadn't saved him; he died in the Philippines.

Capt. Joseph V. Iacobucci's name was not inscribed on the memorial. I knew it would not be. I knew Joe had not survived the war, but he did not die in the Philippines. He had made it to Japan. I asked if anyone in the hotel room knew what had happened to Joe once he was in Japan. Joe Warren, who was also part of the 228th Signal Operations Company, told me how Joe had died: of pneumonia and starvation, with Warren at his side. Like Pfaff and James, Joe had also been on one of the "hell ships" bound for Japan, but his transport made it to Moji, even after being torpedoed by a U.S. submarine. He ended up in Fukuoka Sub Camp Number One on Kyushu, which was Warren's camp. Joe was not well. He had suffered starvation, bombing attacks (he had been on two ships that had been sunk), and massive crowding on the voyage to Japan; once there, he developed pneumonia. Soon after he arrived, he said to Warren, "I don't think I'm going to make it." And he didn't. On 14 March 1945, Joe died in Warren's arms.[1]

To this day, I still weep when I think of Joe. The world endured a loss when Joe Iacobucci died at the age of twenty-eight. He was one of the finest men I have ever known.

Joe's wife, Phyllis, survived the war; she was released from Santo Tomas when the Americans retook the islands. She remarried several years after learning that Joe had died and was still alive as of this writing. We exchanged Christmas cards for years.

I hoped to see Walter Maddock at one of our reunions, but he never appeared. Immediately after the war, once back in the States, I tried many times to contact Maddock, but all of my letters sent to a post office address in California were unanswered or returned. Virginia and I went to his hometown in California in 1946, but we couldn't find him. I have wondered how big a motorcycle he bought on returning home, how far he went on his back pay. I have always suspected that Maddock somehow got himself killed once he was home; I even heard a rumor that this was his fate. But I do not know what happened to him.

Bracky returned to Britain. I have learned little else of him, for we too lost touch. I only know he died in 1979, some thirty-four years after his liberation from a prisoner of war camp. If ever a man deserved a happy life after his imprisonment, it was Lieutenant Brackstone, our Bracky.[2]

Bracky turned out to be right in his concern about the ex-POWs once they were back home. After returning to their various countries, many POWs faced the problems that Bracky had predicted as the war ended. Once we were released, each former POW received his back pay, an amount which, after four years, was quite a bundle all at once in those days. But when the money was gone, many men had a difficult time adjusting to the work world. Some quickly married, or returned to married life, and found themselves confused by the responsibilities suddenly demanded of them from wives and children. Without a clear enemy to work against, many of the ex-POWs didn't know how to face the challenges of their lives. And many former POWs were not entirely healed after returning from the Pacific. Much of the abuse they had endured while prisoners continued to haunt them once they were expected to lead normal lives. The suicide rate among us is higher than that of the general population. I myself have never blamed a former POW for surrendering to despair. We have seen what people should not see.

In 1946 I RETURNED to Tokyo to testify at the War Crimes Trials. In retrospect, I realize that my testimony helped free me from the hatred that some former POWs still carry toward the Japanese. While in Japan, I testified against the men who had abused us: Kambe, Nichizawa, Chisuwa, Ikeda, and other vicious camp personnel. Many others testified or wrote affidavits against these same men, and the accused were punished, either with prison sentences or, as happened to Kambe and Nichizawa, execution. Kambe and Nichizawa were hung. Kambe received two death sentences. One sentence was based on his abuses in our camp (he helped Nichizawa beat several POWs to death); the other was because of his murder of two B-29 pilots— he took them to the top of a high building in the B-29 POW camp and pushed them off. Nichizawa was proven guilty of numerous murders in our camp because of his beatings and neglect of POWs. I believe that many former POWs would have buried their animosity toward the Japanese people if they had been able to point an accusing finger at their persecutors as I and other officers were able to do. It was a vindication, though a tedious and painful one.

I also wrote out an affidavit against Inaki and the personnel at Kamaishi Prison Camp, but I don't believe much came of those trials. Unlike Nichizawa and Kambe, Inaki was a man with some good traits, even if he was pedantic in his attention to army regulations. Inaki was tyrannical because of the chaos of the war, not because of a genuine evil in him. Taking his sword from him was especially cathartic for me; when I did that, the sting of being a powerless POW for so long was soothed.

I have thought of the other Japanese people I encountered as a POW: the Yale-trained interpreter who consciously or unconsciously helped save my life by ordering me to Tokyo; the young sergeant who shared a beer with me on a transport ship bound for Japan; the woman on a Tokyo-bound train who fed me breakfast; the young soldier who bounded from that same train and bought me and my buddies some ice cream. As each of these noble individuals remained nameless to me, I cannot know their fates. But I remember them and honor each of them.

I do know of Okimoto's fate. I saw him when I returned to Japan to testify; I met his wife and daughter. During that visit, Okimoto told me that he had long considered himself more American than Japanese, and yet he was expelled from his adopted country and then required to consider his fellow Americans as enemies. He never did return to the United States; he stayed in Japan and eventually died there.

I am very lucky that I did not die in Japan; I am lucky I did not die as a POW. I cannot take much credit for it. My survival was instinctive; it was luck. Other men, good men like Joe Iacobucci, had the instinct but not the luck, and they perished. The capricious nature of my survival still troubles me, for purely arbitrary factors kept me alive. I am not tall, thus I did not intimidate our guards. I was an officer, so I avoided severe beatings. I happened to know something about U.S. cryptographic machines and methods that the Japanese thought worthwhile, so I was sent to Japan two years before U.S. craft patrolled the Pacific and unwittingly fired upon their imprisoned allies. And when our POW camp was destroyed by an American ship, no shell had my name written on it. When all these arbitrary factors were added to the fact that I had friends by my side in the camps, caring and crafty friends, I survived. I was thus able to walk onto a U.S. ship after the war's end instead of being transported home in a small wooden box containing my ashes, or worse, left behind in a forgotten grave thousands of miles from my home. I thank fortune, or God, or both; I do not know which it was that saved me.

Some final legacies of my captivity? I feel a mingled sense of pride and relief whenever I see an American flag. I cannot listen to "Sentimental Journey" without a handkerchief. I often weep when I think of my years as a POW, and I am not ashamed of my tears; I have learned that courage has nothing to do with a "manly" repression of feeling. I also have never been able to take my liberty and comfort for granted. I move about freely; I eat well; I sleep in a soft bed; I am doctored by concerned professionals; and I spoil a former stray cat that is better fed as our pet than I was as a prisoner of war under the Japanese. I am a lucky man.

The final legacy of my years as a POW is perhaps surprising: I am an optimist. My belief is that though our world is a hectic and troubled one, this life is worthwhile. I am fully aware of the lethal potential of the human race, but more deeply entrenched in my mind is the human capacity for great good. Thus I can only look with hope toward the future and advise those who follow me to carry on with trust and forbearance, for I learned in the bleak and tormented world of several prisoner of war camps that human life is worth preserving.[3]

Notes

Chapter 1. Manila: December 1941

1. Louis Morton, *The War in the Pacific: The Fall of the Philippines* (Washington, D.C.: Center of Military History, U.S. Army, 1953), 48–50, 42–43. Morton offers a detailed account of the Philippine forces and the battles waged there.

2. Ibid., 44.

3. The service personnel in the Philippines were not the only ones who expected the Japanese to attack the Philippines first. When President Roosevelt and his aide Harry Hopkins heard the news that Pearl Harbor was under attack, Hopkins said, "This can't be true, this must mean the Philippines?" John Costello, *The Pacific War* (New York: Rawson, Wade, 1981), 2.

Colonel Grady's reference to the previous war is to the *Lusitania* incident when, on 7 May 1915, a German U-boat sank the British civilian ship, killing 1,200 people, 128 of whom were Americans. Almost two years later, the Germans attacked another British civilian ship and three U.S. freighters, all of which helped catapult America into the war against Germany. Virginia Bernhard et al., *Firsthand America: A History of the United States,* vol. 2, 1st ed. (St. James, N.Y.: Brandywine, 1991), 706–7. Many U.S. military personnel assumed a similar series of events would draw the U.S. into war with the Japanese in 1941.

4. For more information on cryptographic and cryptanalytic practices before and during World War II, see David Kahn, *The Codebreakers: The Story of Secret Writing* (New York: MacMillan, 1967), and Edward J. Drea, *MacArthur's ULTRA: Codebreaking and the War against Japan, 1942–1945* (Lawrence: University Press of Kansas, 1992).

5. Colonel Grady could not remember exactly which day he saw this message; it was either 3 December or 5 December.

6. The message that Colonel Grady saw appears to be related to the famous Japanese transmission of 19 November 1941 that informed Japanese diplomats how Tokyo would warn them of a break in diplomatic relations. That message said that if international communications were cut off, Tokyo would send a message out in a Japanese shortwave weather report saying "HIGASHI NO KAZE AME" [east wind rain]; this

would mean that Japanese–U.S. relations were in danger, and that diplomatic personnel should destroy all code papers (see Kahn, 32).

7. The uncoded message—and all messages transmitted by U.S. communications personnel—would still have been in Morse code, the traditional means of transmitting radio messages in 1941. Usually, U.S. messages were translated into an intricate code with cryptographic machines and then transmitted via Morse code; it took awhile to decode them. The uncoded messages from Honolulu required no decoding because Sollenberger transcribed them directly from Morse code.

8. Peter Calvocoressi, Guy Wint, and John Pritchard, *Total War: The Causes and Courses of the Second World War,* rev., 2d ed. (New York: Pantheon, 1989), 957.

Chapter 2. Retreat

1. Morton, 81–83.

2. Ibid., 84.

3. Historians are uncertain as to why no one at Clark Field received the warning that the Japanese bombers were coming. Colonel Grady remembered the rumor that the pilots and radio operators were at lunch, thus they missed the warning. Morton corroborates that this was a possible reason for missing the alarm; he also offers other possibilities for the error (85).

4. Iba Field was an auxiliary airfield west of Clark Field on the Zambales coast. Fort Stotsenburg was an army base about fifty miles north of Manila.

5. Morton, 88.

6. Calvocoressi, Wint, and Pritchard, 955–57.

7. Morton, 104.

8. Costello, 196–97.

9. Eric Morris, *Corregidor: The End of the Line* (New York: Stein and Day, 1981), 31–32.

10. Morris, 261.

11. Ibid., 262.

12. My thanks to Frank A. Iacobucci, Captain Iacobucci's brother, for providing me with an account of the wedding; it confirms Colonel Grady's story, but Colonel Grady had forgotten the wedding date.

13. Colonel Grady's report of this event is contradictory. In one account, he says he sent MacArthur's message in which he refused to leave the Philippines, while in another interview, it wasn't so clear that Colonel Grady sent the message. Because Colonel Grady cannot clear up the confusion for me, I have drawn on Morton's account of MacArthur's initial refusal to go to Australia (357–58).

14. Colonel Grady did not remember the lieutenant's name.

Chapter 3. Bataan and Corregidor

1. John Toland, *But Not in Shame: The Six Months after Pearl Harbor* (New York: Random House, 1961), 266.

2. E. Bartlett Kerr, *Surrender and Survival: The Experience of American POWs in the Pacific, 1941–1945* (New York: William Morrow, 1985), 49–50.

3. Kerr, 25–27.

4. Morris, 411.

5. I have drawn on Donald Knox's detailed account of the Bataan Death March to verify Colonel Grady's reports of the march. See Knox, *Death March: The Survivors of Bataan* (New York: Harcourt Brace Jovanovich, 1981). Thanks also to Richard Francies and Joe Warren for their accounts.

6. Kerr, 52, 59–60.

7. Morris, 430.

8. Costello, 284.

9. Colonel Grady remembered the gist of Wainwright's surrender message but not the specifics. I recorded this message from Wainwright's account of his experiences during the war. Jonathan Wainwright, *General Wainwright's Story* (Garden City, N.Y.: Doubleday, 1946), 122–23.

10. I consulted Morton (565) to find out how many pesos were destroyed that night in the Tunnel. Colonel Grady was not certain how many they destroyed, but he said it took several men several hours to rip or cut all of it. They did indeed destroy two million pesos.

11. I confirmed the wording of this message by consulting the *New York Times,* 1 June 1942, p. 4. Mr. Strobing's rank is unclear. Colonel Grady called him a staff sergeant. In a listing of the 228th Signal Operations Company, he is listed as a corporal. And the *Times* calls him a private.

Chapter 4. From the 92d Garage to Bilibid

1. Morton, 573. Colonel Grady had forgotten the names of the northern Luzon commanders; Morton's book supplied them for me.

2. Ibid., 572.

3. Kerr, 71. Colonel Grady thought the number of prisoners in the 92d Garage area was nine thousand, but Kerr says twelve thousand. As Colonel Grady was estimating the number, I defer to Kerr's number.

4. Colonel Grady had forgotten the exact date of their removal to Manila. See Kerr for more details of the crossing to Manila (74–75).

Chapter 5. Cabanatuan

1. Colonel Grady had forgotten the commander's name—I am grateful to Kerr for supplying it (79).

2. Kerr, 96.

3. Kerr provides a detailed description of the hospital and Zero Ward at Cabanatuan (see 93–105).

Chapter 6. Betrayal

1. Mindanao is the other main island of the Philippines; it is south of Luzon.

2. Colonel Grady had forgotten Rutherford's name. Kerr provided it for me (96).

3. Richard Francies was one of the telecommunications technicians whom the Japanese put to work fixing the telephone system after the Philippines were in Japanese hands; they were indeed billeted in decent hotels in Manila while they did the work. But according to Mr. Francies, the U.S. technicians engaged in more sabotage than anything else; his work detail also supplied the Filipino guerrillas with equipment whenever they could. As Mr. Francies says, "We did ruin more than we fixed for them. . . . We did a lot of good on that detail for everybody but the Japanese" (personal interview, May 1985).

U.S. cryptographic technology during World War II was among the best in the world; the code machines that Colonel Grady worked with produced codes that were unbreakable (see Cipher A. Deavours and Louis Kruh, *Machine Cryptography and Modern Cryptanalysis* [Dedham, Mass.: Artech House, 1985], 10, 35–91). Without the deciphering abilities of the U.S. code machines, Colonel Grady and his colleagues could not have broken any of the high-security U.S. codes; even a medium- or low-security code would have been extremely difficult for them to break. But one doubts they would have tried very hard to break any ciphers for the Japanese.

4. Colonel Grady and Captain Iacobucci both handled sensitive communications crossing the Pacific. Occasionally, top secret messages came through with instructions that they were to be encoded-decoded only by the officer-in-charge, Colonel Grady. Lieutenants Pfaff and James would have encoded-decoded messages of lesser importance. Enlisted personnel in the cryptographic section seldom did the final encoding-decoding of any message—they turned over messages to an officer before the final decoding. But anyone working in the cryptographic section had considerable knowledge of U.S. cryptographic technology that the Japanese military would have found interesting in 1942.

Chapter 7. Manila: November–December 1942

1. According to Kerr, Bilibid Prison was made into a "hospital and transient center"; it was staffed by U.S. naval medical personnel, which explains why there were fewer POWs there when Colonel Grady returned in November 1942. Most of the POWs had been transferred out to camps near Cabanatuan and Tarlac, a town west of Cabanatuan (78–81).

2. The seventh of Colonel Grady's group from Cabanatuan remained a stranger to them. They never did learn much about him, though Colonel Grady assured me he was a friendly man. Colonel Grady had forgotten his name and rank and never learned of his fate in the Philippines.

Chapter 8. Transport North

1. Even if the ship had been full of POWs, the Japanese probably would not have marked it as a POW ship. They did not do this later, and as a result hundreds of U.S. POWs perished in the tightly packed ships that were bound for Japan in 1943–45. The ships were not marked as POW ships, so U.S. craft fired on them, sinking several. The prisoners were packed (and sometimes locked) into the ships; thus escape was difficult or impossible.

2. It is unclear whether this rumor was true. Wainwright says nothing in his account about being forced to wave to his former troops as they passed on their way northward to Japanese POW camps, but he was in Formosa in January 1943. He was later held in a prison camp on the Chinese mainland, in Manchuria (see Wainwright).

3. Soon after he arrived at the Yokohama camp, Colonel Grady learned of Col. James Doolittle's April 1942 bombing raid on Tokyo; all cities were under blackout orders after that.

Chapter 9. Yokohama Camp Number One

1. Numerous prisoner of war camps were in the Tokyo area. The Shinagawa Camp was a headquarters and hospital for those POW camps.

2. Yokohama is a huge city that sits next to Tokyo on the south, but also on Tokyo Bay. Although Yokohama is technically a separate city, Colonel Grady's Yokohama camp was considered part of the Tokyo POW camp system.

3. The official name of the camp was Number One Detached Camp, Tokyo Prisoner of War Camps. But Japanese personnel and the POWs referred to the camp as Yokohama Camp Number One.

4. Many of the names and descriptions of punishments in this and subsequent chapters on Yokohama Camp Number One come from Colonel Grady's testimony during the War Crimes Trials after the war's end.

Chapter 13. Bombs over Tokyo

1. The someone who had changed America's bombing strategy was Gen. Curtis LeMay of the Army Air Force. See Costello, 593–94.

2. Ibid., 597–98.

3. Calvocoressi, Wint, and Pritchard (1175) place the dead at somewhere from 70,000 to 140,000. Because of the crowded conditions in Tokyo's shitamachi district (it was the most densely populated place on earth when the bombing took place), it is impossible to put an accurate number on those killed. Costello says that official U.S. death estimates of Tokyo fire were 80,000; he puts the number at 100,000. One million people were left homeless by the fire (Costello, 598).

4. These rumors were true—hundreds of U.S. POWs perished on unmarked ships bound for Japan.

Chapter 16. Rising from Ashes: August 1945

1. According to Eric Marsden, James Downs also refused to take morphine when medics first approached him after the shelling; he requested that a Dutch prisoner be treated with the little morphine that was left.

Chapter 17. Freedom

1. These names are from an affidavit Colonel Grady provided for the War Crimes Trials held in Japan in 1946. The name Ch. Vermeulen is written as it was spelled in the transcript.

2. According to John Costello, more than 165,000 people were killed when the nuclear bombs were dropped on Hiroshima and Nagasaki (642–43).

Epilogue

1. I am beholden to Frank A. Iacobucci, Captain Iacobucci's brother, for the name of the camp Captain Iacobucci died in and the date of his death. After the American Defenders of Bataan and Corregidor reunion in Albuquerque, Colonel Grady knew that Joe Iacobucci had been on one of the hell ships and that he had died in Japan, but

he didn't know exactly when or where. I also thank former POW Joe Warren for the information he provided about Captain Iacobucci's death.

2. Lt. Vivian Ernest John Brackstone was awarded the M.B.E. because of his efforts to help his fellow POWs in the camps he was in; Capt. Eric Marsden recommended him for the award.

3. Coauthor's note: Lt. Col. Frank John Grady, beloved husband of Elizabeth Grady, devoted father of Mary Virginia Grady and Huntley Chamberlain, and a dear friend and mentor to me, died 4 May 1991. I believe those who loved him would agree with me that until his death he lived for the day, one day at a time, as he had learned to do while a prisoner of war.

Index

About the Authors

Frank Grady was born in 1913 in Illinois. He joined the Army Air Corps in 1935. After completion of Signal Corps training, he was assigned to the Philippines; he arrived there in 1936. He was later appointed head cryptographic officer for Gen. Douglas MacArthur. He became a POW of the Japanese in May 1942. After his release at the end of the war, MacArthur requested that Grady return to Japan to testify at the Japanese War Crimes Trials. After giving his testimony, Grady did a tour of duty in Japan, then was transferred to Texas and later to Europe; he served as squadron commander at the American Air Force base in Lansdale, Germany. After a transfer to Maryland, Grady attended night school and received a B.A. from the University of Maryland. After retiring from the military, Grady moved to Colorado and worked as a computer analyst for Martin Marietta for ten years. He served as deputy secretary of state of Colorado from 1976 to 1978. He also served as area supervisor for the U.S. Census in 1980. In 1982, he returned to the Philippines to receive from President Ferdinand Marcos a medal of valor for helping to defend the Philippines; he was one of three men to receive this award. Frank Grady died in May 1991.

Rebecca Dickson teaches writing and literature at the University of Colorado.

The **Naval Institute Press** is the book-publishing arm of the U.S. Naval Institute, a private, nonprofit, membership society for sea service professionals and others who share an interest in naval and maritime affairs. Established in 1873 at the U.S. Naval Academy in Annapolis, Maryland, where its offices remain today, the Naval Institute has members worldwide.

Members of the Naval Institute support the education programs of the society and receive the influential monthly magazine *Proceedings* and discounts on fine nautical prints and on ship and aircraft photos. They also have access to the transcripts of the Institute's Oral History Program and get discounted admission to any of the Institute-sponsored seminars offered around the country.

The Naval Institute also publishes *Naval History* magazine. This colorful bimonthly is filled with entertaining and thought-provoking articles, first-person reminiscences, and dramatic art and photography. Members receive a discount on *Naval History* subscriptions.

The Naval Institute's book-publishing program, begun in 1898 with basic guides to naval practices, has broadened its scope in recent years to include books of more general interest. Now the Naval Institute Press publishes about 100 titles each year, ranging from how-to books on boating and navigation to battle histories, biographies, ship and aircraft guides, and novels. Institute members receive discounts of 20 to 50 percent on the Press's nearly 600 books in print.

Full-time students are eligible for special half-price membership rates. Life memberships are also available.

For a free catalog describing Naval Institute Press books currently available, and for further information about subscribing to *Naval History* magazine or about joining the U.S. Naval Institute, please write to:

Membership Department
U.S. Naval Institute
118 Maryland Avenue
Annapolis, MD 21402-5035
Telephone: (800) 233-8764
Fax: (410) 269-7940
Web address: www.usni.org